Min Zhou
The Transcription of Identities

Cultural Studies | The series is edited by Rainer Winter | Volume 43

Min Zhou (PhD) is professor of English at Shanghai International Studies University. Her research interests include British and American literature, Cultural Studies, and Media Studies.

Min Zhou

The Transcription of Identities
A Study of V. S. Naipaul's Postcolonial Writings

[transcript]

Bibliographic information published by the Deutsche Nationalbibliothek
The Deutsche Nationalbibliothek lists this publication in the Deutsche Nationalbibliografie; detailed bibliographic data are available in the Internet at http://dnb.d-nb.de

© 2015 transcript Verlag, Bielefeld

All rights reserved. No part of this book may be reprinted or reproduced or utilized in any form or by any electronic, mechanical, or other means, now known or hereafter invented, including photocopying and recording, or in any information storage or retrieval system, without permission in writing from the publisher.

Cover layout: Kordula Röckenhaus, Bielefeld
Typeset by Justine Haida

Printed and bound in Great Britain by
Marston Book Services Limited, Oxfordshire

Print-ISBN 978-3-8376-2854-8
PDF-ISBN 978-3-8394-2854-2

Contents

Acknowledgements | 7

Abbreviations | 9

Introduction | 11
V. S. Naipaul: A Controversial Position | 13
Problematizing Identity | 25

Chapter One An Exile at Home
A House for Mr. Biswas | 41
A Life Out of Place | 45
Houses as Shifting Signifiers | 57
A Colonial's Aporia | 68

Chapter Two An Exile between Islands
The Mimic Men | 79
Lost in the Metropolis | 84
Shipwrecked at Home | 93
Conflicting Identities | 106

Chapter Three An Enigmatic Identity
The Enigma of Arrival | 117
Articulation of Identity | 122
Deconstructing Englishness | 131
Toward a Hybrid Identity | 148

Chapter Four The Historical Perspective
A Way in the World | 157
Uncertain History | 163
Rewriting History | 175
Diasporic Identification | 186

Conclusion | 201

Works Cited | 211
Primary Sources | 211
Secondary Sources | 212
Works in Chinese | 222

Acknowledgements

The completion of the present volume is the fruit of many people's wisdom and love. It owes a number of debts that are difficult to trace. Of the ones that are apparent, I am particularly grateful to Professor Jihai Gao, Prof. Fengzhen Wang, and Professor Huimin Jin, for their insightful conversations and critical comments during the process of writing. Professor Jianhua Yu, Professor Tom Cohen and Professor Weiping Li's thoughtful and sustained support have been crucial to the completion of this book. Special thanks are due to Professor Rainer Winter and Professor Christina Schachtner for their great friendship and intelligence. I thank my family for their unfailing love and support, which has been a constant source of encouragement.

Abbreviations

As V. S. Naipaul's works are frequently cited in the book, the following abbreviations are used for convenience's sake. For full bibliographic information, please refer to the Works Cited section.

AB	*Among the Believers*
AD	*An Area of Darkness*
BR	*A Bend in the River*
EA	*The Enigma of Arrival*
FC	*Finding the Centre*
HB	*A House for Mr. Biswas*
IFS	*In a Free State*
IMMN	*India: A Million Mutinies Now*
IWC	*India: A Wounded Civilization*
LED	*The Loss of El Dorado*
LBFS	*Letters Between Father and Son*
MM	*The Mimic Men*
MP	*The Middle Passage*
MS	*Miguel Street*
MSKC	*Mr Stone and the Knights Companion*
Mystic	*The Mystic Masseur*
OB	*The Overcrowded Baracoon*
REP	*The Return of Eva Perón*
SE	*The Suffrage of Elvira*
TS	*A Turn in the South*
WW	*A Way in the World*

Introduction

> I belong to more than one world. I am a Palestinian Arab, and I am also an American. This affords me an odd, not to say grotesque, double perspective. In addition, I am of course an academic. None of these identities is watertight; each influences and plays upon the other. [...] It should be obvious that I cannot identify at all with the triumphalism of one identity because the loss and deprivation of the others are so much more urgent on me. (Said 2000:397)

The experience of exile, whether imposed or voluntary, is by no means rare through the course of human history. As an imaginative representation of reality, literature is fraught with works focusing on exile, from Homer's *Odyssey* and *The Old Testament* of the Bible to V. S. Naipaul's *A Way in the World*, to name but a few. The past century witnessed the most turbulent and vicissitudinous era of human history hitherto—the two World Wars, the Cold War between the East and West, and the subsequent economic and cultural globalization process, that exiled millions upon millions of people from their homes. The experience of exile not only draws the subject from his homeland, from all that is familiar, it also breaks the once solid orientation of identity. This shattered identity emerges with many new layers and facets that modulate each other, and invariably cause the subject to wonder who he really is, where he belongs or should belong, culminating in difficulties with understanding his place in the world.

According to Kobena Mercer, "identity only becomes an issue when it is in crisis, when something assumed to be fixed, coherent and stable is displaced by the experience of doubt and uncertainty" (1990: 43). In our increasingly diverse and fragmented world, many people are faced with the problem of identity because identity has become a vibrant, complex, and highly controversial concept. Some might argue that we need to find our "true identities" while others maintain that we are in an era of "identity crisis". Regardless, we experience cultural identity at global, national, local, and personal levels in very real ways. The same unifying power of identity that creates cohesive communities also makes people go to war. Yet cultural identities are non-summative. One cannot simply quantify and separate the aspects of identity associated with culture, race, class, gender, or sexuality. Cultural identities cannot be cleanly dissected and compartmentalized into separate display windows. If anything, they can be paradoxical. When we express who we are in terms of our cultural identity, we create the illusion of belonging to a distinct category with shared beliefs, behavioral norms, and cultural practices. In fact, however, individual differences as well as our various belongings and their inherent social responsibilities, pull us toward many, sometimes conflicting identities.

In the wake of the polemics on postcolonialism, there emerges a proliferation of studies about exile and identity in critical poetics. Literature is in constant interchange with reality. Exile, and its ensuing identity crisis will undoubtedly find their representations in literary works, among which Naipaul's have gained special attention from literary critics because his biographical history has long had "a symbiotic and self-consuming relation" with his writing (Hughs 1988: 11). As a writer who has always and only lived from his writing, Naipaul's life is determined by writing, and dominated by visions of a world undoing itself. Naipaul's lifelong writing career can be seen as an identity-seeking journey navigating between worlds. He was exiled from his ancestral culture by virtue of being born in the New World. The culture most familiar to him was English because of his colonial background. A brief sketch of Naipaul's life is therefore an indispensable entry point to studying Naipaul's novels, and the postcolonial subjects' quest for identity they represent.

V. S. NAIPAUL: A CONTROVERSIAL POSITION

Vidiahar Surajprasad Naipaul, the 2001 Nobel Laureate of Literature, was born on August 17, 1932, in Chaguanas, an impoverished, rural, Hindi-speaking area of Trinidad, a Crown Colony before acquiring its independence in 1962. Most Trinidadians are not natives, and the coming of independence created mutual fears of dominance between opposing ethnic groups: the Africans, the Indians and the Creoles. Naipaul's ancestors immigrated to Trinidad from India as indentured laborers between 1845 and 1917 to relieve the labor shortage in the sugar plantations after the abolition of slavery. Termed East Indians in the West Indies, this predominantly rural population adhered strongly to the traditions of their native land, and remained largely distinct from the urban and creolized Afro-Caribbean majority, who resented them for depressing agricultural wages. Both groups tended to view the other's culture as uncivilized, and the build-up to independence exacerbated these hostile feelings. Naipaul lived his childhood in poverty, among an almost completely isolated community of East Indians. At the age of 18, in 1950, with a hard-earned scholarship to Oxford University, Naipaul left Trinidad and went to England. He has remained in England, where he has written almost thirty books, won many literary prizes and was knighted for his services to English literature in 1990.

Naipaul's background marks him as a typical product of multiculturalism, a legacy of colonialism, a man of no single nation, and a writer in exile. Naipaul's exile is threefold: an exile from the Hindu tradition, an exile from Caribbean cultural heritage, and an exile in Britain. This complicated background gives Naipaul the advantage of viewing postcolonial society from both within and without, near and at a distance. It also sharpens his sensibility to the "true wonder" that Naipaul deems essential for a writer because in his eyes, "the world we inhabit, which is always new, goes by unexamined, made ordinary by the camera, unmediated; and there is no one to awaken the sense of true wonder. That is perhaps a fair definition of the novelist's purpose, in all ages" (REP 1981: 227). Influenced by his father, Seepersad Naipaul, a Trinidadian journalist and writer, Naipaul made up his mind to become a writer at the age of 12. Now author of 30 books, among which fiction and nonfiction are almost evenly divided, Naipaul has realized his childhood dream, and has firmly established his position as one of the best English writers of contemporary world literature. Remarkably, he has blurred the boundary between fiction and non-fiction, and has successfully found ways to express the postcolonial subjects' experiences in today's world of cultural mutation. Many of his works, like *The Enigma of Arrival* and *A Way in the World*, are mixtures of autobiography, fiction, history, and travel writings. Naipaul has literally lived by his writing alone, and has followed no other profession. His dedication to writing has been "complete to the point of complete self-absorption, notwithstanding the fact that his writing has been outward-bound in its fascination with the observed and recorded lives of many others" (Barnouw 2003: 30). Indeed, we can see the shadow of Naipaul himself in most of his fictional characters.

When awarded the 2001 Nobel Prize in Literature, Naipaul had already won almost every literary prize in England. Few readers doubted that he was a suitable recipient of the world's grandest literary award, one for which he had been nominated many times before, in spite of some disagreement over its timing.[1] The Swedish Academy commends Naipaul's extensive literary domain, which extends far beyond the West Indian island of Trinidad, his place of birth and

---

1 | Critics' doubt mainly stems from the timing of the prize, which was announced one month after the September 11 attacks on the United States because Naipaul has written two controversial and sharply diatribed books on Islamic fundamentalism, *Among the Believers* (1981) and *Beyond Belief* (1998). Kumar even claimed that the prize was given to Naipaul by a "grateful West" for his "anti-Muslim" stance (140).

first subject, to now include India, Africa, America from south to north, the Middle East, and England. A "literary circumnavigator", as he is called by the Swedish Academy, Naipaul's oeuvre ranges from the impact of colonialism, its molding and destructive power on the minds of marginalized colonials of the former European empires, to the resulting disordered reality upon decolonization in newly independent states in the Caribbean, Asia, and Africa. As "a modern philosphe", Naipaul has "united perspective narrative and incorruptible scrutiny in works that compel us to see the presence of suppressed histories" (Swedish Academy 2001); and with his vigilant style, he "transforms rage into precision and allows events to speak with their own inherent irony" (Swedish Academy 2001).

However, perhaps no significant contemporary writer's works have been so acclaimed, and, at the same time, so condemned. In spite of his gift for provoking extreme admiration, Naipaul's works also stimulate disagreement. Since he began writing, and through the development of his literary career, both Naipaul the writer and his works have been the target of acrimonious criticism. Critics from the Caribbean, South Asia, Arab, Africa, and Latin America excoriate him for being "a despicable lackey of neo-colonialism" (Singh 1969: 85), "a cold and sneering prophet" (Roach 1967: 5), and "a smart restorer of the comforting myths of the white race" (Achebe 1980: 113). He is criticized for traveling "to confirm his Eurocentric prejudices" (Winokur 1999: 11), and for being "England's favorite 19th-century Englishman" (ibid: 11).

The negative criticism hints at postcolonial critics' annoyance at the "Eurocentric" standpoints they believe revealed in Naipaul's writing. To them, it represents a betrayal of Naipaul's identity as a Third World writer from the ex-colonies. In contrast to other postcolonial writers who have built their writerly identity on the celebration of their cultural inheritance, Naipaul seems to be more critical, not only of the multiracial, multiethnic island of Trinidad, but also of his ancestral homeland of India. As we have already seen, Naipaul is a Trinidadian by birth, an Indian by blood, and a Briton by citizenship. His identity is therefore far from transparent. He has refused to be identified as a West Indian writer, instead, he call himself a "citizen of the world" (IFS 1981: 11). The label "a citizen of the world" actually highlights Naipaul's own perplexity over his identity in that it forever postpones a reconciliation of the tension between what is local and what is global in whom and what he is. Metaphorically one can be a citizen of the world, but in reality one has to face the choice of locality, at least in one's passport. Identity for Naipaul is thus an inevitable dilemma. Reflected in his novels, many of Naipaul's characters are also faced with this dilemma, which naturally results in their identity crisis. As "crisis" connotes a "new beginning", "crisis of identity" can therefore be read as the beginning of one's identity quest. With Naipaul, writing is the way by which he defines himself as a subject in the world. Since literature is in constant exchange with reality and, as an imaginative act, has its roots in life, Naipaul's literary works naturally reflect his aporia in identity. As Landerg White observes, Naipaul's "whole career is centered on the uncertainties of his own position" (1975: 2). This uncertainty of position mirrors Naipaul's abiding perplexity in identification. Meanwhile, Naipaul's books are fraught with characters who write, want to write or pretend to write; they are filled with parodies of bad writing, and with people who out of ignorance confuse serious literature with letter writing, bad journalism, pamphlets, who mistake prominence in the cultural industry, broadcasting or occasional book reviewing, as being a writer. All these writing efforts reflect the characters' endeavors to define themselves in the world and construct their identity.

Naipaul often revisits people and places in his books, his Indian trilogy being the best example. In addition, most of his works incorporate an important element of autobiographical material, which is indicative of uncertainty in his identity, as well as of his efforts at identity construction. Indeed, Naipaul's career as a writer actually parallels his life's quest to seek and construct an identity. A new perspective to Naipul's works would likely emerge from analyzing them from the perspective of the dynamic route to his identity against the background of the different cultures he has encountered.

This might lead to a better understanding of the formation of postcolonial subjects' search for identity since it would necessarily be involved with the study of the identity of postcolonial subjects in general. Criticism focused on his identity has been largely based on the reading of an isolated book, which is understandable given that Naipaul is a living writer. However, such isolated criticism runs the risk of oversimplifying the complex meaning of the texts, and with it, the formation of Naipaul's identity. This book will therefore try to offer a comprehensive study of the journey of identity construction through a close reading of major novels written at different periods of his life. Before delving into the labyrinth of Naipaul's journey, it may be helpful to briefly review commentaries about Naipaul and his works.

Western scholars in particular, commend Naipaul's achievements in shedding light on the misery of the Third World. He has been acclaimed for penetrating the chaos and dysfunction of postcolonial societies, and especially the suffering and deprivation experienced by victims of traumatic exploitation. Naipaul is praised for "writing with a strict refusal of romantic moonshine about the moral charms of primitives or the virtues of bloodstained dictators" and for being "the scourge of our disenchanted age, as free of colonialist bias as of infatuation with Third World delusions" (Feder 2001: 2), as well as "one of the finest living novelists writing in English" (Swedish Academy 2001), and "unarguably the most brilliant interpreter in English (perhaps in any language) of the maelstrom of the Third World" (qtd in Nixon 1992: 4). Naipaul is also singled out as "far and away the most talented, the most truthful, the most honorable writer of his generation" (Epstein 1987: 15).

Obviously, western scholars seem to agree that Naipaul's works truthfully represent the situation in the postcolonial world. With a comprehensive study of Naipaul's autobiography, his travel writings and fictions, Lilian Feder concludes that the central theme of Naipaul's fictions is a "lifelong process of self-creation, an individual narrative of a search for truth that incorporates the historical and social framework in which it is enacted" (2001: 20). In *Naipaul's*

Strangers, Dagmar Barnouw explores how Naipaul, whose works were profoundly shaped by his cultural background, has raised questions that go to the core of cultural (ethnic) plurality, the most important and difficult challenge to late modernity. She argues that he has learned to understand and document the difficulties of other cultures through his own difficulties in understanding his own multiethnic background, and has made their "disorienting strangeness intelligible" (Barnouw 2003: 2-4). In the second edition of *V. S. Naipaul*, Bruce King voices his support for Naipaul against charges by some critics that he has failed to see injustice and the effects of colonialism. He stresses that what Naipaul has done instead is to treat these themes with a complexity that acknowledges the rich, apprehensive and truthful ambivalence of the postcolonial reality, thus revealing it more acutely because "Naipaul does not choose sides, he observes what happens" (King 1993: 195). In general, in the eyes of Western critics, Naipaul's depictions of the society and people of the Third World are trustworthy, and he is therefore an honest, objective and candid photographer and spokesman for the Third World.

Naipaul's career and achievement can be seen as part of the worldwide political and cultural changes that have produced significant postcolonial writers such as Chinua Achebe, Wole Soyinka, and Derek Walcott. True, Naipaul writes mainly about ex-colonies and developing countries, which may contribute to his being labeled a postcolonial writer. But he cannot be grouped with those postcolonial writers who idealize their ethnic culture and write from a conscious nationalistic perspective. In contrast, Naipaul is often accused of taking the point of view of Westerners, and looking down upon his ancestral Indian culture, and the place of his birth. In addition, Naipaul is not popular among fellow West Indian writers such as Derek Walcott and George Lamming, who glorify their homeland and find Naipaul contemptuous of the land of his birth. Naipaul is rebuked as a literal and political ingrate who has internalized colonial denigrations of the Third World, and holds a self-loathing view of his own country. In George Lamming's *Pleasure of Exile*, there is a much-quoted diatribe against Naipaul:

What holds [Samuel] Selvon and myself together is precisely what could hold Indians and Negroes together in Trinidad. It is their common background of social history which could be called West Indian: a background whose basic feature is the peasant sensibility. Neither Sam nor I could feel the slight embracement about this; whereas Naipaul, with the diabolical help of Oxford University, has done a thorough job of wiping this out of his gust. (1991: 224-225)

Some postcolonial critics have also portrayed Naipaul as a traitor to the cause of the victims of colonialism, with whom they think he should have sought solidarity. In his scathing review of Naipaul's *Beyond Belief*, Edward Said rebukes Naipaul as "a man of the Third World who sends back dispatches from the Third World to the implied audience of disenchanted Western liberals who can never hear bad enough things about all the Third World myths—national liberation movements, revolutionary goals, the evils of colonialism" (Said 2000: 101). After reading *Among the Believers: an Islamic Journey*, Said further observes that Naipaul has become "the celebrated sensibility on tour" (ibid: 113), who shows an "unexamined reverence for the colonial order" (ibid: 114). The "deep emptiness in Naipaul the writer," according to Said, causes him "to promote an attitude of distant concern and moral superiority in the reader" (ibid: 117). Following Said's steps, Nixon titled his monologue on Naipaul, *London Calling: V. S. Naipaul, Postcolonial Mandarin*, and maintains that what sets Naipaul apart from other controversial writers are the lines of the dissent: the rift between the "the United States and Britain, on the one side, from [...] the Third World, on the other" (1992: 3).[2]

---

2 | Bruce King, in his *V. S. Naipaul*, has similar discoveries: "Behind most criticism of Naipaul, no matter how qualified by disclaimers, is the tendency to divide the world into such opposing polarities as center (England, imperialist, Western civilization) and margins (colonies, Third World, black)" (195). His conclusion, nonetheless, is contrary to Nixon's in that he thinks that those against Naipaul are "usually nationalists, on the political Left, and tend to read literature as politics." (195) Early in the 1980's, Selwyn

While ruminating on the gulf between Naipaul's reputations, Nixon warns that we should avoid the error of viewing Naipaul simply as a writer, instead, according to Nixon, we must realize that drawing on the advantage of his exilic condition, and with the rhetoric of displacement, Naipaul has successfully made himself a "buff on postcolonial politics" and is treated as "a mandarin possessing a penetrating, analytic understanding of Third World societies" (ibid: 4-16). Ostensibly, Said and Nixon's criticism centers on the political dimension of Naipaul's work.

Other critics believe that Naipaul sacrifices the truth of postcolonial reality to achieve an aesthetic impact, and that he writes from an Orientalist perspective. Homi K. Bhabha holds that Naipaul is so profoundly impressed by "the triumph of the colonialist moment in Conrad's texts of the civilizing mission" that he "'translates' Conrad from Africa to the Caribbean in order to transform the despair of postcolonial history into an appeal for the autonomy of art" (Bhabha 1994: 107). Fawzia Mustafa, drawing on Bhabha's reading of Naipaul, concludes in her monograph on Naipaul that "if a particular 'civility' and the 'autonomy of art' are indeed the grids whereby Naipaul constructs his narratives of the Caribbean and the greater Third World, then his relation to history is aesthetic rather than historiographical, and predetermined rather than explorative" (1995: 5). For Mustafa, Naipaul has failed to "historicize" the Caribbean experience since he has not seen it through the "transformative lens of colonialism" as has Fanon, because he is not involved in "the process of "decolonizing the mind", where the alienation fostered by colonization becomes the site from which writers posit a "liberation" (ibid: 5-7). According to Mustafa, "Naipaul's investment in the 'Novel' is deeply rooted in anxiety about 'cultural' rather than historical

---

R. Cudjoe contended that "a reading of V.S. Naipaul's texts is, by definition, a political act" (4). Cudjoe draws a similar dividing line between those idealistic readings of Naipaul's works from his materialistic reading, with a conclusion similar to that of Nixon.

authenticity," and, with "his bookishness can with justification be read as Orientalist" (ibid: 6-7).

Besides those postcolonial readings of Naipaul's works, the element most pointed out is his positioning of exile, and the consequent sense of rootlessness and homelessness. Many critics have talked about Naipaul's feeling of congenital displacement, of having been born a foreigner, a citizen of an exiled community on a colonized island. He has no natural home except for India to which he often returns, only to be reminded of his distance from his roots, a sentiment evidenced by a quick scan of review titles of his work: *Writer without a Society, V. S. Naipaul, Man without a Society, Without a Place, Writer without Roots, Historicity and Homelessness in Naipaul, Exile's Story, No Place: V. S. Naipaul's Vision of Home in the Caribbean, Nowhere to Go*. To be an exile is to be a stranger. The position of an exile, is, as termed by Julia Kristeva's, a "secret wound" that pushes the stranger into his wandering (1988: 13).

Despite the consensus among critics about Naipaul's feelings of alienation, paradoxically, Naipaul's position of exile has been given quite contradictory interpretations. Timothy F. Weiss posits that "for Naipaul, exile has been both an outsiderness and a state in-between different cultures and worlds" (1992: 222). Weiss reasons that Naipaul's art of exile explores cultural shocks and collisions, and enables us to better understand ourselves, as well as others. It is therefore "about all of us in a world radically changing and in our awakening to the stranger without and within" (ibid: 225). For Weiss, given the radical changes of today's world, the state of rootlessness is universal, and Naipaul's position as both an outsider and a person between different cultures, makes his writing an exemplary guide to understanding others and ourselves. Selwyn R. Cudjoe, and Rob Nixon, in their commentaries on Naipaul, also pay attention to his positioning of exile, albeit with completely opposite conclusions. For Cudjoe and Nixon, exile for Naipaul is but a strategy he deploys to shed prejudices against postcolonial societies, and to win favor from Western critics. For Nixon, Naipaul applies the rhetoric of displacement and alienation to emotional advantage. Thus, British and American critics are won over by the dramatic appeal in Naipaul's account of his uprootedness (1988: 20-21).

Beyond the disputes surrounding Naipaul and his works, as suggested by Nixon and King, there lies a lingering tendency to divide the world into the dichotomy of the occident and the orient, the center and the margin, the First World and the Third. As a matter of fact, we can relate the polemics around Naipaul's writing to the debate between Aijaa Ahmad and Fredric Jameson. Jameson in his "Third World Literature in an era of Multinational Capitalism" claims: "What all third-world cultural productions have in common, and what distinguishes them radically from analogous cultural forms in the first world [is that] as third-world texts are necessarily [...] allegorical, and in a very specific way: they are to be read as what I will call national allegories, even when, or I should say particularly when, their forms develop out of predominantly western machineries of representation, such as the novel" (Jameson 1986: 67). He goes on to say: "Third world texts, even those which are seemingly private and invested with a properly libidinal dynamic, necessarily project a political dimension in the form of national allegory: the story of the private individual destiny is always an allegory of the embattled situation of the public third-world culture and society" (ibid: 67).[3] Ahmad disputes Jameson's tendency to judge literature against an over-determined binary world-view. He argues that "the ideolog-

---

3 | An allegory is "a Symbolic narrative" in which the major features of the movement of the narrative are all held to refer symbolically to some action or situation. Allegory has long been a prominent feature of literary and mythic writing throughout the world, but it becomes particularly significant for post-colonial writers for the way in which it disrupts notions of orthodox history, classical realism and imperial representation in general. Allegory has assumed an important function in imperial discourse, in which paintings and statues have often been created as allegories of imperial power. Consequently, one form of post-colonial response to this has been to appropriate allegory and use it to respond to the allegorical representation of imperial dominance. (Ashcroft at el. 1998: 9)

ical conditions of a text's production are never singular but always several [...] there are more and more texts which cannot easily be placed within this or that world" (Ahmad 1992: 122), for this reason, Jameson's ambition to construct a "cognitive aesthetics" for Third World literature can only be an impossible mission (ibid: 123). While stereotyping Third World literature, Jameson is actually attempting to suppress the prevailing existence of differences, and maintains a binary division comprised of the First and Third Worlds. There exists, therefore, a totalizing and universalizing tendency in Jameson's argument. Stephen Slemon suggests that what is really wrong with Jameson's argument is that he takes a Eurocentric literary notion of allegory and applies it to colonized societies. Since allegory has always been a dominant mode of colonial representation, as Slemon argues, we can see allegory as "a function of the conditions of post-coloniality" (qtd. in Ashcroft et el. 1998: 9), which may function as forms of counter-discourse. A deep analysis of the argument between them lies beyond the scope of this book, yet the idea that informs our discussion is that we should not read Naipaul's works simply as a betrayal of the Third World nationalism and decolonization movement, nor should we think that since he comes out of the Third World, his depiction of those places must necessarily be true to fact. Following Ahmad's argument that we cannot homogenize Third World literature as "national allegories", we should not homogenize postcolonial literature and condemn Naipaul's work only because he presents a picture different from that of nationalist writers. Neither the Euro-centric nor the nation-centric point of view is appropriate to the reading of Naipaul's work.

Naipaul is becoming a hot topic in China as well, especially upon winning the Nobel Prize for Literature in 2001. By the end of 2013, 14 of his novels (*The Mystic Masseur, The Suffrage of Elvira, Miguel Street, A House for Mr. Biswas, Mr. Stone and the Knights Companion, A Bend in the River, Magic Seeds, The Mystic Masseur, A Flag on the Island, In a Free State, Guerrillas, The Enigma of Arrival, Half a Life, and Magic Seeds*), his Indian trilogy (*An Area of Darkness, India: A Wounded Civilization* and *India: A Million Mutinies Now*), and a collection of letters between Naipaul and his father during his days at Oxford (*The Letters Between Father and Son*) have been translated into Chinese and published. Chinese scholars are showing increasing interest in Naipaul's work. In mainland China, dozens of doctoral dissertations have been devoted to the study of Naipaul, focusing respectively on the postcolonial, political, cultural, and spatial dimension of his writing. More than 100 academic literary reviews have been written about his work. Among Chinese critics, the division between those in favor or against Naipaul's writing is not as obvious as in international circles, but there also exist two voices: Naipaul as a truthful spokesman of the postcolonial predicament, and Naipaul as a racist and traitor to the postcolonial nationalist and decolonization movement.

Setting aside the more complicated motivations behind the disputes surrounding Naipaul, which, I am sure, are plentiful, diverse and may lead to quite a different kind of study, the key element, in my view, that initiates such debates is the issue of Naipaul's complex identity. In defense of the accusation that Naipaul has been Anglicized, especially after publishing *The Enigma of Arrival*, Brent Staples writes:

> Few writers of V.S. Naipaul's stature have been so consistently and aggressively misread on account of ethnic and racial literary politics. Much of the criticism stems not from what Mr. Naipaul writes but from expectations about what he *ought* (emphasis original) to write, given that he is a brown man (of Indian descent) born into the brown and black society that is Trinidad. Alas, after a 40-year-voyage as a writer, Mr. Naipaul has arrived at a time when his work is too often viewed through the filter of race. This would seem an impoverished way of seeing in any case. In V.S. Naipaul's case, a strictly racial reading amounts to no reading at all. (Staples 1994: 1)

I think the reason Naipaul's works tend to be read through the "filter of race" is due to a misreading of his complex identity. Unfortunately, the problem of Naipaul's identity/ties has not been studied in any depth. A comprehensive study of Naipaul's identity based on a close reading of his works is therefore necessary to better understand both his writing and him as a person. At the same time, as a Brahmin-cum-Englishman in Trinidad, a European in India, an Indian in London, Naipaul is a typical legacy of colonialism, a product of multiculturalism, a postcolonial subject and a blend of Eastern and Western philosophy. His view of the world and experiences in life have shaped the vision of his work, and a study of his identity with regard to his own writing would probably shed new light to our understanding of the question of identity, especially that of the postcolonial subject.

PROBLEMATIZING IDENTITY

Identity is important because it gives us a place in the world. It gives us an idea of who we are, and functions as a link between us and the world. Identity marks our way in the world, and provides a way of understanding the interplay between our subjective experience of the world and the cultural and historical construction of our subjectivity. What is identity then? According to *The New Key Words: A Revised Vocabulary of Culture & Society*, identity has "to do with the imagined sameness of a person or of a social group at all times and in all circumstances; about a person or a group being, and being able to continue to be itself and not someone or something else" (Bennett et al. 2005: 172). In other words, our identity marks the ways in which we are the same as those who share that designation, and the ways in which we are different from those who do not because it is usually defined by what it is not, and frequently constructed in terms of oppositions such as woman/man, black/white, culture/nature, self/other etc. (Woodward 1997: 2). As Hall puts it, "Identity is a structured representation which only achieves its positive through the narrow eye of the negative. It has to go through the eye of the needle of the other before it can construct itself" (Hall 1990: 21). Therefore, identity is "an unstable effect of relations which define identities by marking differences" (Hall 1996: 89). In recent years, there has been a "veritable discursive explosion" (ibid: 1) around the concept of identity. As such, it has become a word "in common currency" (Woodward 1997: 1). The concept of identity is now subject to a searching critique because most contemporary discourses are critical of an "integral, originary and unified identity" (Hall 1996: 1).

The OED says that the 17th century was the first time that the concept of identity was used with respect to the individual. What Stuart Hall calls the "Enlightenment subject" based on "the conception of the human person as a fully centered, unified individual, endowed with the capacities of reason, consciousness and action" came into existence at this time. During this period, the essential center of the self was a person's identity (Hall 1992: 275). What Hall describes is individual identity, although there exists another dimension, a collective identity that concerns particular ways of imagining and instituting social groups and group belonging. With collective identity, as well as with individual identity, the principles of unity and continuity are at the fore. "The logic of identity has worked in favor of integrity and coherence with reference to what came to be figured as the collective self" (Bennett et al. 2005: 173). When the community is conceived of as a unitary and homogeneous entity with a shared substance, the internal diversity and the complexity of the group is disclaimed. Meanwhile, to solidify the unity of the group, it resorts to its heritage, memories, value systems and particular uniqueness and thus, as a consequence, historical change and discontinuity is denied. The "imagined community" (Benedict Anderson 1983) of the nation state is the most typical of this kind of collective identity. In the framework of this "imagined community", the question of identity has been restricted to the dimension of belonging. "Belonging to such a community—a culture in common—has been regarded as the fundamental condition for self-expression and self-fulfillment" (Bennett et al. 2005: 173). Taking advantage of a person's need for a sense of belonging and self-fulfillment, politicians have tried to essentialize this kind of collective national or ethnic identity, fascism being the most tragic example in human history. This idea of collective identity banishes or erases differences, and it motivates people towards "processes of interconnection in which individuality is renounced or dissolved into the larger whole represented by a nation, a people or ethnic group" (Woodward 1997: 304).

The question of identity—both individual and collective—has become increasingly salient as a consequence of migration, displacement and the social and cultural transformations associated with globalization. There thus emerges a proliferation of pertinent theories, all attempting to decipher this reality. According to Hall, there are three possible consequences to globalization with regard to identity. First, globalization contests the settled contours of national identity and exposes it to the pressures of difference, "otherness", and cultural diversity. Second, globalization strengthens local identities, which are seen in the defensive reaction of those members of dominant ethnic groups who feel threatened by the presence of other cultures. And thirdly, it may also lead to the production of new identities. Globalization, therefore, contests and dislocates centered and "closed" identities. Its impact on identity is pluralizing, producing a variety of possibilities and new positions of identification, and making identities more positional, political, plural, and diverse (Hall 1992: 304-309).

In face of the decolonization movement and globalization, Hall observes that a new kind of postmodern subject and identity is now emerging. Hall argues that "the subject assumes different identities at different times, identities which are not unified around a coherent 'self.' Within us are contradictory identities, pulling in different directions, so that our identifications are continuously being shifted about" (ibid: 277). Besides the postmodern subject, according to Hall, there exist two other concepts of identity: the Enlightenment subject and the sociological subject. The Enlightenment subject is based on the concept that people are fully centered, unified individuals, endowed with the capacities of reason, consciousness and action. This subject remains essentially the same throughout an individual's experience. The sociological subject has been formed in relation to "significant others", those who mediate the values, meanings, and symbols—the culture—of the worlds he inhabits. The notion of sociological subject does not believe in an autonomous and self-sufficient subjectivity. Identity, in the sociological conception, sutures the subject into a structure, bridging the gap between the personal and public worlds (ibid: 275-277).

Scott Lash and Jonathan Friedman periodize identity into pre-modern identity, modern identity and post-modern identity. Pre-modern identity can be understood as externally determined, and is defined by kinship-ordered cosmologies. And in the archaic civilizations of world religions, the nominating powers emerge as a transcendental godhead, a pantheon or a hierarchy of deities. In modern times, with the demise of God, social space opens up the way for an autonomous definition of identity. Modernist identity recognizes two temporal elements: first, responsibility in modern times means responsibility for the consequences of one's actions, a more and more difficult task in an increasingly complex society; second, identity has to do with the temporality of our existence. Modernist identity "privileges the cognitive and moral over the aesthetic and the libidinal, the ego over the id, the visual over touch, and discursive over figural communication. It gives primacy to culture over nature, to the individual over the community" (Lash and Friedman 1992: 5). The individual is "closed" instead of open, obsessed with self-mastery and self-domination. Two stances on post-modern identity are proposed by Lash and Friedman. The pessimistic outlook holds that postmodern landscapes function as mechanisms of social control and effectively constitute identities to function in the reproduction of transnational postindustrial capital. These landscapes take on the status of signifiers, of sign-values functioning in the reproduction of capital. "Responsibility for social control—and its definition and normalization of identities—has passed on such an account from the modern norms of Foucault's social to the postmodern simulacra in Baudrillard's astral empire of signs" (ibid: 7). The optimistic rendering of post-modern identity is aware of the identity choice since identity formation is freed from the sphere of production of consumption and leisure in the transition to postmodernism. Individuals can therefore consciously experiment with identity (Lash and Friedman 1992: 8). Postcolonial critics like Hall and Bhabha seem to view postmodern identity from an optimistic perspective, and stress its capacity to produce new identities. With Hall, globalization is more likely to produce new "global" and new "local" identifications. Yet Hall also points out that the proliferation of identity choices is more extensive at the "centre" of the global system than at its peripheries (Hall 1992: 304-305).

Discourses on identity can be roughly categorized as essentialist and anti-essentialist. The debate between the social constructionists and the essentialists goes back to the argument between the Sophists and Plato. Following Plato's argument, essentialist, reductionist rationality reigned until recently, when the postmodern turn reintroduced a different kind of logic based on the acknowledgement that things are local, inherently temporary, mutable, multiple, fragmented, and indeterminate. According to the essentialist view, identity is ascribed, natural, and fixed. Essentialists believe that one's identity is the expression of some inner essence or property. The essentialist view is based on a belief that there is a sense of selfhood through which we can measure ourselves against the hectic upsets, discontinuities, and ruptures of history. Related to this understanding, lies the comforting idea that "around us history is constantly breaking in unpredictable ways but we, somehow, go on being the same" (Hall 1997: 42-43). Anti-essentialist discourse, however, emphasizes the socially constructed status of all identities. For the anti-essentialists, identities are not self-sufficient but socially and historically constructed. Therefore, identities are subject to continuous change and reconfiguration, and they are "in fact instituted through the play of differences, constituted in and through their multiple relations to other identities" (Bennett et al. 2005: 173). The essentialist view is now being replaced by the anti-essentialist premise that identity is constructed and historical.

In addition, some scholars also think that instead of preserving the binary division between the essentialist and the anti-essentialist, we should uphold a dialectic viewpoint toward identity. With these scholars, identity is a matter of "being as well as of becoming" (Hall 1990: 223). Taking Spivak as an example, she employs the term "strategic essentialism", suggesting a "strategic use of positivist essentialism in a scrupulously visible political interest" (Landry and Maclean 1996: 214). Similarly, to mediate the paradox of the relationship between essentialism and anti-essentialism, Satya P. Mohanty posits the "post-positivist realist" approach to identity, claiming that identities can be both real and constructed, both politically and epistemologically significant on the one hand, and variable, nonessential, and radically historical, on the other (qtd. in Moya and Hames-García 2000: 29-43).

Indeed, the question of identity has been at the fore of British cultural studies since the 1960's. The continuing migrations of labor since the post-war period also served to accelerate the decline of the concept of Englishness. Following the two world wars, more and more ex-colonials immigrated to England, making the concept of Englishness no longer unquestionably clear and transparent. For centuries, white identities in Britain have been rooted in a sense of superiority derived from the power exercised over "racialised others" (Hall 2000). Yet Britain no longer has an empire and has now become, in a very particular sense of the term, a post-colonial nation. Decolonization in the former colonies brought many colonials back to England: "When finally Britain conceived itself it had to decolonize, it had to get rid of them, we [people] from ex-colonies all came back home" (Hall 1997: 24). This home is not just England. Immigrants tend to seek the very center of England—London—as the home they are after. V.S. Naipaul's very presence in London is a reflection of this phenomenon.

Paul Gilroy outlines three important themes that underpin the theoretical development in British cultural studies' engagement with identity. The first is identity as subjectivity. Religious and spiritual obligations once defined subjectivity. Yet, there has been a loss of internal moral and spiritual certainty governing social interaction with the move from a religious to secular society. Digital technologies have now produced a "culture of simulation", which has brought about fundamental shifts in our experience of what constitutes individual identity. Then there is the idea of "sameness". Recognition of one's similarity to and difference from others drives us to think about collective or communal identity instead of the formation of the individual subject's identity. If the first approach is subject-centered, the second concerns the inter-subjective dynamic. Differences appear within the self because it is no longer a unitary entity but changes constantly in its interactions with others. The third theme is "solidarity", where connectedness and difference form the foundation for social actions to be produced (Woodward 1997: 313-318). Politically enabling, the focus of the third theme is on the "social structures which both limit and produce specific identities within specific historic conjunctures" (Turner 2003: 216).

Originally from Jamaica, Stuart Hall first went to England in the 1950s. His experience is similar to that of Naipaul, and his cultural theory on identity is especially informative to our understanding of Naipaul's identity. When Hall first went to London, he thought he was going *home*, only to find that he was but an immigrant—the same feeling experienced by Naipaul and his protagonist in *The Mimic Men* and *The Enigma of Arrival*. While in Jamaica, Hall said he had never heard the word "black" because everybody was more or less black. It was only in the wake of the Civil Rights movement, the wake of de-colonization and the nationalistic struggles of the 1970s, that he began to hear the word "black" used (Hall 1997: 54-55). Inspired by his own experiences, Hall broaches that identity is not something pre-ascribed, waiting for us to discover, rather, it is identification we have to learn to see when we measure ourselves against others (Hall 1996: 4). Like Hall, Naipaul's awareness of identity undergoes a similar journey. He went to study at Oxford in 1950, the period right after World War II, and observed "the beginning of a great movement of peoples after the war, a great shaking up of the world, a great shaking up of old cultures and ideas" (EA 1988: 159). Those people were driven by a "restlessness and the need for a new idea of self" (ibid: 159).

Hall argues that on account of the five ruptures in the discourse of modern knowledge, the concept and nature of identity is shifted from the Enlightenment concept of identity to a modern "de-centered" and "dislocated" identity (Hall 1992: 274-275). The five ruptures are as follows.

First of all, Marxism denies the universal essence of man, and contends that man cannot act without the historical conditions created by others. He is able to use only the resources provided to him by previous generations. Marx denies that there is a "single" and "real" subject because, for him, man exists in social relations, defined as modes of production, the exploitation of labor power, and the circuit of capital (ibid: 286). Marxist theory holds that the role of the material, and the relations of production and of collective action, especially class solidarity, are very important in forming social identities. Later developments within Marxism, represented for example by Althusser's work, have given more emphasis to symbolic systems rather than material factors. For Althusser, the symbolic system, or ideology, to put it differently, interpellates the individual into the subject position unconsciously.

The second rupture in the development of modern discourse, according to Hall, happens in the field of psychoanalysis concerning the function of the unconscious. With Freud, identity is formed through the unconscious when a child looks at the "other". The child enters the system of symbolic representation, such as language, culture and sexual difference at a given moment. Based on this concept, Lacan posits that entering of symbolic representation is the beginning of a split subject in that by entering into the symbolic system, the child encounters contradictory and unresolved feelings, such as the splitting of love and hate for the father. These contradictory feelings will remain with a person for life and leave him divided. As such, identity is not something born with us, but an ongoing process developed unconsciously. It "arises not so much from the fullness of identity which is already inside us as individuals, but from a *lack* of wholeness which is 'filled' from *outside us*, by the ways we imagine ourselves to be by others" (ibid: 287).

Thirdly, Ferdinand de Saussure's structuralist thinking claims that we are not absolute "authors" of what we say because language pre-dates us. We can only use language to produce meanings by positioning ourselves within the rules of language and the systems of meaning of our culture. By using language, we enter a symbolic system. The meanings of words are not fixed in a one-to-one relation to objects or events in the world outside language, but are instead decided by the differences and connections between signs. Hall's reading of Saussure seeks to help us notice the analogy between language and identity. According to Hall, "I know who 'I' am in relation to 'the other' (e.g. my mother) whom I cannot be" (ibid: 288). Influenced by Saussure and the "linguistic turn", many modern philosophers believe "despite his/her best efforts the individual speaker can never finally fix meaning—including the meaning of his or her identity" (ibid: 288).

Michel Foucault's concept of "disciplinary power" articulates the formation of the subject by showing that a person, along with his moral and physical health, his sexual practices, and family life, is placed under strict discipline and control by the governing power. Its basic objective is to produce "a human being who can be treated as a docile body" (ibid: 289). Where there is power there is resistance. And there is likewise resistance on the part of the disciplined. The more collective and organized the institutions of the "late-modern", the greater the isolation and individuation of the subject. This is the fourth rupture.

The fifth rupture concerns feminism, which, along with other social movements, paves the ways for identity politics. In the language of feminism, gender identity is not given but constructed through ambivalence. Feminism challenges the notion that men and women were part of the same identity—"mankind"—replacing it with the question of sexual difference (ibid: 290).

These ruptures reflect the increasing complexity of the modern world. Through them, we become aware that the subject in itself is no longer autonomous and self-sufficient. In *Who Needs Identity*, Hall further explores this idea and posits that "it is only through the relation to the Other, the relation to what is not, to precisely what it lacks, to what has been called its *constitutive outside* that the 'positive' meaning of any term—and thus its 'identity'—can be constructed" (Hall 1996: 4-5). Hall also claims that cultural identity is both a matter of "being" and "becoming" (Hall 1990: 223) and it belongs to the future as well as to the past because it has histories and is subject to constant transformation.

To understand cultural identity, Hall suggests we should approach it from two perspectives. First, we can understand it through our collective and shared cultural background, derived from a shared history and ancestry that provide us with "stable, unchanging and continuous frames of reference and meaning" (Hall 1990: 223). The other way of defining cultural identity is to realize that apart from a common heritage, there exist significant differences. These constitute what we are and what we have become. Cultural identity in this second sense is a matter of both "becoming" and "being", for it "belongs to the future as much as to the past" (ibid: 224).

According to Hall, it is only through the second perspective that we can understand the "traumatic character of the colonial experience" (ibid: 224). The dominant power of the imperial regimes positions the colonial to see himself as an "other". This "otherness" is inscribed in the colonial by the colonial discourse. According to Bhabha, the identification of the colonial is neither that of the colonist "self" nor the colonized "other", but "the disturbing distance in-between that constitutes the figure of colonial otherness (Bhabha 1994: 45). It is in this "third space" of in between that the colonial constructs his identity. For colonials, the place of identification is a "space of splitting" (ibid: 45). They become neither the colonialist "self" nor the colonized "other", which seems an impossible object, yet "It is in relation to this impossible object that the liminal problem of colonial identity and its vicissitudes emerges" (ibid: 45). Meanwhile, "the question of identification is never the affirmation of a pre-given identity, never a self-fulfilling prophecy—it is always the production of an image of identity and the transformation of the subject in assuming that image" (ibid: 45). Identification, as is suggested here, involves transformation of the subject.

Thus the issue of identity is naturally more complicated for the colonial. The moment he desires the identity of the colonizer, the splitting begins because while he transforms himself in order to claim the image of identity he produces for himself, the displacement of the self happens simultaneously. The traveling of this self between the original place and the place it longs to occupy will produce what Bhabha calls a "hybrid" identity. The difference between Bhabha's hybrid identity and Fanon's colonials with black skin and white masks is that the hybrid identity is a breaking of the binary division of people into white and black. It is more optimistic, and can become a subversive political strategy for the colonial. The trajectory of this identification begins with the negation of the original identity, and undergoes a stage of mimicry before it acquires a hybrid identity. In mimicry, if the untranslatable chunk were to remain, it in turn would lead to the hybrid form of identity. The very notion of hybridity breeds a vernacular cosmopolitanism, for as Hall argues, globalization, instead of obliterating localism, more than ever encourages the flourishing of difference.

The reader should beware that important as the theory of identity is to the study of Naipaul's novels, it will not be used in this book as a theoretically privileged approach, nor a better alternative, but instead as a means of exploring Naipaul's identification more comprehensively. It is hoped that this exploration, tentative rather than dogmatic, will help reveal the route of postcolonial subjects' identification.

***

Literature has always been concerned with questions about identity, and literary works sketch answers, implicitly or explicitly, to these questions. According to Jonathan Culler, the theoretical treatment of identity may seem reductive in comparison with the subtle explorations done in novels, which are able to finesse the problem of general claims by presenting singular cases while relying on a generalizing force that is left implicit (Culler 1997: 108). Naipaul's fictions can therefore make a very concrete example for the construction of identity of the postcolonial subjects, just as *The Empire Writes Back* demonstrates:

Naipaul's position is a deeply ambiguous one in that his writing does not always carry the conviction of [a coherent] perception. The result is a curious ambivalence when the novel considers the authenticity of the margins. Yet such an ambivalence is by no means disabling, for it provides the tension out of which emerges a rich and incisive reconstruction of post-colonial experience. (Ashcroft et al. 1997: 91)

Salient in this "rich and incisive reconstruction of post-colonial experience" is Naipaul and his characters' efforts at identity construction. The ambivalent position from which Naipaul projects his writing is an important element for the reading of Naipaul's work because of the identity perplexity this position causes. This study of Naipaul's writing is therefore limited to how Naipaul and his characters find their way in the world. It is my contention that Naipaul's identification trajectory runs parallel to his writing career because writing is the only means Naipaul has used to learn about the world and himself. Through the study of identification in Naipaul's characters, it may be possible to see how Naipaul, a typical postcolonial subject, orients himself in a rapidly changing world. Another reason to approach Naipaul from the perspective of identity is that this problem looms large in current identity politics. In addition, as the accelerated force of migration and globalization make the sense of rootlessness and perplexity of identity a universal issue, the study of identity of a writer with a typical colonial history background, displaced from his ethnic culture and home country under the guide of globalization, will not only be meaningful and valuable to a better understanding of the writer and his work, but may offer a new exploratory space for cultural identity.

This book attempts to explore Naipaul's major novels along this line of reasoning, because for Naipaul, as well as for his protagonists, identity is a problem they must face and make choices about. My study will be based on a close reading of Naipaul's major fictions from his early, middle, and late periods: *A House for Mr. Biswas*, *The Mimic Men*, *The Enigma of Arrival* and *A Way in the World*. I choose these four novels because I observe in them the common manifestations of how a postcolonial subject constructs his identity. Written early in Naipaul's career, *A House for Mr. Biswas* is the author's first work dealing explicitly with a colonial man's search for independent identity in a colonial society. The house on Sikkim Street that Mr. Biswas finally purchased embodies a paradox by which "achievement and failure are aspects of a single experience typical of a world which is shot through with contradictions" (White 1975: 98). The evolution of Naipaul's oeuvre shows the movement outward from the West Indian settings of his early work in the metropolis, to his ancestral India, and finally to the rest of the postcolonial world. After *A House for Mr. Biswas*, Naipaul wrote two travelogues, *The Middle Passage* and *An Area of Darkness*, the first about the bleak reality of West Indian society, and the second about India. While traveling in India, Naipaul wrote of an English character in an English setting, *Mr. Stone and the Knights Companion*. The novel is about the English man's futile attempt to change the pattern of events, and assert the individual's importance. Disappointment with both colonial society and the metropolis finds its expression in *The Mimic Men*, in which the protagonist travels between his colonial island and London to assert an independent identity. An important factor of mimicry in the identification of the colonial is elaborated in the novel. In 1987, after much traveling and writing, Naipaul published his autobiographical work, *The Enigma of Arrival*, in which he reflects on his own life in England, and the journey many years prior that took him to London from Trinidad. Intended as a summary of Naipaul's life and writing, the book offers much to help us understand how Naipaul constructs his identity as a postcolonial subject, thus necessitating a detailed study. In *A Way in the World*, Naipaul's vision becomes even broader. Ruminating on how colonial history is written, and on how historical figures assert their independent identities, Naipaul finally achieves a diasporic vision of identity against a global background. The works selected for discussion are those that best exemplify the process of a postcolonial subject's journey of identification. In this way, I hope to map Naipaul's path in the world—how he negotiates and translates his political and cultural identities through a journey that runs parallel to his literary career.

It is true that in addition to novels, Naipaul has also produced a large number of very valuable travel writings and reportages. I choose to base my study mainly on his novels motivated by Naipaul's own conception of fiction: "An autobiography can distort; facts can be realigned. But fiction never lies: it reveals the writer totally" (REP 1981: 6). During an interview, Naipaul once said that he regarded novel writing as engaging a truer part of himself (Wheeler 1977: 537). Also, as Naipaul says in *Among the Believers*, "people can hide behind direct statements; fiction, by its seeming indirections, can make hidden impulses clear" (AB 1985: 47). Recalling the years when he worked on *A House for Mr. Biswas*, he ruminates on the process of writing and believes the "novel called up its own truth" (HB 1983: 22). For him, the "wonder" of fiction lies in "the unsuspected truths turned up by the imagination" (ibid: 22).

I chose to approach Naipaul's identity in a chronological reading of his novels instead of by categorizing elements affecting his identity's formation, i.e., the act of writing, his understanding of history, the influence of Hinduism, etc., because, to use Hall's words, "identities are (that) which discursive practices construct for us. [...] They arise from the narrativization of the self" (Hall 1996: 4-6). A chronological reading facilitates a sharper view of "points of temporary attachment to the subject positions" (ibid: 5). In addition, this approach may help clarify the path Naipaul has lived. The novels I chose are intended to represent the key moments that led to Naipaul's identification. The spectrum of these moments reflected in fiction should provide a more vivid image of Naipaul along the way, as well as a better grasp of how his identification changed and developed during different periods of his life. At the same time, based on a general understanding of identity formation as a process, and taking into account the fact that Naipaul is a living writer, the chronology of his identification can only be left open to interpretation.

I agree with Dagmar Barnouw's claims that critical readings of Naipaul's work have generally been divided into two groups: a strongly focused postcolonial critique of his indebtedness to Western cultural values that does not address textual complexity, and literary studies of his fictional and non-fictional texts that do not address representational complexity, i.e. the texts' connectedness to social and political realities (Barnouw 2003: 1). By locating the present study in a socio-cultural context, this book mainly adopts an eclectic approach to V. S. Naipaul based on a close reading of his novels in combination with his travel writings when necessary.

This book consists of four chapters as well as an introduction and a conclusion.

Chapter one applies Lacan's theory to the study of *A House for Mr. Biswas*. The premise of the novel is that the main character, Mr. Biswas is doubly marginalized in colonial society because he was born into a symbolic system that is alien to his cultural heritage. Independent identity, as such, can only be a fantasy for him. The jerry-built house he finally acquires is an all-encompassing symbol of his struggle, as well as of the compromise he makes with his social and historical contexts. It is a departure from the postcolonial subject's route of identification, rather than a symbol of the realization of an independent identity.

Chapter two discusses mimicry in *The Mimic Men* as a means to the colonial's identification. Feeling shipwrecked in his colonial homeland, Singh goes in search of his identity in London as expected by colonial discourse. Mimicking the colonizers, however, does not prove fruitful in his quest for identity. In contrast to Bhabha, Naipaul is critical, satirizing colonial mimicry. He does not believe that it is the way out of the colonial's identity crisis.

Modern theories of autobiography view it as a process through which the author attempts to construct one or several identities. Chapter three examines Naipaul's heavily autobiographical work *The Enigma of Arrival,* and demonstrates how, through the process of writing

Naipaul, deconstructs the notion of Englishness, reconciles with his homeland, and establish for himself a positive hybrid identity.

Chapter four is a detailed examination of *A Way in the World*. In this book, Naipaul deconstructs the accepted history of the colonial, as written from a Euro-centric perspective, and rewrites it as a means to de-re-constructing the colonial's identity. For Naipaul, then, history becomes a steppingstone beyond the land of one's birth, beyond ethnicity and nationalities, in an attempt to reach for spiritual and intellectual development, and to start afresh by embracing a diasporic identification that privileges "route" over "root".

The concluding remarks briefly summarize the route of the postcolonial subject's identification and presents an analysis of the three factors affecting Naipaul's identification: colonialism, his notion of history, and the course of his writing career. The final conclusion is that writing for Naipaul serves both as mimicry and revolution in the quest to assert his identity. This book also exemplifies how reading literature may provide a method to better understand world reality, whether directly or indirectly.

Chapter One An Exile at Home
A House for Mr. Biswas

> The exile is a universal figure. The proximity of our lives to the major issues of our time has demanded of us all some kind of involvement. [...] We are made to feel a sense of exile by our inadequacy and our irrelevance of function in a society whose past we can't alter, and whose future is always beyond us. Idleness can easily guide us into accepting this as a condition. Sooner or later, in silence or with rhetoric, we sign a contract whose epitaph reads: To be an Exile is to be alive. (Ashcroft et al. 1998: 12)

Inadequacy and irrelevance of function in a society bring about a sense of exile. This is especially true of colonial people when they are deprived of the opportunity to assert their subjectivity and identity as a consequence of having no knowledge of their past and no say in their society. Yet, their desire for independent identity is not easily daunted despite not always being able to enjoy the fragrant taste of the fruit of their struggle. Published the year of Trinidad's independence from Britain (1961), *A House for Mr. Biswas* describes the long process through which Muhun Biswas attempts to construct an independent identity, an identity that comes in the form of "a house that is at once a literal and ramshackle physical structure and the grandest of metaphors" (Gorra 2004: 372). Unlike Naipaul's earlier stories,[1] the unifying factor in *A House for Mr. Biswas* is of a single integrating metaphor: a house. Reflecting on the writing in this novel, Naipaul says that it is the "story of a man's search for a house and all that the possession of one's own house implies" (FC 1985: 22).

While it is an imaginative and fictional recreation of Naipaul's childhood, the protagonist of the novel is based on Seepersad Naipaul, V. S. Naipaul's father, who introduced him to the garden of literature,[2] and encouraged him to be devoted to the art of writing.

---

1 | *A House for Mr. Biswas* is the fourth book of Naipaul and the one that establishes his fame as a writer. It is still unarguably one of the best works by Naipaul and one of the best in contemporary English literature. His earliest written yet the third to be published book is *Miguel Street*, a collection of short stories told by a boy about the life in the Port of Spain, in which each character has an eccentricity that raises him out of the rut of ghetto life and imparts to him a stylized and special identity. The first published work of Naipaul, *The Mystic Masseur*, is united around a central thesis of how Ganesh rises to fame. Ganesh represents the meeting place of the old East Indian world and the new, Euro-American world, combining the spiritualism of the former and the materialism of the latter. *The Suffrage of Elvira*, the third book written by Naipaul, is a tightly-knit story about the mixed-up equation of money-mindedness, profit, and enfranchisement in a predominately East Indian community.

2 | During his childhood, Naipaul read his father's early articles as "memorials of a heroic time I had missed." (FC 1985: 25) His father read to him "Charles Kingsley's story of Perseus, chapters from Dickens's novels, stories by O'Henry, and, when he was only ten, Joseph Conrad's "The Lagoon." In an essay on Conrad written in 1974, Naipaul records his lasting response to the atmosphere "of night and solitude and doom" and his later feeling for the Conradian "passion, the abyss, solitude and futility and the world of illusions" that his brief story creates (REP 1981: 224). In addition, while working as a reporter for *Trinidad Guardian*, Seepersad also began to write fictions to relieve himself from anger and depression. Naipaul was asked to engage in the process. By listening to these stories as they were created in

In his early days at Oxford, when young Naipaul was dismayed at the hardships he needed to overcome to write, his father encouraged him by saying: "Don't be scared of being an artist. D.H. Lawrence was an artist through and through; and, for the time being at any rate, you should think as Lawrence" (LBFS 1998: 23). From time to time, Naipaul talks about his father: "My father was extremely important to me in my childhood: nearly everything that I am is because of this great link I felt with him, and a lot of my work—especially my early work—I meant to be dedicated to him" (Bingham 1972: 306). *A House for Mr. Biswas* is, without a doubt, a son's eulogy to his father, not only for contouring his father's life, but also by the very composition of the story. In *A House for Mr. Biswas*, Naipaul draws on memories of the world he left behind, as well as his father's stories. For Naipaul, this is his "father's book. [...] written out of his journalism and stories, out of [...] knowledge he had got from the way of looking (that) Macgowan [former managing editor at the *Trinidad Guardian*] had trained him in. It was written out of his writing" (FC 1985: 60).

From Mr. Biswas's life story, we get a clear picture of the difficulties experienced in Naipaul's early life, and his frustration with writing. According to Naipaul, the victory of *A House for Mr Biswas* is due to its subtle representation of "the fear of destitution", from "a vision of the abyss [...] that lies below the comedy of this book" (Naipaul 1983:22). Repeatedly, over decades, Naipaul refers to the disadvantages of growing up in the colonial society of Trinidad, which he said he was born into by accident and could not feel as his own. In response to his father's wish for him to return to Trinidad after graduating from Oxford, he wrote, "I know and can understand your wish for me to settle in Trinidad. But let me explain why, if I did so, I shall die from intellectual starvation" (LBFS 1998: 35). He describes his experience in Trinidad as living in an "eclipsed" world, caught between "two spheres of darkness that had become my subject" (Jus-

---

version and giving advice when asked, Naipaul got his first taste of writing and learned a great deal about the craft.

sawalla 1997: 78).³ Therefore, what lies beneath the "comedy of the book", which actually constitutes the drive of the novel, is the son's fear of what would have happened to him had he not managed to leave.

Mr. Biswas's unfinished story *Escape* signifies not only his desire to escape from the stifling colonial society that deprives him of subjectivity, and from the trap of a loveless, unhappy marriage, but also of Naipaul's own angst that this same fate might well have befallen him. This book is, therefore, a justification for Naipaul's "escape" from Trinidad, as well as a symbol of Mr. Biswas's struggles for a house of his own, an objective correlative which symbolizes a displaced and disoriented colonial's quest for independence, identity, freedom, inner wholeness, order, and the dignity of an individual. However, as we will see in a moment, this beautiful and alluring dream of owning a house, after so much painstaking and heartbreaking effort, can only be partially realized, if at all, just as signified by Mr. Biswas's cracked, mortgaged house on Sikkim Street.

Based loosely on his father's life story, this book is about the "little man" Mr. Biswas, a tragicomic hero who "achieves through his undaunted quest for independence, a victory for the human spirit" (Nightingale 1987: 44). At the same time, Mr. Biswas's ambition to have a house of his own has been read as "a metaphor of the quest for identity of the colonial individual" (Hawle 2001: 305). Similarly, Mr. Biswas becomes a symbol of the colonial society struggling toward independence and freedom (Nightingale 1987: 53), and his life a success story of immigrant life and New World assimilation (King 1993: 47). Furthermore, as Naipaul's first novel to reach beyond Trinidad, this work is thought to address universal human problems, and is "open to all those whose identity is at odds with their society, who understand homelessness and the threat of disorder, and who are ready to sympathize with struggle and failure and triumph" (White 1975: 126).

---

3 | See also *Conversations*, 75-92; *Letters Between A Father and Son*, 1953, Oct., 8; *Sir Vidia's Shadow*, 326; *Reading and Writing*, 34.

Most readings of *A House for Mr. Biswas* focus on the concept of a displaced immigrant, a colonial's "successful" attempt at asserting an individual identity. In contrast, I draw on Lacan's theory of the development of the human subject, and explore the complex and ambiguous essence of Mr. Biswas's struggle, and the author's ambivalence toward it, hoping to reveal the paradox embedded in the very notion of individual identity for a displaced colonial caught between tradition and reality.

A Life Out of Place

Homi Bhabha says in an article that Naipaul's "infantile yearning to be a writer emerged from the anxiety and shame of profound cultural loss" (Bhabha 2001: 11). Indeed, as an East Indian born in the West Indians, the beginning of Naipaul's life is marked by a profound sense of lack—a lack of a cultural heritage he can claim and anchor his identity to. Similarly, Mr. Biswas's beginnings in the world are characterized by one loss after another.

At the beginning of the novel, shortly before he is born, Mr. Biswas's mother Bipti walks in the hot sun, all the way to his grandmother's village because of a quarrel with his father Raghu. At midnight that evening, he is born at his grandmother's house, six-fingered and breech. An inauspicious birth by all accounts. Significantly, he is born away from his father's house and in the darkness of night. Mr. Biswas's horoscope seems to be against him from the beginning. His enchantment with the stream fulfills the pundit's prophecy and leads to his father's death. After fulfilling all the prophecies of the astrological almanac about how he might "eat up his own mother and father" (HB 1984: 16), with his mother's parents dead, his father dead, his brothers on the estate at Felicity, his sister Dehuti as a servant in his aunt Tara's house, and himself rapidly growing away from his mother, who herself is broken, Mr. Biswas has to leave "the only house to which he had some right" at the age of six (ibid: 40). The "pastoral" period of Mr. Biswas's childhood comes to an end. If, as Naipaul's title for the first chapter indicates, the early setting is "pastoral", it is "pastoral" only in the sense that the setting is rural, and that Mr. Biswas enjoys some right to his father's hut made of mud and grass. It is actually "pastoral" lost for Mr. Biswas since his subsequent history is a history of displacement, accompanied by a sense of psychic fragmentation. It is also an impoverished place of marginal existence, where, if it were not for his transgression, Mr. Biswas could at most have lived out his life as an illiterate labourer in the sugarcane fields, the same as his father and grandfather before him. All that is familiar severed and removed from his place of origin, Mr. Biswas is thrown into a world that is alien to him.

From that point forward, Mr. Biswas can never say exactly where his father's hut stands. Many years later when he returns as a reporter, trying to find the place he spent his early years, he finds nothing but "oil derricks and grimy pumps, see-sawing" (ibid: 52). His grandparents' house has also disappeared. "His naval-string, buried on that inauspicious night, and his sixth finger, buried not long after, had turned to dust" (ibid: 54). With the past destroyed, Mr. Biswas is dispossessed of his origins and becomes rootless. Even his birth certificate is an after-thought and the date of his birth guesswork. Mr. Biswas's attempt to acquire a house can therefore be read as his quest for a place on the earth to call his own, as well as his desire to leave some marks on a world that "carried no witness to Mr. Biswas's birth and early years" (ibid: 41). Later, when trapped in the Hanuman house, he ponders his feelings of futility because he cannot claim any house he has resided as his own:

He had lived in many houses. And how easy it was to think of those houses without him! [...] In none of these places he was being missed because in none of these places had he ever been more than a visitor, an upsetter of routine. Was Bipti thinking of him in the back trace? But she herself was a derelict. And, even more remote, that house of mud and grass in the swamplands: probably pulled down now ploughed up. Beyond that, a void. There was nothing to speak of him. (ibid: 131-132)

Chapter One An Exile at Home: *A House for Mr. Biswas*

To have a house of his own symbolizes his need to have something to be spoken of, and to fill the "void" of the past. The past that Biswas has been deprived of is, nevertheless, a past of darkness: he was born at the darkness of midnight, his father dies in the darkness at the bottom of the pond, and in darkness the hostile villagers destroys Bipti's garden. Brooding over his own sense of the past in *An Area of Darkness*, Naipaul writes:

To me as a child the India that had produced so many of the persons and things around me was featureless, and I thought of the time when the transference was made as a period of darkness, darkness which also extended to the land, as darkness surrounds a hut at evening, [...] And even now, though time has widened, though space has contracted and I have travelled lucidly over that area which to me was the area of darkness, something of darkness remains, in those attitudes, those ways of thinking and seeing, which are no longer mine. (AD 1981: 32)

The darkness of both the colonial reality and the Hindu heritage render Mr. Biswas' early life into what Jacques Lacan calls the condition of "lack", a life made up of constant losses. According to Lacan, humans are born into a condition of "lack" and are driven by our desire to overcome this condition. As we look back, we continue to believe that the union with our mother was a moment of plenitude, which is *l'object petit a*, an object that is desired but forever out of reach, a lost object, signifying an imaginary moment in time. As we have already seen, Mr. Biswas's "pastoral" period never actually exists; even proof of his early existence is buried in oblivion. This pastoral time, therefore, is like Lacan's *Real*, a time of plenitude that is forever irretrievable and may not have existed at all. Yet the subject believes in the existence of such a period, the same as Naipaul's treatment of Mr. Biswas's childhood. No one can return to his mother's womb, nor relive that happy real time. By naming a destitute childhood "pastoral", the author appears foreboding about the prospect of subjectivizing colonial people. The subject of Lacan walks into alienation as soon as he is born into the world, and this is more so for colonial people who are doubly alienated and marginalized. The independent identity that Mr. Biswas endeavors to achieve in the form of a house is made questionable by the author himself before he goes on his way.

According to Lacan, the development of human subjectivity has three stages. The first stage is the "mirror phase", the second the "fort-da" game, and the third the Oedipus complex. Lacan's infant starts out as something inseparable from its mother in a mythical moment of plenitude, a time when there is no distinction between self and other, and between the baby and mother (at least, from the baby's perspective). This period is called "the real" by Lacan and is followed by a period experienced as one of "fragmentation", which is "beyond the constant satisfactions of the womb, and dependent on the intermittent satisfactions of the breast" (Storey 2004: 75). Lacan says that at some point in this period (between the age of 6 and 18 months), the baby will see itself in a mirror. It will look at its reflection, then looks back at a real person—its mother, or some other person—then look again at the mirror image of himself. At this stage, on the basis of this recognition or, more properly, misrecognition (not the self, but an image of the self), the child will begin to see itself as an integrated being and a person as a whole. Yet the self that the child thinks itself to be is but a "misrecognition". In other words, what the child sees is an image in a mirror, yet he mistakes the image as "me". It is in fact, *not* the child, but merely an image. The "mirror phase" heralds the moment of entry into an order of subjectivity, what Lacan calls "the imaginary". According to Terry Eagleton, "the imaginary for Lacan is precisely this realm of *images* in which we make identifications, but in the very act of doing so are led to misperceive and misrecognize ourselves" (Eagleton 1983: 165). With each new image we will attempt to return to the time before "lack", to find ourselves in what is not ourselves, yet each time we are bound to fail. To Lacan, ego, or self, or identity, is at some level, a fantasy and an identification with an external image rather than the internal sense of a separate and whole identity. As the image the infant sees in the mirror is not his real self, Mr. Biswas's pastoral past, as endowed by the author, is not actually a happy pastoral time, but instead a time of loss and lack.

The second stage is the "fort-da" game period, originally named by Freud after watching his grandson cast a cotton reel away and then pull it back again through an attached thread. The child casts the reel and says "fort", which is a German word for "gone". He pulls the reel back and says "da", which in German means "here". Lacan rereads the "fort-da" game as a marker of entry into language, through which the subject enters what Lacan calls the Symbolic. It is Lacan's contention that language is always about loss or absence because we only need words when the object we want is gone. If the world were all fullness, with no absence, then there would be no need for language. The "symbolic order" pre-dates us, Lacan maintains, and is already there, waiting for us to take our places. The "symbolic order" produces our subjectivity, yet "it is forever outside our sense of being, belonging to others in the same way as it belongs to us" (ibid: 76). Our senses of self and otherness are composed from the language we speak, as well as from the cultural repertoire we encounter. Language enables us to think of ourselves as subjects, without which "we would have no sense of self, and yet within language our sense of self is continuously slipping away—fragile and threatening to fragment" (ibid: 76).

The "mirror phase" and the "fort-da" game shed some light on our understanding of both Naipaul and Mr. Biswas's identity given that they share a colonial background. If Lacan's subject is born into a continual process of alienation, it is more so for colonials because the "mirror" that offers the fantasy of being a whole person is not singular. As one's identity is constituted largely by culture, a colonial's identity is naturally more complicated due to his unique position between his cultural heritage and the host culture. The moment the colonial is born, he is born into the colonizer's "symbolic order", and must speak a language not his own. The path to identity for a colonial is therefore bleaker and harder. He is not only made to be an "other" in the colonizer's code of culture, but is alienated from his own heritage. In other words, a colonial man is a double "other", whose position is like that of a woman, who is an "other" in the symbolic world as well as in a world that is mostly in the hands of men. As reflected in Mr. Biswas's story, the tension arising between what is suggested by the title "pastoral" and the actual "darkness" that permeates the scene is also indicative of Naipaul's hesitant and ambiguous attitude toward his Hindu heritage. Unlike his father, Seepersad Naipaul, who experienced the Hindu-Muslim rural culture of Trinidad as a whole culture, close to India, by the time Naipaul came of age, that culture had begun to weaken; the time of wholeness was as far away as India itself, and almost lost in time.

The opening of the novel not only vividly evokes the ambience of a Hindu world, but also undermines it. Accordingly, Naipaul's representation of the Hindu rituals in the Indian village is dotted with a satirical as well as a poetic attitude. The very fact that all the prophecies about Mr. Biswas's inauspicious fate come to pass, demonstrates Naipaul's unconscious justification of Hindu tradition. During childhood, Naipaul came to know the rituals through his father's stories. This "gave beauty (which in a corner of my mind still endures, like a fantasy of home) to the Indian village life I had never known" (FC 1985: 42). These early memories may later prove to motivate Naipaul's poetic, revealing, and moving descriptions of Hindu rituals. After Raghu's death, Bipti prepared herself according to Hindu tradition for the funeral:

> Bipti was bathed. Her hair, still wet, was neatly parted and the parting filled with red henna. Then the henna was scooped out and the parting filled with charcoal dust. She was now a widow forever. Tara gave a short scream and at her signal the other women began to wail. On Bipti's wet black hair there were still spots of henna, like drops of blood. (HB 1984: 32)

The bathing, the charcoal dust, and the blood remind us of the Biblical description of rituals of sacrifice and lamentation for the loss of loved ones. The almost pious description of the Hindu ritual immediately reveals Naipaul's reverence and nostalgia. How we look at our past affects the image with which we seek to identify. Heritage is thereby crucial to the constitution of our identity. The way we look at it will inevitably leave marks on our identity. For Lacan's subject, there is a time of plenitude before he is born. Yet the colonial men are in fact both uprooted from their own cultural heritage, and severed from the host culture of the colonizer. They are, in a sense, floating subjects marginalized by both their own heritage and the colonizer's culture. The "symbolic" they enter condemns them as a colonized other and outsider the moment they are born.

The identity problem caused by the loss of the past is a recurring theme in Naipaul's writing. In *India: A Wounded Civilization*, for example, he writes about a journalist who "had lost the key to a whole world of belief and feeling, and was cut off from his past" (IWC 1985: 70). Indian identity for the journalist is not dynamic or changing, but instead fixed, an idealization of his own background, the past he feels he has just lost. "Identity was related to a set of beliefs and rituals, a knowledge of the gods, a code, an entire civilization. The loss of one's past equals the loss of identity" (ibid: 72). Such remarks show Naipaul's critical attitude to the idea of attaching identity to heritage. However, as one critic insightfully observes, using conciliatory and intimate third-person narration, *A House for Mr. Biswas* balances the "sympathetic 'inside' and evaluative 'outside' views of the main character" and resolves "provisionally" the tension between Naipaul's Trinidad past and his London present (Weiss 1992: 47). Likewise, from both the satirical and poetic delineation of the Hindu rituals, we can also see Naipaul's acceptance, as well as judgment of his Hindu heritage.

This "pastoral" chapter sets the social and historical background for Mr. Biswas and the East Indian villages built by indentured workers in the 19th and 20th centuries. With the abolition of the slave trade in 1807, planters turned to East Indians for labor to work on the sugarcane estates. Nearly half a million East Indians immigrated to the Caribbean as indentured workers[4] between 1838 and 1924

---

4 | An indentured worker, according to Eric Williams, is a free man, not a slave. "He came to the Caribbean on contract, generally for five years. [...]

(Williams 1984: 348). From 1845 to 1917, 143,939 Indians had immigrated to the Caribbean (Brereton 1981: 102). Mr. Biswas's grandfather, like Naipaul's maternal grandfather, was probably one of these workers. Mr. Biswas's father, Raghu, is naturally also a laborer belonging to the lowest social strata. The social identity Mr. Biswas inherited from his father is thus that of a worker-laborer, which Mr. Biswas himself tries to dispel. Later, when Mr. Biswas finds that in his daughter's birth certificate, his occupation is given as "laborer", he is furious and shouts at his wife: "Look. Occupation of father: Labourer! Me! Where your family get all this bad blood, girl?" What he would like to call himself is a "proprietor" (HB 1984: 163). To be a proprietor means, to some extent, to have the right to enjoy independence, safety, and dignity.

The end of the "pastoral" life for Mr. Biswas marks the departure from his life as a dependent. From that point on, he must move from place to place to obtain food and shelter. This life is like the stage of the "fort-da" game in Lacan's development. According to Lacan, not only does the language we speak produce our subjectivity, we are in reality subject to its structural processes. Furthermore, Lacan maintains that our unconscious is also constructed from our contact with language, a language of the other. Thus, "our sense of self and our sense of otherness are both composed from the language we speak and the cultural repertoire we encounter in our everyday existence" (Storey 2004: 76). In Mr. Biswas's case, as he moves from place to place, he comes into contact with a colonial reality that is a mixture of both the colonized and the colonizer's culture. Mr. Biswas's journey of identification is condemned to move from one difficulty to another.

The contract specified that the Asian labourer was to have a free passage to the West Indies before 1898, a free return passage in the case of males, two-thirds in the case of females. [...] The contract further provided for medical attention during his employment, and housing accommodation at the expense of the employer." (Williams 1984: 351-352)

During the eight months in his uncle Bhandat's house, Mr. Biswas is sent to study with Jairam to train as a pundit. He is ultimately driven away after desecrating the flowers of the oleander tree that Jairam uses in the *Puja*, with the excrement he throws out of a window in a handkerchief. As Thieme insightfully points out, this interlude is particularly important in that it demonstrates both the distance that already separates Mr. Biswas from orthodox Hinduism, and the extent to which his destiny is intertwined with such Hinduism (Thieme 1987: 67). Once again, Naipaul's ambiguous attitude toward his Hindu heritage is revealed. It may provide a certain sense of safety and dignity but it constrains people, even the most natural human needs can be considered a defilement.

Before marrying into the family of the Tulsi, Mr. Biswas lives in a mud hut behind his uncle's home. At the time, "it would have pained Mr. Biswas if anyone from the school saw where he lived, in one room of a mud hut in the back trace. He was not happy there and even after five years considered it a temporary arrangement" (HB 1984: 48). This sense of temporariness in a time of poverty shows Mr. Biswas's inner humiliation by his background; it is also indicative of the subject's dissatisfaction with his identity. This sense of temporariness becomes the impetus for wanting to be somewhere else and something better, and for the construction of a new identity. It is also a symptom of the fragmentation of identity because an important element in one's identity is the continuity of the self. Moreover, cut off from the past, and with no future to hope for, the situation in which Mr. Biswas finds himself in is indeed a gloomy one. His sense of temporariness, thereby, symbolizes his hope of ending his displacement, asserting his identity. It is in the flux of the displaced life that Mr. Biswas begins to dream of a house of his own. In addition to its many other symbolic meanings, like culture, order, safety, dignity, to name a few, for Mr. Biswas, a house represents a life of independence and rootedness.

After leaving the Bhandat's store, Mr. Biswas finds a job as a sign painter at the Tulsi store in Arwacas. There he meets Shama, one of the Tulsi family daughters, who later becomes his wife in keeping with his caste: a Brahamin. After their marriage, Mr. Biswas and Shama live in Hanuman House with the other Tulsi sons and daughters and their families. Built by pundit Tulsi, the Hanuman House is like an enclave of Indian culture in the Caribbean, adhering to many of the Hindu rituals and rites while at the same time utilitarianly appropriating impending Western ideas as per the family members' interest. They send the younger generation to Christian schools so that they can have better prospects. One of the two sons in the family is even sent to study medicine in England. Mr. Biswas, with his defiance of tradition and a spirit longing for independence, clashes with the Tulsis from time to time because he is not satisfied as a dependent deprived of his own rights and individuality the same as the other sons-in-law of the family, and paradoxically, he is contemptuous of the Tulsis' utilitarian adoption of Western ideas. Eventually he leaves the Hanuman House and begins to work as a shopkeeper at a Tulsi store in a village called the Chase, a settlement of huts located in the heart of the sugarcane area. For six years, in a life of "boredom and futility", his days disappear in an undifferentiated tedium as a shopkeeper. This he also deems only a temporary stay. His strong sense of temporariness immediately reveals Mr. Biswas's reluctance to accept his reality, as well as his perpetual longing for something more meaningful and decent.

In the end he must abandon the indebted shop. He reluctantly takes a job as a driver on the Tulsi sugar estate in Green Vale, while his wife and children remain at Hanuman House much of the time. In an effort to escape his depressing living quarters and his inherited identity as the "son of a labourer", he hires a carpenter to build him a house away from the workers' huts. The house proves to be a folly, and is finally burnt down by the workers he superintended. Broken and homeless, he is taken back to Hanuman House to recuperate.

With a wife and four children to support, Mr. Biswas finds himself in a position not unlike that when he was seventeen, with no vocation and no reliable means of earning a living. He is still at the mercy of the Tulsis for his and his family's sustenance. After recovering his health, he has little choice but to leave again. "He was going out into the world, to test it for its power to frighten. The past was counterfeit, a series of cheating accidents. Real life, and its special sweetness, awaited; he was still beginning" (HB 1984: 305). Leaving the Hanuman House, Mr. Biswas goes to Port of Spain, acquires a profession there and finally buys himself and his family a house. Each of these accomplishments, however, has its qualifying and ironic aspect. Initially he works as a sign writer at the Trinidad *Sentinel* and later gets a chance to be a reporter for the newspaper. With writing, Mr. Biswas finds an outlet for his creativity and a way to define his subjectivity. From the beginning of his life as a journalist, Mr. Biswas takes pleasure in writing sensational articles like "I am Trinidad's Most Evil Man" as part of a series on superlatives about the island's "richest", "poorest", "tallest", "fastest", "strongest" persons. These articles seem to provide an imaginative channel to express his fears as well as dreams artistically. These writings turn him into the *Sentinel*'s star reporter. Unfortunately, his glory comes to an end when Mr. Burnett, his mentor and protector, is fired, and he himself transferred to "court cases, funerals and cricket and matches," where reporting is drudgery. There he works in constant fear of being "sacked" (HB 1984: 346). Even with some success, Mr. Biswas's independent identity is still ambiguous or uncertain because of the social forces, or to use Lacan's term, the "symbolic order" he is in, and because of the contradiction inherent in that a colonial's independent identity stems from the very structure of the colonial society. In the last section of this chapter, we will look in greater detail at how colonialism makes the colonial's effort at identity a quest in vain.

Nevertheless, Mr. Biswas's status as a reporter improves his standing among the Tulsis. He takes his wife and children away from the Tulsi family, and moves to the city of Port of Spain. During this time, Mr. Biswas acquires a professional identity and achieves a certain independence from the Tulsis. At the flush of his ambition to become a writer,[5] Mr. Biswas attempts repeatedly to write a short story appropriately entitled *Escape*, which he never manages to finish. It remains an unfinished manuscript and a fragmented story without an end. The title of the unfinished story suggests Mr. Biswas's desire to be freed from the "symbolic order" in which he is made an other, yet the fact that he is never able to get it finished indicates that independent identity can only be a fantasy, just as Lacan maintains.

Mr. Biswas dies at the age of forty-six in his shaky house on Sikkim Street. Shortly before he dies, he imagines for his obituary a gallant, half-mocking, un-self-pitying headline: "ROVING REPORTER PASSES ON" (ibid: 589). The very word "roving" not only vividly depicts the life Mr. Biswas has led, but also shows his undaunted spirit in the face of all that life has given him: the loss of his father at an early age, dependency on others for food and protection most of his life, an unhappy marriage, an unsuccessful profession and, in the end, dying in a house full of flaws. However, after his death, the actual notice reads: "JOURNALIST DIES SUDDENLY" (ibid: 589). The difference between the two headlines—the one fanciful, the other matter-of-fact—encapsulates Mr. Biswas's life story: "fantasy rejected or revised by history" (Weiss 1992: 51).

According to Lacan, the mirror stage establishes the self as fundamentally dependent upon external objects, on an "other". As the subject matures and enters into social relations through language, it enters the stage of the "fort-da" game. The subject experiences language, which allows him to communicate with others, although it also intensifies his sense of "lack". The entry into language, the "symbolic", actually opens up a gap between the need for the origi-

---

5 | In the "Foreword" of *The Adventures of Gurudeva,* Naipaul writes that he is not quite sure how the wish to be a owriter came to his father. "But I feel now, reading the stories after a long time and seeing so clearly (what was once hidden from me) the Brahmin standpoint from which they are written, that it might have been the caste-sense, the Hindu reverence for learning and the word, awakened by the beginnings of an English education and a Hindu religious training" (see in Seepersad 1976: 12-13).

nal moment of plenitude and the promise and failure of language; it is in this gap that desire emerges. For Mr. Biswas, in his life doubly alienated from both his Hindu heritage and the colonizer's culture, he simplifies his desire for identity, a fantasy he doesn't realize, into a house, without knowing that it is but a signifier that is far from the signified.

HOUSES AS SHIFTING SIGNIFIERS

At the "mirror phase", it is through an external medium (a mirror) that the child is made "whole", and this foreshadows the improbability of subjectivity in its real sense. The "fort-da" game period leads the child into the "symbolic" and further alienates the subject. Following the "mirror phase" and the "fort-da" game period is the Oedipus complex. Drawing on the Greek myth of Oedipus as dramatized by Sophocles in the tragedy *Oedipus the King*, Freud describes the Oedipus complex as a stage in a child's development in which the child experiences an erotic attachment to one parent and hostility toward the other. Lacan rewrites the Oedipus complex in terms of language. The Freudian father is then replaced by the "name of the father", or, the "law of the father". To enter the "symbolic order", one has to submit to the rules of language itself—the "law of the father". In other words, to become a speaking subject, one has to be subjected to, or must obey, the laws and rules of language. The Oedipal movement from the imaginary to the "symbolic" leaves the child moving from one signifier to another. The Oedipus complex determines not only the subject's future relations with itself, but also with others. Realization of desire will therefore always be an impossibility. It is like "the process or pursuit of the fixed signified, always forever becoming another signifier—the incessant sliding of the signified under the signifier" (Storey 2004: 77). Born into the "symbolic order" of a colonial society, Mr. Biswas obeys the laws of the Western language when he desires an independent identity, casting aside the Hindu tradition that advocates group identity. However, as

Lacan maintains that it is impossible for the subject to attain subjectivity in the "symbolic", Mr. Biswas's incessant struggle for a house of his own then becomes a chain of signifiers, ever distant from the signified. Mr. Biswas has been transferred from place to place, and for thirty-five years he has no house to call his own. In the midst of the insecurity and humiliation caused by the displacement, caught between the Hindu culture in which he is raised and the Western culture that surrounds him, Mr. Biswas holds on to the Western view of individuality without realizing that he is acting according to the "law of the father", which, tragically, is not his. His dream of subjectivity remains a mere fantasy!

While working as a driver in Green Vale, Mr. Biswas makes his first attempt to build a house. Arriving at the Green Vale, "as soon as he saw the barracks, Mr. Biswas decided that the time had come for him to build his own house, by whatever means" (HB 1984: 206). Mr. Biswas thinks deeply about the house, and knows exactly what he wants. It must be "a real house, made with real materials" (ibid: 210). The longing for something "real" indicates his reluctance to deem his previous life of dependence on others for food and shelter meaningful, and that he holds an optimistic view of a life that is "made with (the) real materials" of independence and dignity.

The fact that he has to live in the barracks, the same as the labourers, further strengthens his desire to escape and to have his own house. Mr. Biswas's unwillingness to live in the barracks with the labourers under his supervision is a clear sign of his wish to be rid of the class identity he was born to. He doesn't want to work as an agricultural labourer, as do his brothers, father and grandfather, and does everything he can to escape this inherited social identity. In the nineteenth and early twentieth century, the socioeconomic rung of the East Indians was the lowest in Trinidad (Brereton 1981: 110-111). What Mr. Biswas seeks to escape is the degradation of agricultural labourers. While trying to assert his individuality, Mr. Biswas endeavors to shake off the identity of "indentured labourer" and strives to attain a position equal to the colonizer, seeking to share the same privacy, order of life, dignity, and all that a house of one's own symbolizes. Yet it is the colonial's discourse that instills the value of individuality into the mind of the colonized. This is what Bhabha means by the ambiguity of the colonial discourse: it colonizes the mind of the colonial, but simultaneously plants the seed of self subversion—the colonized is now no longer satisfied with being the silenced Other under the bondage of epistemic violence.

Before building his real house, Mr. Biswas buys his daughter Savi a doll's house as the Christmas gift costing more than a month's wages. It is such a wonderful house: "Every room of the doll's house was daintily furnished. The kitchen had a stove such as Mr. Biswas had never seen in real life, a safe and a sink" (HB 1984: 216). The house and kitchen stand for the most basic human needs for shelter and food. Naipaul's emphasis on them highlights Mr. Biswas's "lack" of them, and sharpens his humiliating condition: he has no house and little money, his wife and children cannot even stay with him. On the other hand, it also represents Mr. Biswas's unconscious desire to provide food and shelter to his children on his own, that is to say, to assert his fatherhood.

For Mr. Biswas, the gift of a doll's house for Savi also symbolizes his effort to recover from the traumatic experience of his fatherless childhood. As described in the novel, Mr. Biswas's inauspicious birth causes his father's premature death. Later, when he gets back to his mother for comfort and love after being beaten up by Bhandat and receives none, he grieves, "You see, Ma. I have no father to look after me and people can treat me how they want" (ibid: 67). As is known, father is the symbol of protection and root. The premature death of Mr. Biswas's father is indicative of the colonial's lack of protection and roots. Raised in the context of the "borrowed culture" of the colonizers, colonials like Mr. Biswas speak the language of the colonizer, are taught with the colonizer's culture and values, and deprived of knowledge of their own history. By negating the history of the colonized, the colonizer hopes to inscribe the image of the "other" in the psychology of the colonials themselves. To put it differently, the colonized is made to internalize his standing of an "other" and becomes what Fanon calls a man of black skin wearing the mask of the white. Yet Mr. Biswas is not so much a brown man with "white masks" as an early colonial who is anxious to assert his own identity.

By giving the exuberant doll's house to Savi, Mr. Biswas provides his child with the memory of a "father"—a symbol of protection and roots. However, this gift, extravagant and over-determined in its symbolism, provokes the bitterest of all his quarrels with the Tulsis. Mrs. Tulsi rebukes him for showing favoritism to his own child, and the affront to the Tulsi sisters at this display of individualism. To appease the Tulsi sisters' contempt, Shama destroys the doll's house. When Mr. Biswas returns to the Hanuman House the next Saturday, he finds:

> There, below the almost bare branches of the almond tree that grew in the next yard, he saw it, thrown against a dusty leaning fence made of wood and tin and corrugated iron. A broken door, a ruined window, a staved-in wall or even roof—he had expected that. But not this. The doll's house didn't exist. He saw only a bundle of firewood. None of its parts was whole. (ibid: 218)

Such demolition foreshadows the obstacles Mr. Biswas is to encounter, and the bleak future of his identity construction as measured by a house of his own. Since the doll's house for the moment stands for his existence as a father, Mr. Biswas reacts in the only way possible to him. He takes Savi to Green Vale, to the trap and darkness of his life there. On their way there, they are stopped by the police because Mr. Biswas's bicycle does not have license and lights, which symbolizes that at the present stage Mr. Biswas is not capable of taking the role of a father to lead his child into a life of light when he himself is still in the void of darkness. Savi spends the following week at Green Vale with Mr. Biswas, but she is not happy there. Both Mr. Biswas and Savi look forward to the coming of Saturday, when Seth will take her back to Hanuman House. From that point on, Mr. Biswas begins to feel that he is "trapped" in a "hole" and gradually he descends into a nervous breakdown: "He was rocking hard on the creaking board one night when he thought of the power of the rockers to grind and crush and inflict pain, on his hands and toes and the tender parts of the body" (ibid: 229). Such fears vividly reveal that Mr. Biswas unconsciously begins to doubt the feasibility of his dream, and comes to dread the destructive power of society.

Finally Mr. Biswas decides that he cannot wait any longer, and reasons that unless he begins his house immediately, he never will. Without a house, "his children would stay at Hanuman House, he would remain in the barrack room, and nothing would arrest his descent into the void" (ibid: 237). Yet Mr. Biswas begins the house not only as an attack on the darkness, an attempt to "arrest his descent into the void", but also as a reaction to the laborers whom he is supposed to be overseeing and whose open mockery he is powerless to discipline. That is to say, for Mr. Biswas, the house he is to build is not only important in itself, but also a matter pertinent to his dignity. In addition, the doll's house has served to involve his children in his dream of a house, and thus the house project is also for their sake, to free them from the bondage of Hanuman House. Thus, the house becomes a symbol of his ability to leave a mark in the world as a father, as someone more than a rebel, a clown, and instead someone with identity and dignity.

He begins the construction of the house with exuberance. The site he has in mind is like a "bower", an enchanting word used by Wordsworth as read in the *Royal Reader*. The actual place, however, is far from poetic, with trees blocking the road and a shallow damp depression that runs with muddy water after rain. Like the difference between the beautiful word "jasmine" and the dull vegetation[6],

---

6 | In *Jasmine* Naipaul recounts an incident in the 1950s when he visited an elderly lady of a distinguished Christian Indian family in whose veranda he smelt a flower he has known since his childhood in Trinidad but the name of which he never found out. He asked the lady for the name of that flower and she told him it was called "jasmine". As a youth in Trinidad he was familiar with the scent of the flower. But he never could link the dull vegetation to the beautiful and romantic name of "jasmine", which was "a word in a book, a word to play with, something removed from the dull vegetation" (OB 1987: 19). "The old lady cut a sprig for me. I stuck it in the top buttonhole the romantic word "bower" creates a feeling within Mr. Biswas that the reality of his house and its location seem to betray. The final product—because of all the necessary compromises in scope and materials—is a mockery of his dream. The lack of money for the house he envisions requires that every step be revised. It has to be built on wooden pillars instead of concrete, as he desires; instead of boards separating the ceiling and roof, branches are put in place; instead of a new roof, an old, bent, rusty, hole-ridden used one is installed. The house turns into an embarrassment, and is ultimately burnt down by the laborers.

Although never finished before it is finally burnt down, the house at Green Vale serves to connect Mr. Biswas to his son, Anand. Significantly, during the construction process, Anand objects to using the rusted corrugated iron purchased cheaply from the Tulsi family. He confides to his father how carelessly the stuff is loaded. To a certain extent, the construction of the house parallels the construction of Mr. Biswas' identity as a father. Anand's comment marks the turning point in Mr. Biswas' attitude toward the house. It is Anand who in another tense scene resolves to stay with his father, not because of the crayons, but because, as he tells his father "they was (sic) going to leave you alone" (HB 1984: 279). The father and son have some happy moments together. But more often, their time together in the unfinished house is plagued with terror. Mr. Biswas has been suffering from psychological problems since the beginning of the construction of the house. Haunted by fear, Mr. Biswas feels forsaken and extremely lonely. It seems to him that every man,

---

of my open shirt. I smelled it as I walked back to the hotel. Jasmine, jasmine. But the word and the flower had been separated in my mind for too long. They did not come together" (ibid: 19). Both "bower" and "jasmine" are names only belonging to the British textbooks, the romance of which being separated from the dull reality of the colonial island. It takes more than education to bridge the gap between the signified and the signifier. A lot more actions are needed to be taken, like the construction of a house on the site of "bower".

even the whole world is an enemy who seeks to cheat him and take his life. His dog Tarzen is killed one evening. Anand, terrified by the killing of Tarzan, and by the black asphalt snakes, numbering in the thousands, hanging from the roof as if to bite whomsoever they might find below, wants to go back to the Hanuman House. The father and son's fears culminate in a storm one evening that not only destroys the roof of the wall-less and floor-less house, but also brings about Mr. Biswas's complete collapse. Mr. Biswas's first attempt to build his own house, despite the compromises and good intentions, winds up in total failure.

And yet, under the patronage of the Tulsi family, with no means to support himself or his family, Mr. Biswas finds himself unable to earn his own identity and establish his identity as a father. As mentioned above, the roof of the house is made up of iron sheets cheaply purchased from the Tulsi family, bent, warped, richly rusted, and with nail-holes everywhere. Shabby and humble as it is, the roof from Hanuman House, the symbol of the enclave of Indian culture, an important part of his identity, provides a place under the sky for Mr. Biswas. It cannot, however, stand in the face of the storm both in life and nature. A house symbolizing independent identity cannot be built while its owner remains dependent. Even during the process of construction, Mr. Biswas begins to feel the house as a burden, and suffers nervous breakdowns from time to time. Intended as a means to arrest his descent into the void, the construction of house has never been finished before it was burnt down by the laborers. The irony is that the house is built partly to show Mr. Biswas's difference from, and superiority to, the laborers who despise him because they know he is but a laborer working for the Tulsi family. That the disintegration of Mr. Biswas's house at Green Vale happens simultaneously with his nervous breakdown is indicative of Mr. Biswas's complicated psychology: he longs for independent identity yet wonders whether he is capable of assuming it. Significantly, when Seth brings him the news that the house is burnt down by the laborers he feels "an immense relief" (ibid: 301). Poor Mr. Biswas! What he has been fighting is a battle that is doomed from its inception. The claim is premature, but at least it has been made, and Mr. Biswas never loses hold of his children again.

Mr. Biswas's second attempt at his own house happens after he gets a job as a reporter in Port of Spain. This time he finds the site as he always wanted: "isolated, unused and full of possibilities" on a low hill buried in bush and well back from the road, as "wild and out-of-the-way as he could have wished" (ibid: 423, 424). Unlike his situation in the construction of the Green Vale house, this time Mr. Biswas is able to afford building materials, and builds the house as he likes. Unlike the Green Vale house, whose roof is taken from Hanuman House, this Shorthills house is completed with no help from the Tulsi family. But problems soon appear: his wife Shama has over a mile to walk to the shops; water has to be brought up the hill from a spring in the cocoa woods; he has to cycle a long distance every day to go to work; children have to walk a long way to catch the Tulsi family car to go to school. In addition, the new house "imprisons the children in silence and bush (ibid: 425). The children are not happy because choosing Mr. Biswas encompasses city life in Port of Spain. As a symbol of Mr. Biswas's identity as a father, the house that denies his responsibility as a father is no longer relevant. Like its predecessor in Green Vale, the Shorthills house goes up in smoke soon after it is completed, though this time it is Mr. Biswas who accidentally sets it afire while clearing bush and forest.

The Shorthills house, however, helps Mr. Biswas to fulfill his duty as a son to his mother Bipti. For so long he has told her—since he was a boy in the back trace—that she would stay with him when he had his own house. When they are together, Shama shows the great respect due her as an Indian daughter-in-law by touching Bipti's feet with her fingers. Bipti is also very friendly and helps with the housework and works on the land. An affectionate connection between Mr. Biswas and his past seems to be reconstructed, and the lost loving relation between mother and son is restored. Later, when Mr. Biswas remembers Bipti, he thinks less of his childhood and the back trace, than of this fortnight with her at Shorthills. After Bipti's death, he recalls returning home from work to find that "in the setting sun, the sad dusk, with Bipti working in a garden that looked, for a moment, like a garden he had known a dark time ages ago, the intervening years fell away" (ibid: 427). Bipti now becomes a symbol of the Eden-like past of pure Indianess, directly connected to the land. For Mr. Biswas, this brief visit by his mother leaves memories much sweeter for him than those of his childhood in Pagotes. It seems that Mr. Biswas is now able to appreciate Bipti's motherly love. Her seemingly rude and cold treatment to him in childhood when he was driven out of the priest Jairam's home is now understandable. Naipaul's writing seems to suggest this analysis here: "He did not see at the time how absurd and touching her behavior was: welcoming him back to a hut that did not belong to her, giving him food that wasn't hers" (ibid: 57). What appeared rude and rough, mere fun or fury, may hide a secret flow of tears. Life is often like that. A laborer who had lost her own land, Bipti at that time couldn't assure her son of home comfort, because she had no home, and was herself deprived of all the solace of a shelter. Now in Mr. Biswas's house, her love for him is expressed through what she can do for him and the house. The house therefore becomes a place for mother and son to reconcile, and a place to make up for the lost childhood: his traumatic memory of a loveless childhood is now replaced by a loving and caring mother living in the same house.

Soon after the fire accident, transportation to Shorthills becomes impossible and the adventure at Shorthills comes to an end. Mr. Biswas is now relieved of the Shorthills house that denies his responsibility as father and husband and moves back into the Tulsi family house in Port of Spain. With Owad's return from England, however, Mr. Biswas is once again in danger of losing the room he presently inhabits. It seems that his children are now more and more involved in his dream of a house. Before building the Shorthills house, because of the quarrel with Chinta, the girls urged Mr. Biswas to move out of the house they shared with other members of the Tulsi family. This time it is Anand, who after a conflict with Owad, appeals to him to move out. The humiliation the father has experienced is now being repeated in the new generation. Mr. Biswas is no longer alone in his sufferings. With the children on his side, and a job as a reporter, once again, Mr. Biswas sets off to look for a house.

This time Mr. Biswas buys a house. What makes the purchase possible is the four hundred dollars he receives in exchange for the materials from the Shorthills house. The house in the bush which fulfills all he has hoped for as an individual but which denies his responsibilities as father and husband now makes it possible for Mr. Biswas to buy a house to save his family from the humiliation of the Woodford square. As if to symbolize the flourishing of his dream, Mr. Biswas plants a romantic laburnum tree in the house's yard.

The house is, for Mr. Biswas, a "ready-made world" of his own, not just a victory over the Tulsis family, and over the solicitor's clerk's plans to cheat him of part of his land, but the climax of a life's vision, a place that had been hollowed out by time, by all that he has lived through. The house is not only significant to Mr. Biswas. For his children, it is a center of security, and the cozy home that their father never enjoyed as a child. It becomes for Shama a place where she learns new family loyalties to both the children and Mr. Biswas, and a possession that she can boast to the Tulsis. Although both Mr. Biswas and his family have already discovered many obvious flaws in the house, very soon they accommodate themselves to "every peculiarity and awkwardness of the house" and accept the house as it is (ibid: 12). And for Mr. Biswas:

[...] bigger than them was the house, his house.
How terrible it would have been, at this time, to be without it: to have died among the Tulsis, amid the squalor of that large, disintegrating and indifferent family; to have left Shama and the children among them, in one room; worse, to have lived without even attempting to lay claim to one's portion of the earth; to have lived and died as one had been born, unnecessary and unaccommodated (ibid: 12-13).

To die among the Tulsis would mean he had no independence, to leave this family unaccommodated would mean that he failed to fulfill his responsibility as a husband and father, most importantly, however, to die homeless and without trying to lay claim to his portion of the earth, would mean that he had no subjectivity and identity. Yet a house can speak against all those charges. It is a claim to a life in which he can feel "necessary", and that he is accommodated not only by a literal roof over his head, but by the subjectivity and identity that the house symbolizes. If we read Mr. Biswas's dream of a house as his quest for independent identity, the children's joining him signifies the prevailing trend to long for independence among colonial people. In addition, the children's memory of the past made up of "cheating accidents" will not be as frightening and disheartening because they will have a future to look forward to. For the children, therefore, the house on Sikkim Street serves not only to make up for the trials and chaos of the past, but also as a bridge connecting the gap between the present and the past. Mr. Biswas's biggest dream in life is thus realized, and its significance magnified. All the frustration and anxiety accrued from failures with other houses seem to disappear in the security of this last one. And despite his initial disenchantment with its imperfections, his progressive disappointment that it constantly needs repairs, Mr. Biswas sees the house "bridging the gap between expectation and completion, as the grand symbol of his freedom, personal independence, pride and dignity; and sees it too as redeeming all his past trials, perhaps the very past itself" (Morris 2002: 35).

In spite of the victory, however, Mr. Biswas dies not long after he buys the shaky and heavily mortgaged house, which immediately undermines the glory of his success. What is more, the author does not forget to remind the reader that Mr. Biswas is actually duped by the solicitor's clerk into paying too much for the house. Put together, all the houses constitute a line of signifiers, referring to the signified: independent identity. Yet just as Lacan's subject in the Symbolic, the desire for which is structured by the discourse of the Other, and is forever shifting in the form of signifiers, the houses Mr. Biswas has tried to build at different times and in different places suggest the impossibility of his independent identity.

A Colonial's Aporia

The story of Mr. Biswas is generally based on Naipaul's father's life, who also died young. Mr. Biswas's premature death, however, is not just a faithful reproduction of Seepersad's life. The pattern of the story lends itself to interpretation as an allegory of the search for identity in colonial men. Unlike traditional English fictional biography as diverse as *Robinson Crusoe*, *Tom Jones*, *Jane Eyre* and *Great Expectations*, which follow the protagonist's fortunes from birth or early childhood through some kind of difficulty to adult success, Mr. Biswas's story is not of success because the society in which he is born is incapable of providing opportunities for success in a real sense. The social context in which the story is set makes it impossible for the author to give a neat resolution to the hero's struggles. Therefore, though Mr. Biswas finally gets his house before death, the culmination of his quest is "irretrievably mortgaged" and jerry-built.

Colonialism moves people away from their original spaces and brings them into contact with alien cultures, causing difficulty in identification. In the West Indies, and Trinidad in particular, it first moved American Indians from their home island, and then Africans from Africa to be sold as slaves, and Asians, especially sub-continental Indians, to work as indentured laborers. These colonial people suffer an acute sense of alienation because they are deprived of their root culture, and are raised in a Creole culture that they cannot really accept. For a third generation Indian, such as Naipaul and Mr. Biswas, the sense of alienation becomes more complicated because they do not feel attached to Indian culture the way their grandparents and parents did. They become culturally rootless people in the real sense. Actually, Naipaul refers to the place where he grows up as a "half-Indian world", mysterious to him with "its language not even half understood, its religion and religious rite not grasped" (EA 1988: 111). In 1971, when interviewed by Ian Hamilton, Naipaul talked about his feelings as a colonial thirteen years before, exactly at the time when he set about writing *A House for Mr. Biswas*. He said,

"To be a colonial is, in a way, to know a total kind of security. It is to have all decisions about major issues taken out of one's hands. It is to feel that one's political status has been settled so finally that there is very little one can do in the world" (qtd. in Jussawalla 1997: 14). But it seems that Mr. Biswas wants to get away from that colonial mentality. Instead of idling away life like other sons-in-law under the patronage of the Tulsi family at the cost of individual identity, he incessantly fights for his freedom and never gives up his struggles to overcome his sense of alienation by way of constructing a house of his own.

The longing for a house reveals Mr. Biswas's anxiety for a cultural heritage. A heritage that can serves as potent means for the colonial to flush away the sense of alienation caused by colonialism. Although they are insulated from India and hold an ambivalent attitude toward Hindu rites and rituals, the anxiety of cultural heritage lingers at the heart of both Mr. Biswas and Naipaul. In *An Area of Darkness*, Naipaul writes that though the Indian culture he had been exposed to in childhood had been "cut short and rendered invalid so soon, ...[it had] left so deep an impression" (AD 1981: 36). He says that he has grown up "rejecting tradition; yet how can I explain my feeling of outrage when I heard that in Bombay they used candles and electric bulbs for the Diwali festival, and not the rustic clay lamps, of immemorial design, which in Trinidad we still used" (ibid: 36). Paul Theroux, in his book about his friendship with Naipaul, says that "It had taken me a long time to understand that Vidia was not in any sense English, not even Anglicized, but Indian to his core—cast conscious, race conscious [...]" (Theroux 1998: 344). But as Naipaul's own realization that "culture is ever developing" (OB 1987: 38), even in the place of its origin, cultural heritage may have already been changed, just as Naipaul finds in his first trip to India. For a colonial like Mr. Biswas, the third generation of indentured laborers from India, growing up in an Indian enclave among the hybrid culture of the Caribbean, identification with a cultural heritage is crucial to his identity construction. His act of buying a doll's house for Savi at Christmas, a Western festival, not only reveals his desire for a house of his own to provide shelter for his children, but also divulges his unconscious wish for admission into the colonizer's Symbolic order. The doll's house also symbolizes his longing to leave the offspring with some cultural heritage as a father. However, as we have already seen, Mr. Biswas's life is one that is always out of place, one that is already uprooted. For Mr. Biswas, as well as for Naipaul, root (cultural heritage) searching can only be a fantasy and a doomed enterprise.

In his analysis of Caribbean identities, Hall points out the three kinds of "presences" which constitute the complexity of Caribbean identity: Présence Africaine, Présence Européenne, and Présence Americaine. Présence Americaine refers to the "New World" presence. It does not posses as much power as ground, place, or territory. The "New World" presence is "the beginning of diaspora, of diversity, of hybridity, and difference" (Hall 1990: 116-119). The situation Naipaul and Mr. Biswas are born into is this very space of diversity, hybridity and difference, which is made up of the presence of African culture, European culture, and Indian culture. Amid such a hybrid and diverse form of culture, the role of cultural heritage in the construction of one's identity is particularly important. As an East Indian in the West Indies, however, where can they look for their cultural heritage in the vicissitudes of their life? To India, a place their grandfathers left almost a century ago? To the Caribbean, where they were born and brought up? Or, to London, long thought to be the center of the metropolitan world? Naipaul's later fictions and travelogues show that in none of these places can they find a cultural heritage to which they can cling. Many of the Naipaulian characters therefore choose to escape Trinidad's stifling society, as does Mr. Biswas's son Anand.

Nevertheless, Naipaul's attitude toward cultural heritage is not unquestionably embracing. Mr. Biswas's relationship with Hanuman House, the symbol of Hindu cultural heritage in Trinidad, is indicative of his ambiguous attitude. Entering the Tulsi family by marrying one of the Tulsi daughters, Mr. Biswas quickly discovers that the price for such an accommodation is the loss of his independent identity: "Their names were forgotten; they became Tulsis." He feels "lost, unimportant and even frightened. No one particularly noticed him" (HB 1984: 96). The moment he come into Hanuman House, Mr. Biswas is in constant conflict with the Tulsi family. He rebels through clowning, speaking English instead of Hindi, and espousing the cause of the reformist Aryan missionaries.

Mr. Biswas, therefore, seems to be an individual locked in a struggle with traditional Hindu values. However, despite his iconoclasm, while amid the Tulsis, Biswas repeatedly falls back on Hinduism in moments of crisis. Every time, after an unsuccessful attempt at asserting independence, after his failure at the Chase, Green Vale, Shorthills, and when he first goes to Port of Spain, Mr. Biswas goes back to Tulsi family for shelter and protection. Significantly, all four of his children are born in Hanuman House. After his life at the Chase grinds to a halt, returning to Hanuman House, Mr. Biswas admits, the house "was a world, more real than the Chase, and less exposed; everything beyond it was foreign and unimportant and could be ignored" (ibid: 128). The "ordered" and "real" life is exactly what Mr. Biswas wants to achieve in life. Paradoxically, the house with which he has always been in rivalry contains order, and it seems to him more real a world than his own at Chase. After his breakdown at Green Vale, he feels "secure to be only a part of Hanuman House, an organism that possessed a life, strength and power to comfort which was quite separate from the individuals who composed it" (ibid: 205). Later, after Mr. Biswas develops a profession in Port of Spain, when Anand is humiliated at school because Mr. Biswas is only a journalist, Mr. Biswas tells him: "I don't depend on them for a job. You know that. We could go back any time to Hanuman House. All of us. You know that" (ibid: 302).

In spite of the excitement and romance surrounding the fancy, modern house on Sikkim Street, the narrator remains sober and does not fail to remind readers that it is a house with a rickety staircase, ill-fitting doors and windows, and that there are numerous other cracks. The paradox of the house is thus maintained, which reflects on all that the house represents. If Mr. Biswas has triumphed, we are left with little doubt about how little has actually been won. If his dependent life before is but a "counterfeit", his newly achieved independence remains tenuous, for he is still heavily in debt. Significantly, the debt is to Tara, "the champion of the old ways" (White 1975: 109). The money with which Mr. Biswas bought the house is obtained partly from his salary as a journalist, partly from the selling of the house on the Shorthills, and partly from a relative from his Hindu past. As the central image of Mr. Biswas's longing for independence and identity, the various sources of money for the house constitute a meeting place of heterogeneity and diversity. Same as the house, Mr. Biswas's identity is therefore a meeting place for his Hindu past, western thoughts, as well as his own subjectivity. It is what Hall calls the meeting point, the point of "suture", between on the one hand the discourses and practices which attempt to interpellate, speak to us or hail us into place as the social subjects of particular discourses, and on the other hand, the processes which produce subjectivities, which construct us as subjects that can be spoken. Identities are thus points of temporary attachment to the subject positions that discursive practices construct for us. They are the result of a successful articulation or "chaining of the subject into the flow of the discourse" (Hall 1996. 6). That is to say, the suturing of the subject to a subject-position entails both the discourse's "hailing" of the subject, and the subject's engagement in the position, a two-way process. In other words, both the structure and the agent are involved in the construction of identities: points of temporary attachment to subject positions. Identity is thus identification and root searching should be replaced by the routing of identification.

However, the power that "interpellates" Mr. Biswas into a social subject is not singular. As a child of Indian heritage, he grows up in a Hindu culture environment, and is educated in Hindu religion by a pundit. As a boy, Mr. Biswas spurns Hindu rituals, yet in his most severe moment of crisis, while in Green Vale, he chants "Rama Rama Sita Rama" to relieve the terror that threatens to overwhelm him. As a colonial, however, he is more often exposed to the colonizer's culture and values. Colonialism impinges on the mind of the colonials most directly through its educational systems, and the orientation of their curriculum is essentially foreign to the colonials.

Since *Miguel Street* and *The Mystic Masseur*, an important theme in Naipaul's work has been the irrelevance of the imported education conferred on the colonials. Elias studies "litricher and poultry" at Titus Hoyt's academy, and ends up driving a scavenger's cart (MS); Ganesh teaches at a school whose function is to form, not inform (MMS); in *The Mimic Men*, Singh attends Isabella Imperial, a private world from which the island is excluded, and where any mention of local events draws satiric laughter. In addition, Mr. Biswas reads many English books, literature as well as philosophy: Marcus Aurelius's *Mediations*, Epictetus' *Discourses*, Bell's *Standard Elocutionist*, Hawkins' *Electrical Guide*, Collins' *Clear-Type Shakespeare*, *Reform the Only Way*, *The Super Sensual Life*, *Arise and Walk*, *Newspaper Management*, *How to Write a Book*, and novels by Samuel Smiles. These readings make the stifling world of Trinidad all the more abhorrent to him, increasing his yearning for metropolitan romance.

A tug of war emerges between Hindu heritage and Western thought in the battlefield that Mr. Biswas becomes, bringing about difficulty in his identification. Like the characters in Naipaul's early stories, Mr. Biswas is of the middle generation of Indians, that unique group displaced between a shrinking Indian past and a disordered Creole present. A pure and fixed identity is a sheer impossibility because as a crystallization of unique experiences of people, identity is not so much an inheritance as a social construction (Said 1995: 32). For a colonial like Mr. Biswas, the complexity of disordered Creole society to which he is born, predetermines the difficulty of his identification.

Writing is the major avenue Mr. Biswas uses to construct himself as a "spoken" subject. However, in learning writing, the very act that establishes his subjectivity, he exposes himself to another type of cultural colonialism when he enrolls at the London Ideal School of Journalism correspondence course. He is instructed to write on subjects as common as the four seasons. The irony is that in Trinidad there are no distinct seasonal divisions; the island lies practically at the equator, and seasons are the privilege of colder climes. Apart from the sensationalized snippets for the *Sentinel*, two of Mr. Biswas's writings are mentioned in particular in the novel. One is the prose poem written after his mother Bipti's death, celebrating the reimagined sweetness of the past between him and his mother. Here he exaggerates the affectionate feelings between them at the time when he was driven home by the pundit. The poem signifies Mr. Biswas's effort at constructing a history, as well as his efforts to produce his identity by establishing his subjectivity through writing. In following with Jonathan Friedman, the construction of history is a way to produce identity in terms of its representation of a relationship between what is assumed to have happened in the past and the present condition of events. For an individual subject, the construction of history is the construction of a meaningful world made up of events as well as narration (Friedman 1994: 177). The writing of the poem is also a catharsis for Mr. Biswas, as the narrator realizes, "The writing excited, relieved him; [...] The poem written, his self-consciousness violated, he was whole again" (HB 1984: 484). Significantly, however, "there is no title" for the poem (ibid: 484). The lack of a title reveals Mr. Biswas's hesitation or bewilderment as regards the true meaning of the past and his relationship to it. Although the past is unsettled, one thing is sure: he wants to escape from the trap of life and the sterility of the society he finds himself in.

Another writing mentioned in the novel is a many-versioned, yet never finished story "Escape": "their theme was always the same. The hero, trapped into marriage, burdened with a family, his youth gone, meets a young girl. She is slim and dressed in white. She is fresh, tender, unkissed; and she is unable to bear children" (ibid: 344-345). The slim girl in white in the story is the symbol of Mr. Biswas's dream: a life full of hope and with no burden. However, just like the girl who is "unable to bear children", his dream is illusive and can lead him nowhere. The only chance for escape lies in education, and only through education can the colonials hope to escape to the metropolis, where, their education tells them, lies the hope of freedom, individuality, wholeness, and everything good. The title of the story thereby expresses Mr. Biswas's yearning to get away from his burdened life. The fact that it is never finished suggests the impossibility of escape. In addition, as Weiss points out, the unfinished story also signifies Mr. Biswas's unrealized dream of becoming a writer, and Naipaul's apprehensive vision of what might have become of his own career had he stayed on that West Indian Island (Weiss 1992: 47).

For Mr. Biswas, as well as for Naipaul, being an Indian in the West Indies, living between a dwindling Indian heritage and Western colonial education, influenced by the colonial discourse of Western progress, freedom and individuality, the crisis of identity is their inevitable fate as there is nothing stable or fixed for them. And for Mr. Biswas, the idea of owning his own a house gives his life direction, and in some way becomes his reason for existence. Yet, the construction of selfhood is never an individual event. It must first of all be put into the context of the history and society the self finds itself in. The individual becomes social through language, which in turn constructs the individual as a subject. The binary division between the individual and society is not the nature of reality. Yet, conflicts between society and the individual often result in an identity crisis. In other words, when historic norms and regulations that shape and evaluate the self exist in discord with the definition of the self, identity crisis follows. Therefore, as Hall elaborates, identities are

subject to a radical historicization, and are constantly in the process of change and transformation. We need to situate the debates about identity within all those historically specific developments and practices which have disturbed the relatively 'settled' character of many populations and cultures, above all in relation to the process of globalization, which I would argue are coterminous with modernity and the processes of forced and 'free' migration which have become a global phenomenon of the so-called 'post-colonial' world. (Hall 1992: 4)

In his article "Who Needs Identity?" Hall further maintains that identity is a "meeting point", the point of "suture", between discourse and practices. They attempt to "hail" people into place as social subjects of particular discourses, where the processes that produce subjectivities, that construct us as subjects can be "spoken" (Hall 2005: 5-6). What Hall refers to is the reality confronted by all human beings. For the colonial, however, this can be more complicated because within the discourse that tries to interpellate them as subjects, they begin already marginalized; they begin as the other in the Symbolic made up of the language of the colonizers. In other words, as Mr. Biswas's society lacks a coherent and dominant discursive practice, it affects the processes of subjectivization. As such, Mr. Biswas's self realization is doomed to be a partial one in that what he has is a half-made colonial society that can't offer more opportunities. In view of this, Naipaul seems to be suggesting that escape is the only way, although this route has become impossible for Mr. Biswas.

If we read the house as the symbol of identity, Mr. Biswas's moving from house to house can be interpreted as a colonial's trajectory of identification. Although Mr. Biswas has resided in different houses, he never lives in any one for very long—his stays in those houses are always temporary. This is a situation typical of the colonials, who are just like grafted fruit: they are similar to, but not quite the same as the original plant. Indeed, a colonial's way to identification will naturally be contingent, uncertain, and even contradictory.

Mr. Biswas actually never owns the house before he dies at the end of the novel. In this sense, for Mr. Biswas, the colonial's dream of independent identity is not truly realized as most critics contend. Significantly, Anand, Mr. Biswas's son and hope in life, leaves the island and never returns before Mr. Biswas's death and the end of the novel. What is different between the father and the son is that the father, unable to escape, dies with his dream of an independent identity, epitomized in the image of a mortgaged house, yet the son has achieved an identity that enables him to write for and about Mr. Biswas by escaping from the colonial island.

Chapter One An Exile at Home: *A House for Mr. Biswas*

***

Similar to earlier works with Trinidad as their settings, the protagonist of *A House for Mr. Biswas* never leaves the place of his birth—Trinidad. As a colonial, however, Mr. Biswas is an exile at home in that his homeland does not offer the environment needed to develop a sense of belonging. The life led by Mr. Mohun Biswas is a life out of place, a life always on the move, during which he leaves the poverty of his father's house, moves from humiliation at Hanuman House to temporary autonomy at the Chase, from the boredom and frustration at the Chase to fresh independence at Green Vale, from collapse and submission at Green Vale to the willed adventure in Shorthills, and at last to the mortgaged house on Sikkim Street. Mr. Biswas's journey through life is a journey into dispossession. Once he has left his mother's house, "the only house to which he had some right" he finds himself "a wanderer with no place he could call his own" (HB 1984: 37). His quest for a house of his own in this state of displacement enacts scenarios of colonial disorientation, loss, and uncertainty.

Mr. Biswas's story is also the response of an East Indian to the New World. In his life of displacement, disorientation, and chaos, Mr. Biswas tries to find his way through a confused Indian world and a chaotic colonial New World. To a great extent, he struggles against forces that he cannot fully understand. The house he finally acquires becomes an all-embracing symbol of his struggle, as well as a bargain he has to make with his social and historical environment. Seen in this light, the house Mr. Biswas finally purchases on Sikkim Street becomes the point of departure of the colonial's path to identification, rather than the target of identity itself. Independent identity is impossible on the colonial island. Instead, colonials must leave and go to the metropolitan center, as dictated by colonialism. Comedy and tragedy, satire and pathos, success and failure coexist in close proximity in the novel which, while offering the most minutely detailed portrait of a colonial to have appeared anywhere in the Third World, also has universal application. The novel, like most of Naipaul's subsequent work, dramatizes the hero's sense of alienation from a pure landscape to which he can never return. The house Mr. Biswas finally acquires thus becomes a symbol not only of his successful struggle, as many critics have pointed out, but more importantly, of the true emblem of a colonial's identity: seemingly whole yet fissured within—as the fragile condition of the house reveals.

As the interface between subjective positions, and social and cultural situations, identity derives from a multiplicity of sources such as nationality, ethnicity, social class, community, gender, and sexuality, among other factors, that may conflict in the construction of identity, and lead to fragmentation (Woodward 1997: 1). Just as the house Mr. Biswas buys on Sikkim Street is built with various materials the contractors gathered here and there, Mr. Biswas's Trinidad society is a meeting place where Indian, Muslim, Black, European, and American culture co-exist. In addition, Cudjoe observes that Mr. Biswas lives in the transitional period between the rural, feudal Hindu society and the capitalist urban one (Cudjoe 1988: 13), with the Hindi tradition dwindling and western thought blooming and gradually shaping people's lives. A *House for Mr. Biswas*, together with his early "social comedies", can be read as a vindication for Naipaul's escape from the colonial world, and the point of departure to finding his way in the world.

In the next chapter, I take the story of Ralph Singh to discuss whether a colonial can build an identity by moving from a peripheral colonial island to the metropolitan center.

Chapter Two An Exile between Islands
The Mimic Men

> Faced with a loss of roots, and the subsequent weakening in the grammar of "authenticity", we move into a vaster landscape. Our sense of belonging, our language and the myths we carry in us remain, but no longer as "origins" or signs of "authencity" capable of guaranteeing the sense of our lives. They now linger on as traces, voices, memories and murmurs that are mixed with other histories, episodes, encounters. (Chambers 1994: 19)

Just as the shaky and heavily mortgaged house on Sikkim Street Mr. Biswas buys before his death symbolizes the impossibility that a colonial can claim an independent identity in a "half-made" colonial society, *A House for Mr. Biswas*, along with other stories in Naipaul's early work, ends with both Naipul and Mr. Biswas's belief that hope of independent identity resides in London. It is thereby expected that nearly everything Naipaul writes in that period culminates in a celebration of escape—escape from Miguel street, from Elvia, and from Mr. Biswas's Port of Spain.

Indeed, it is the colonials' strong belief that the center of the world lies in the metropolis, and that it is also regarded as the source of standard language and the focus of order. The colonies, in contrast, are thought of as the periphery of the world, crowded with "shipwrecked" people living fragmented lives in disorder. In

The Mimic Men, Naipaul clearly incorporates an extreme version of the opposition between the metropolitan centre and the colonial periphery. It "contrasts the metropolitan centre, which is the location not only of the power which comes from the control of language but also of order itself, with the periphery of the colonial world, in which only the illusion of power exists and in which disorder always predominates" (Ashcroft et al. 1989: 87-88). More significantly, via a detailed description of Ralph Singh's disheartening experience in London, Naipaul shows us that the "reality", "truth", "order" and "power" of the center are illusive as well. Thus "the idea of the centre as permanent and unrefractory is endlessly deferred" (ibid: 89).

In the eyes of Ralph Singh, although people on Isabella island pretend to be real, learning, and preparing themselves for life, they are actually "abandoned and forgotten" people shipwrecked on the colonial island and are but "mimic men of the New World, one unknown corner of it, with all its reminders of the corruption that came so quickly to the new" (MM 1984: 146). As Bald observes, it is the logical progression of "colonized intellectuals" to become "English" in order to get rid of the "abandoned" state (Bald 1995: 84). To assert his identity, upon the initial negation of colonial identity, as is hoped by the colonizers, a colonial usually undergoes an inevitable stage of mimicry in identification. Yet, rather than helping him assimilate the master code of the dominant culture, it only serves to intensify his sense of alienation and marks the inerasable difference between the colonial and the colonizer. The betrayal of the colonial myth that in London he would escape "shipwreck" and "disorder", however, does not result in Singh's total rejection. As Singh writes at the end of the novel, "so this present residence in London, which I suppose can be called exile, has turned out to be the most fruitful" (MM 1984: 248). The crisis Singh experienced in his personal life is nothing more than the crisis that the individual subject undergoes as society moves from a colonial to a postcolonial status. Mimicry, as is represented in the novel, cannot resolve the postcolonial subject's perplexity with identification.

Chapter Two An Exile between Islands: *The Mimic Men*

The Mimic Men is Naipaul's first work to employ a first-person narrator, who is also the central character of the novel. Born of Indian heritage and raised on a British-dependent Caribbean island, Ralph Singh has retired to suburban London, writing his memoirs as a means of imposing order on his chaotic existence. In the course of the novel, the narrator comments on his narration from time to time, and at last acknowledges openly, "It never occurred to me that the writing of this book might have become an end in itself, that the recording of a life might become an extension of that life" (MM 1984: 244). Such comments make us wonder about the relationship between the author and his narrator, an important issue in our study of Naipaul's identification. Critics have different viewpoints as regards the persona of Ralph Singh. With Peter Zazareth, he is an "alter ego" for Naipaul himself (qtd. in Thieme 1987: 114). Angus Calder holds that Singh is "a more limited man than his creator, older, one guesses richer, but almost as close to Naipaul, one suspects, as Marlow is to Conrad" (Niven 1976: 277). In the eyes of Victor Ramraj, however, the problem is more complicated. He makes a distinction between the Ralph who experiences the story and the Ralph who narrates the story: Ralph the character of the story is "a supercilious figure, a poseur and a libertine" while Ralph the narrator a recluse, who tells the story with restraint and coolness" (Ramraj 1972: 134). As for Thime, Ralph is a distasteful and lecherous character who makes the reader feel soiled, and thus fails to arouse sympathy. He thinks Naipaul's attitude toward Singh is ironic because he deliberately makes him expose himself (Thime 1987: 114-116). Landeg White, however, posits that there exists a close identification between Naipaul and his narrator (White 1975: 159). I agree with White and think that the ironies in the novel are not directed toward Singh, and that Singh's gradual understanding concerning the act of writing parallels that of Naipaul's as he states, "[writing], for all its initial distortion, clarifies, and even becomes a process of life" (MM 1984: 251), which is true to Naipaul's writing process. Twenty years later, in his heavily autobiographical book *The Enigma of Arrival*, Naipaul ruminates on the time when he worked on *The Mimic Men*: "my disappointment; and the homelessness, the drifting about, I had imposed on myself. I had as it was—and as had happened often before—become one of my own characters" (EA 1988: 166).

In addition, Singh's disillusion with London is very similar to what Naipaul experienced when he first arrived there. This is clearly shown in the correspondence between Naipaul and his father. Moreover, preceding the writing of *The Mimic Men*, when writing *An Area of Darkness*, Naipaul described his disillusion with London:

I came to London. It had become the centre of my world and I had worked hard to come to it. And I was lost. London was not the centre of my world. I had been misled; but there was nowhere else to go. It was a good place for getting lost in, a city no one ever knew, a city explored from the neutral heart outwards until, after years, it defined itself into a jumble of clearings separated by stretches of the unknown, through which the narrowest of paths had been cut. Here I became no more than an inhabitant of a big city, robbed of loyalties, time passing, taking me away from what I was, thrown more and more into myself, fighting to keep my balance and to keep alive the thought of the clear world beyond the brick and asphalt and the chaos of railway lines. All mythical lands faded, and in the big city I was confined to a smaller world than I had ever known. (AD 1981: 45)

Compare Singh's experience in London:

Shipwreck: I have used this word before. With my island background, it was the word that always came to me. And this was what I felt I had encountered again in the great city: this feeling of being adrift, a cell of perception, little more than that might be altered, if only fleetingly, by any encounter [...] In the great city, so three-dimensional, so rooted in its soil, drawing colour from such depths, only the city was real. Those of us who came to it lost some of our solidity; we were trapped into fixed, flat postures. And in this growing dissociation between ourselves and the city in which we walked, scores of separate meetings, not linked even by ourselves, who became nothing more than perceivers: everyone reduced, reciprocally, to a succession of such meetings, so that first experience and then personality divided bewilderingly into compartments. Each person concealed his own darkness [...] I had longed for largeness. How, in the city, could largeness come to me? How could I fashion order out of all these unrelated adventures and encounters, myself never the same, never even the thread on which these things were hung? They came endlessly out of the darkness, and they couldn't be placed or fixed. (MM 1984: 27)

By quoting the two passages at length here, I intend to show how Ralph Singh and Naipaul have had similar experiences in London. Since a close study of the narrative techniques of the novel is not the objective here, I will simply point out that Ralph Singh's story reflects to a large extent Naipaul's own experience of cultural impoverishment in the West Indians, and cultural displacement in a fictionalized London, and that he identifies with the narrator's comments and discoveries. Singh's search for identity is, therefore, very much that of Naipaul's.

The Mimic Men is a prototypal demonstration of the post-colonial subject's search for identity. Growing up between two worlds, that of the colonizer and of the colonized, Singh struggles to develop a cohesive self from childhood, attempting to reconcile Western values and beliefs with those of his traditional background. It is the colonial myth that London is the centre of the world that first defines the colonial man's sense of shipwreck on the island. In the words of Frantz Fanon, the metropolis is for the colonial a highly charged and quasi-religiously significant place. Citing the Martinicans who travel to, and return from the "mother country" of France, Fanon writes:

The black who arrives in France changes because for him the metropolis represents the Tabernacle; he changes not only because it is from France that he received Montesquieu, Rousseau and Voltaire come from France, but also because France gave him his physicians, his department heads, his innumerable little functionaries [...] There is a kind of magic vault of distance, and the man who is leaving next week for France creates round himself a magic circle in which the words Paris Marseille, Sorbonne, Pigalle become the keys to the vault. (Fanon 1967b: 23)

Singh's experiences in London, however, seems to betray his dream of life in the city.

LOST IN THE METROPOLIS

The Mimic Men opens with Singh's search for identity in London. At the beginning of the novel, shortly after World War II, as a student in an unnamed institution, Ralph Singh finds himself in London, in a boarding house owned by Mr. Shylock. The name of the landlord immediately reminds the reader of Shylock the Jew in Shakespeare's *The Merchant of Venice*. The Jewish name here serves as an allusion to the Jewish experience of Diaspora and of the Holocaust in Europe during the Second World War. Shylock, the Jew's owning of a house and having a mistress in London makes him a model of admiration for Singh, and worthy of emulating. This reveals both the author and the protagonist's longing for rootedness in England, to be accepted by English society, and to become an English man. Yet Mr. Shylock dies swiftly and secretly, foreshadowing Singh's disillusionment with London.

After Shylock's death, Singh witnesses his first snowfall, a moment rich in symbolic significance because as a Caribbean, snow is something he has only heard of and read about. Synecdochic of the colonial's desire for the metropolis, the image of snow and the excitement it causes conversely points to the impossibility of the colonial to feel at home in the metropolitan centre. Moreover, since childhood Singh has dreamed of knightly leadership in lands of horsemen, high plains, mountains and snow. Yet his life on Isabella Island is remote from his childhood dream. Instead of becoming a hero to his ancestral people in the snow-capped mountains he used to dream of, he is now lost in a forlorn London boarding room. Called by Singh his "element", snow becomes the symbol of his predicament between the ancestral culture and the metropolitan landscape. After the first excitement aroused by the snow, Singh climbs to the attic of the boarding house, where Mr. Shylock used to meet his mistress. To his great disappointment, what appeared solid from below now appears heartbreakingly fragile. Observing the city from this height, he felt "the magic of the city go away and have an intimation of the forlornness of the city and the people living in it" (MM 1984: 7). Singh's first experience of snow in London is therefore interlaced with an experience of death. "Let it not happen to me," he prays, "Let my relics be honoured. Let me not be mocked" (ibid: 7). The conclusion he draws from this experience establishes one of the major themes of the novel: "I knew that my own journey, scarcely begun, had ended in the shipwreck which all my life I had sought to avoid" (ibid: 7).

Repeatedly, Singh emphasizes that he comes to London to escape "shipwreck" at Isabella and to seek a real life of "order". But here in London he learns that London revolves around an "order" not of his pursuit: "For there is order of a sort. But it is not mine. It goes beyond my dream. In a city already simplified to individual cells this order is a further simplification. It is rooted in nothing; it links to nothing" (ibid: 36). The refrain image of shipwreck that is originally elaborated to embody all the cultural and social disorder that Caribbean people inherit from their condition of displacement and deracination is experienced again in London because of the protagonist's double alienation from his home, and from London, his long cherished place.

Another memory related to his first snow is the christening of Lieni's illegitimate child and the party that follows, both of which being as chaotic as a farcical nightmare. The Christening of the baby is intended to be symbolic because it embodies the colonial's desire to be accepted by the host culture in a real sense. But the fact that both the christened and the pastor are late for the ceremony is indicative of the impossibility of the realization of this desire. Actually, when Naipaul and Singh came to England, the British Empire has passed its peak and the postwar migration of people has rendered the very notion of Britishness a problem. Britain is recognized as not just a political unit but also as an imagined community. When British identity itself becomes a problem, the colonials who migrate to the metropolis will encounter a more complicated identity crisis:

> Coming to London, the great city, seeking order, seeking the flowering, the extension of myself that ought to have come in a city of such miraculous light, I had tried to hasten a process which had seemed elusive. I had tried to give myself a personality. It was something I had tried more than once before, and waited for the response in the eyes of the others. But now I no longer knew what I was; ambition became confused, then faded. (ibid: 26-27)

Instead of enjoying the "flowering" of himself in London as he has dreamed of, Singh feels that "so quickly had London gone sour on me. The great city, centre of the world, in which, fleeting disorder, I had hoped to find the beginning of order" (ibid: 18). In London, more than anywhere else, colonial people suffer an identity crisis because they experience so little certainty, as Singh notes, he has no guide and there is no one to link his present with his past (ibid: 20). His desire coming to grief, his sense of self breaking into pieces, Singh feels "spectral, disintegrating, pointless, fluid" (ibid: 52).

The intense sense of placelessness experienced by Singh drives the narrative to move at a very rapid pace, and the insistent narrative voice dramatizes the agony of a displaced soul lost in the metropolis. Displaced in the London he has longed for, Singh experiences "the panic of ceasing to feel myself as a whole person. The threat of other people's lives, the remembered private landscapes, the relationships, the order which was not mine" (ibid: 27-28). To overcome his loneliness and isolation, Singh throws himself into relationships with different women. Yet to his disappointment, such efforts prove futile, and he finds that all sexual relationship embodies only "the tragedy of flesh" (ibid: 131). He dreads intimacy and takes it as self-violation. For him, intimacy is a fearful thing, "Intimacy: the word holds the horror [...] Intimacy: it was violation and self-violation" (ibid: 25). Dread of intimacy reflects the colonial's inability to face others as well as himself. According to Peggy Nightingale, Naipaul's Singh is an archetypal colonial person, who is "uncommitted and uninvolved, believing all decisions to be in the hands of the masters. [He is] completely isolated and unable to identify with anyone" (Nightingale 1987: 101). And, Singh prefers to have relations with women whose language he cannot speak because he feels:

> I never wished even in imagination to enter their Norman farmhouses or their flats in Nassjo, pronounced Neshway, or their homes set atop the rocky fiords of geography books. I never wished to hear of the relationships that bound them to these settings, the pettiness by which they had already been imprisoned. I never wanted our darkness, our auras to mingle. Understand the language I use, I am describing a failure, a deficiency. (MM 1984: 25)

Taking them as prisoners of their past with fixed identities, Singh is aggressive toward these women whose language he doesn't want to know, and whose life is meaningless to him. Wishing forever to stay "at a woman's breast", he nonetheless gets "enraged" by "the skin", "the smell of the skin", "the bumps and scratches" (ibid: 25). Singh's relationship with the European women illustrates his difficulties with identity. According to Lacan, our desires are shaped by the Other and the unconscious that speaks from the locus of the Other. Lacan's famous claim about the unconscious is that "The unconscious is structured like a language" (qtd in Leitch et all. 2001: 1281). It does not mean that the unconscious is language, but the unconscious is like a language—a foreign language. Language, according to Lacan, "operates on us much as we operate on it. We follow the signs. Language speaks us. But in the process, we become split between a conscious self and an unconscious self that we repress, deny and repeat" (ibid: 1282). Emphasizing the power of the unconscious, Lacan rewrites Descartes's famous statement of "I think, therefore I am" as "I think where I am not, therefore I am where I do not think" (ibid: 1282). The negation of the European women's language illustrates Singh's subjective action of establishing his true self where he does not think, in the language that he refuses to know. Singh's desire for those European women may therefore be interpreted as his desire to be rid of colonial identity as an other and a woman. Raised with a colonial education, Singh's unconscious is structured by the language of the colonizers. His reluctance to know the language of the women with whom he is having sex, therefore suggests his unwillingness to enter into the symbolic order of their culture. The relationship with those women is also indicative of Singh's efforts to erase his colonial identity, and asserting himself as a master and a man.

We learn of this from Singh's memoir, with which he tries to impose order upon the chaotic events in his life. Like the author Naipaul, Singh does not think his hometown Isabella important, and for him, "to be born on an island like Isabella, an obscure New World transplantation, secondhand and barbarous, was to be born to disorder" (MM 1984: 121). So he looks to the "mother country", England, as a place of hope, order, and independent identity. Yet London does not embrace him as he has expected, and his life in London, as we have seen, is even more confusing. Before coming to London, he dreams that he will be in the centre of things and will enjoy order in life, but ironically, he finds himself still in the periphery, not different from what he felt in Isabella.

The narrative of his memoir moves in a non-chronological sequence between Singh's life in Isabella and London, the past and present, childhood and adulthood, and between his fantasy and actual reality in a matter-of-fact fashion, with the attempt to piece together and clarify the fragments of his life so as to achieve a better understanding of himself and his life. Naipaul once said he was "particularly pleased with *The Mimic Men*" because it deals with his own problem, "the disassociation of a man from the simplicity around him" (Naipaul 1968: 57). *The Mimic Men* creates a centerpiece of Singh's knowledge that London has failed to offer him a life of order and rootedness. The very form of the novel emphasizes this point. The interweaving narration resolutely resists the simplicity of order in chronological succession and appears confusing. Yet the novel is thematically consistent. As Helen Hayward observes, it is "held together by a vision of universal desolation, shipwreck and

Chapter Two An Exile between Islands: *The Mimic Men*

disorder: a consistency of mood and theme links this disparate and fragmentary material" (Hayward 2002: 69). Besides the thematic consistency, the novel also moves around a physical centre: it repeatedly returns to the point at which Singh is writing in the suburban London hotel, offering comments and a new understandings of events. When he received the W.H. Smith award for this novel, Naipaul told Francis Wyndham, "I tried to write *The Mimic Men* three times, then I realized it needed a physical centre—and this would be the place where the man was writing his memoirs" (Wyndham 1968: 32).

It is the colonial myth that London is the centre of the world that first defines Singh's sense of shipwreck on his home island. Yet London proves to be an illusion. Staying in London, he feels it shrinks to a two-dimensional city of separate cells. In the desolation, shipwreck, and disorder of London, Singh tries more than once to give himself a personality. Nevertheless, in London he realizes that he is becoming what he sees of himself in the eyes of the others. That is to say, he is losing his own subjectivity there and becoming a construct of the others. Meanwhile, he finds that in London every person conceals his own darkness. Therefore, instead of offering an escape from colonial disorder, London underlines that disorder more acutely. Disappointed and discouraged, Singh wants to leave and return to Isabella. He does not go back to Isabella by himself, though. Right before returning, Singh meets Sandra, an Englishwoman, and marries her.

Singh is attracted by Sandra's "self-love" (she is particularly proud of her breasts, which she paints), "her rapaciousness", and her ability to experience the city that had reduced Singh to "futility". Singh meets Sandra when she is at her lowest, when "She had no community, no group and had rejected her family. She saw herself alone in the world and was determined to fight her way up" (MM 1984: 44). Therefore the relationship between them grows out of mutual need and "self-defense". In this relationship, Singh is at the passive pole. It is Sandra who asks him to propose while they are together in the canteen of a radio service. So Singh proposes to Sandra and within a month they are married. The norm of their relationship at this point suggests that Singh's seemingly active efforts at identification are still presided over by the colonizer. As is already known, Singh used to have sex with women whose language he did not wish to know. With Sandra, however, he feels that the mere fact of communication is a delight. As the narrative moves on, Singh's excitement fades and after the wedding ceremony at the Willesden registry office, he becomes "truly appalled" and wishes to "get away at once, to reflect, to be alone again" (ibid: 49).

This reaction by Singh after his wedding is reminiscent of that of Mr. Biswas's when he got married. Both are lost, one in colonial society, and the other in metropolitan London. Both are led into marriage by forces out of their control. For Mr. Biswas, it is by the Tulsi family, the symbol of Hindu tradition in Trinidad, and with Singh, by Sandra, an English woman who is equally lost herself and whose personality is equally fragmented in London. Initially searching for an anchor to their identity, both end up in a drab and fearful marriage, both protagonists' experience reveal Naipaul's view of identity at that stage of his life: he is still trying to hold on to the idea of a fixed identity, believing that identity is more a construct of forces beyond the control of the subject, and that the dominant cultural model molds the subject into its framework. Therefore in search of an independent identity, Singh moves first from Isabella to London, and once failed in London, he resolves to look for certainty in his identity back home, the place he escaped. Swaying back and forth, between English culture and his ancestral culture, Singh does not know where to anchor his identity.

Returning to Isabella with Sandra, Singh engages in political activities. Yet the crisis in his political career drives him back to London to seek help. After the failure of his mission in London on the nationalization issue, he is reluctant immediately to return to Isabella and stops in an unidentified city, to which a whole chapter is given in the novel. There he takes a prostitute, who, according to Singh's description, is "ghastly, tragic, a figure from hell with a smiling girl's face" (ibid: 236). In his sexual encounter with this woman, characterized by its lack of human or personal concern, Singh is all but annihilated by the profusion of her flesh. After the failure of his last endeavor to save his political career, it may be appropriate that he experienced the almost total effacement of his being in this sexual encounter:

No damp, flat, smothering embrace came; only the softest of words, the sweetest of breaths, a brushing—of those breasts?—against my nipples, the barest touch of a fingernail circling my areola. I never touched; my hands still lay at my side. Yet I was already turning in on myself; judgement was disappearing. Nails, tongue, breath and lips were the instruments of this disembodied probing [...] The probing went lower; no effort of concentration was now required, no need to shut out the world, the liquid sighs and sounds. Judgement disappeared. I was all painful sensation. Flesh, flesh: but my awareness of it was being weakened. I was turned over on my belly. The probing continued, with the same instruments. The self dropped away, layer by layer; what remained dwindled to a cell of perception, indifferent to pleasure or pain; neutral perception, finer and finer, having validity, existing only because of that probing which, growing fainter, yet had to be apprehended, because it was the only proof of life: fine perception reacting minutely only to time, which was also the universe. It was a moment that was extended and extended and extended. There could be no issue; it was a moment which, when release without fruition came and perception widened again, defined itself as an extended moment of horror. It is a moment that has remained with me. After three years I can call it back at will: that moment of timelessness, horror, solace. (ibid: 282-283)

In *The Mimic Men* there are many descriptions of sex. Apart from the fact that it is aimed at a larger audience,[1] the descriptions here

---

1 | While writing *The Mimic Men*, Naipaul also worked on *A Flag on the Island* for a film company that requested a musical comedy with an American character, and "much sex and much dialogue" (White 1975: 139). The heavy descriptions of sex in *The Mimic Men* may have resulted from the influence of *A Flag on the Island*. In addition, both novels have a narrator of metropolitan origin, and deal with the influence of metropolitan power, even carry with them a deep sense of existential nihilism. This intense revelatory moment is counter posed with the autoeroticism Singh experiences at the beginning of the novel. London becomes for Singh the "greater shipwreck", where memories become trifling and frivolous, and where the future is a dead end. There is permanent division between the self and the others since the individual is reduced to "a cell of perception". The colonial thus becomes homeless both physically and metaphysically. His existence is reduced to that of hollow flesh. In the endlessly extended moment of nihilism, the two human bodies disappear into an image of placelessness, man reduced to anonymous flesh, concerned only with keeping his body intact, and man purchasing physical pleasure to verify his existence in isolated moments and in places unknown. What pure scene of desolation and horror this is! In the city where he invests so many hopes and dreams, he is now hopelessly lost and deprived of all expectations, and even the most basic physical sensation gives way to the agony of total uprootedness. Significantly, in the same evening he dreams of Sally, Sandra, his father, and Lord Stockwell, each of whom has been very important to him in different aspects of his life. They stand for his Hindu heritage and the English host culture, respectively. They are all anxious to come to him as he cannot move toward them. According to Freud, dreams are the suppressed wishes of people, and works of art sublimation of these suppressed wishes. Singh's dream reveals that in the state of desolation and complete abandonment, he longs for something to build his identity upon, and dreads being deserted to this timeless, placeless, and rootless condition. The fact that he dreams of two forces simultaneously moving toward him symbolizes the difficulty he is in as to what to choose between his colonial past and the host culture of the colonizers. Though reluctant, at last he

---

after colonial ties are severed. Most strikingly, however, the same as Singh the narrator, who changes his name while at school in Isabella, in *A Flag on the Island* there is also a writer, Mr. Blackwhite, who changes his name into H.J.B. White. Behind the transformation of the names lies the colonial's dilemma of the anxiety of identity.

chooses to go back to Isabella after the stopover in the unnamed city with the anonymous woman. His life in London inverts his dream of nurture and security. Of London and its imprisoning and isolating effects on him, and other immigrants, Singh grieves:

We seek the physical city and find only a conglomeration of private cells. In the city as nowhere else we are reminded that we are individuals, units [...] but the god of the city was elusive. The tram was filled with individuals, each man returning to his own cell. The factories and warehouse [...] were empty and fraudulent. [...] In the great city, so solid in its light [...] life was two-dimensional. (ibid: 18-19)

SHIPWRECKED AT HOME

The most active period of Ralph Singh's life is spent in his place of birth, the Caribbean Island of Isabella. The name of Isabella is evocative because historically Isabella is the name of the first island settled by Christopher Columbus in the Caribbean Sea. The settlement, however, proves to be calamitous and a failure. Naipaul's naming of the island seems to bear a suggestive correlation that the colonials' effort at decolonization and independence, as well as the protagonist's search to anchor an identity in the island, is doomed. This part of Singh's life includes his bewildered childhood, the unhappy marriage to Sandra, and the sterile political involvement that occupies most of the novel. Nevertheless, Ralph Singh in his memoir calls this most active period in his life a period in "parenthesis" (MM 183), a time between his preparation for life and his withdrawal from it. And it is during this period that he thinks of writing because

It was my hope to give expression to the restlessness, the deep disorder, which the great explorations, the overthrow in three continents of established social organizations, the unnatural bringing together of peoples who could achieve fulfilment only within the security of their own societies and the landscapes hymned by their ancestors, it was my hope to give partial expression to the restlessness which this great upheaval has brought about. (ibid: 32)

The memoir itself, however, is baroque in form, like a patchwork with disorganized episodes, and is constructed anti-chronologically. To this seeming contradiction between intention and practice, Singh in a moment of reflexivity explains: "To impose order on my own history [is] to abolish that disturbance which is what a narrative in sequence might have led me to" (ibid: 243). Obviously, Singh's expression of the restlessness and the deep disorder is not aimed at abolishing the disturbance, the very reality of the colonial island, but to articulate it. As if to represent colonial society more faithfully, the memoir is contrived using parenthetic form, rather than a sequential, or a more systemic and lineal pattern of recollection.

The tension between Hindu heritage and Western education, albeit only implied and not well elaborated by Mr. Biswas, becomes salient in *The Mimic Men*. As a boy, Singh finds himself encountering tensions between his western education and his Aryan origins. Even the memory of his school days becomes confusing: "My first memory of school is of taking an apple to the teacher. This puzzles me. We had no apples on Isabella. It must have been an orange; yet my memory insists on the apple. The editing is clearly at fault, but the edited version is all I have" (ibid: 183). Singh's distorted memory of this childhood episode reveals how colonial education contaminates the minds of the colonials. It is not hard to imagine that what the children learn from school textbooks is all about the metropolis, whereas the reality and history of their own place is intentionally degraded, if not altogether ignored. Thus, education at school is meshed with the lived experience of the colonial, resulting in Singh's "edited" memory of his childhood. While working on *The Mimic Men*, Naipaul also wrote an article entitled "East Indian" for the *Reporter*, in which he wrote: "To be a colonial is to be a little ridiculous and unlikely, [...] To be an Indian from Trinidad is to be unlikely" (OB 1987: 35-36). It is truly unlikely for the colonial to strike a balance between ancestral heritage and the engulfing colonial discourse. Another memory of childhood recorded in Singh's memory is that of the coronation of the English King. Singh says he remembers the weight of the crown: so heavy that he can wear it only a few seconds (MM 1984: 192). Besides alienating the child from the history and reality of the Caribbean Island, experiences related to the Empire are inscribed in the child's memory, intensifying his sense of disdain for the island and a longing for the Imperial centre.

Singh's attitude toward his Hindu background is contradictory. He is at once fascinated with his Aryan origins, and yet maintains an increasingly detached stance. In the novel's subtle representation of a sense of uprootedness against the backdrop of a nostalgic feeling for Hinduism, Singh has fantasized about his Aryan ancestry since boyhood, and feels lost in Isabella. He romanticizes his ancestral heritage, visualizing a mental landscape of snowy mountains and Asian plains, and his mind keeps roving back to a distant past. In order to obtain a better understanding of his ancestry, he goes to the library to borrow *Aryan Peoples and Their Migrations*. Believing himself to be the first person to take the book out of the library, he finds it "not an easy book to read" (ibid: 102). Obviously, it is not easy for the colonial to search for his ancestral past in colonial society. Yet the link with the past cannot be easily severed. To the first snowfall he experiences in London, Singh says directly: "Snow. At Last; my element" (ibid: 8). For a Caribbean Islander who has lived his life in the tropics, but revolves around his snowy ancestral land, snow is enshrined in his quest for cultural autonomy, and with the longing for his lost origins. As Hall elaborates:

It is because this New World is constituted for us as a place, a narrative of displacement, that it gives rise so profoundly to a certain imaginary plenitude, recreating the endless desire to return to "lost origins", to be one again with the mother, to go back to the beginning. Who can ever forget, when once seen rising up out of that blue-green Caribbean, those islands of enchantment? Who has not known, at this moment, the surge of an overwhelming nostalgia for lost origins, for "times past"? And yet, this "return to the beginning" is like the imaginary in Lacan—it can neither be fulfilled nor requited, and hence is the beginning of symbolic, of representation, the infinitely renewable source of desire, memory, myth, search, discovery—in short, the reservoir of our cinematic narratives. (Hall 1990: 227)

What Hall theorizes here is representative of the situation of colonial people who have been deprived of access to their own history. The unfulfillable desire to "return to the beginning" becomes the impetus to represent the source of desire, memory, myth, etc. The past as such is unrecoverable, and can be told only in the form of representation and narration. Ironically, though he clings to his Hindu heritage, and longs for knowledge about it, Singh grows increasingly Anglicized. An extreme example of this is his clandestine name change from his Hindu-connoted name, Ranjit Kripasingh, into Ralph Singh.[2] His paternal grandfather's name is Kripal Singh, and when his father migrated to Isabella, probably as an indentured labourer like Naipaul's grandfather, he put the name Kripal and Singh together to form a surname Kripalsingh. What Singh does at the age of eight is to separate Kripal from Singh and adds Ralph as the first name, and so he creates the signature R.R.K.Singh (Ralph Ranjit Kripal Singh) or simply Singh R. He chooses the name Ralph for the sake of the initial, which is the same as that of his real name Ranjit, so that "I felt I mitigated the fantasy and deception" (ibid: 93). From the age of eight till twelve, he carries this "heavy secret" and dreads being discovered both at school and at home (ibid: 94). However, the secret is exposed when he has to change schools at twelve from elementary school to Isabella Imperial College, when his birth

---

[2] Naipaul's works are fraught with characters who transform their names in the course of their lives. In *The Mystic Masseur*, at the end of the story, we see Ganesh "impeccably dressed", coldly insisting his name is G. Ramsey Muir. In *A Christmas Story*, one of Naipaul's strongest short stories, the narrator changes his Hindu name, Choonilal, to Randolph. And in *A Flag on the Island*, the most interesting transformation is that of Mr. Blackwhite into H.J.B. White so as to be accepted by a Western audience.

certificate has to be consulted. Questioned by the teacher, Singh tells him that Ranjit is his secret Hindu name that is not supposed to be used in public according to the Hindu custom among certain castes. "But this leaves you anonymous" (ibid: 94), the teacher does not understand, "Exactly. That is where the calling name of Ralph is useful. The calling name is unimportant and can be taken in vain by anyone" (ibid: 94), Singh explains. The abandonment of his Hindu name means his denial of the Indianess in his identity, which leaves him anonymous. The English name is useful in that it takes the vacant place caused by the erasure of the Hindu name. Yet the English name is not significant and "can be taken in vain by anyone" (ibid: 94). That is to say, though Singh has denied his Indian identity, he is not pleased with the English identity and considers it unimportant, which suggests the hollowness of the Western identity he invents for himself. In other words, the issue of identity is far from being resolved at this time. Meanwhile, this episode further reflects that at this stage of writing, Naipaul still clings to the idea of a fixed and unified identity, struggling between the conflict of Indian and English identity.

The protagonist's transformation of his name signifies his desire to shake off the identity born to him, and his wish to embrace an identity he thinks more respectable. The yearning for more respectable roots takes shape early in his life. As we have already seen, as a boy at school, he often read about Aryan knights, horsemen and wanderers, and imagined himself living among those heroes (ibid: 98). He likes to think that he and his family are parts of that heroic tribe who only happened to be "shipwrecked" on this island where they now live. Actually, the first mention of the thematic term "shipwreck" is about his father: "I used to get the feeling that my father had in some storybook way been shipwrecked on the island [...]" (ibid: 88). Singh's father is very poor and the relationship between them is not friendly. To imagine his father "shipwrecked" on Isabella Island suggests Singh's unwillingness to identify with his father's depressing situation. To be shipwrecked means to be abandoned, and that something safe and beautiful is lost. With his father, it is the real country of India that is lost. Singh also imagines himself to be the leader of an Aryan tribe who will eventually be beckoned back to his true home among the northern mountains of India. Once alone on a deserted beach, he wonders to himself, "...what was an unmarked boy doing here, shipwrecked chieftain on an unknown shore, awaiting rescue, awaiting the arrival of ships of curious shape to take him to his mountains" (ibid: 111)? What the thematic word "shipwreck" connotes, as we can see from both Singh and his father, is nostalgia for the lost ancestry.

To a certain degree, colonial education also permeates the children with the sense of "shipwreckedness" because it persists in Anglicizing young people like Singh and alienates them from the reality of the island. The children at school are brainwashed by all that is English. When they think of a river, instead of thinking of any river on the island, they think of the Thames. In their compositions they write about visits to temperate farms though it is hot all year round on the island. In contrast to Imperial knowledge, which is foregrounded, knowledge about the island is denied and considered humiliating:

We had converted our island into one big secret. Anything that touched on everyday life excited laughter when it was mentioned in a classroom: the name of a shop, the name of a street, the name of the street-corner foods. The laughter denied our knowledge of these things to which after the hours of school we were to return. We denied the landscape and the people we could see out of open doors and windows, we who took apples to the teacher and wrote essays about visits to temperate farms. (ibid: 95)

It is colonial education that teaches colonial people to be ashamed of their own identity, and opt to become English. In fact, all through the novel, Singh drifts between the longing to be a hero to his ancestral people, and the desire to be an English man. He is practising either-or logic in his choice of identity, except that he is not satisfied with either one. Like the author in his own life at the stage when he

Chapter Two An Exile between Islands: *The Mimic Men*

wrote the novel, Singh has difficulty in accepting multiple identities, instead, he tries to hold on to one unified and fixed identity, be it Indian or English. Only in his later fictions, through much writing, does Naipaul begin to accept the concept of identity formation and enacts theories such as that expounded by Stuart Hall and James Clifford, that identification is a process of becoming, and that identity is multiple, mixed, and changing.

Besides Singh, there are other characters in *The Mimic Men* who struggle with identity seeking. One of them is Hok, Singh's friend and competitor at school. Unlike Singh, who is visually Indian, Hok's background cannot be decided from his physical appearance. Hok's name indicates Chinese ancestry, but he is not pure Chinese. He is multi-racial, a mixture of Chinese, Syrian, or European, and African blood. The culture with which Hok chooses to identify is Chinese. As such, his "secret reading" is in the Chinese section of the library. Hok is ashamed of his blackness and thinks Chinese culture more desirable and respectable. Once, in their crocodile to the Training College, a boy catches Hok avoiding his mother, who is out heading for the market. The mother herself walks past Hok, pretending not to see him—there seems to be a mutual agreement between the mother and son about their relation in the public. Informed by the boy, the teacher demands that Hok go to greet his mother. This is devastating, and Hok is crushed by the demand because his mother is "a Negro woman of the people, short and rather fat, quite unremarkable" (ibid: 95-96). At school Hok is usually the object of admiration, but now he becomes a laughingstock, and has to talk to his mother, an unremarkable Negro woman! It is not so much about having a black mother as about being "expelled from that private hemisphere of fantasy where lay his true life" and about being "totally betrayed" and becoming "as ordinary as the street" (ibid: 97). Singh understands Hok's sadness and feels that he himself "had been given an unfair glimpse of another person's deepest secrets" (ibid: 97). Singh knows that the last book Hok has been reading is *The Heroes* and realizes that "Hok had dreams like mine, was probably also marked, and lived in imagination far from us, far from the island on which he, like my father, like my self, had been shipwrecked" (ibid: 97).

To escape the acute feeling of being "shipwrecked", Singh goes to London. Equally lost there, as we have seen in the previous section of this chapter, Singh returns to Isabella, with an English wife. Singh does not inform his family of his marriage to an English woman. He is aware that his mother will not approve of his mixed marriage because Hindu doctrine forbids even people from different castes to intermarry. In the correspondence between Naipaul and his father while he was studying at Oxford University, Naipaul's parents often reminded him not to marry an English woman. Like Singh, when Naipaul at last married Pat, an English woman, he kept it a secret from his family. It is therefore not hard to imagine the mutual dismay when Singh's mother and Sandra meet each other for the first time at the quay: one in a carefully chosen Western disembarkation outfit, and the other in conventional Indian attire. The rivalry begins as soon as they meet. Not surprisingly, Singh's mother refuses to accept Sandra and acknowledge their marriage. Singh's marriage to Sandra symbolizes his efforts to resolve his crisis of identity. Yet the enmity between Singh's mother and Sandra foreshadows the gloomy prospect of his enterprise. When Singh marries Sandra, he feels that they have come together for self-defence against a hostile world and their common fears. Soon after the married couple returns to Isabella, Singh begins to realize that Sandra is equally lost. Despite Sandra's apparent confidence, she has been relying on Singh to save her from nonentity in England. They become uncomfortable with each other in their house and each of them begins to seek happiness outside the marriage. When his dream of "colonizing" an English woman fails, Singh is left with his vision of being a hero for his ancestral people. When Sandra at last leaves him, Singh remembers his childhood dream: "I am like that child outside a hut at dusk, to whom the world is so big and unknown and time so limitless; I have visions of Central Asian horsemen, among whom I am one, riding below a sky threatening snow to the very end of an empty world" (ibid: 82).

At the beginning of chapter four, the narrator protagonist reflects in a detached tone: "In the active period of my life, which I have described as a period in parentheses, marriage was an episode; and it was the purest accident that I should have entered politics almost as soon as this marriage came to an end" (ibid: 41). Indeed, as soon as his marriage with Sandra is broken, Singh enters politics. He is involved in the turbulent roiling political affairs of the newly independent nation, and throws himself into political movement. It is not in the narrow political sense that Isabella is a typical ex-colony. We learn, in fact, very little about the practical issues Browne's government must address. We are never told how big a majority he has won, whether a two-party system is set up with an established opposition, nor whether it ever becomes necessary to imprison political opponents. Clearly it is not the author's purpose to give us a sample of the decolonization movement in the former colonies.

A leader in the self-governing and nationalization movement, Singh deems his political life an extended "playacting" and what he is doing merely offers "drama" to the island people. His political engagement, beginning with his support of Browne's periodical *The Socialist*, ends with his failed delegation task in London, and his final departure from the island. Recalling the first article he writes for *The Socialist*, he admits that "the article was, deeply, dishonest", while "The writing of this book has been more than a release from those articles; it has been an attempt to rediscover that truth" (ibid: 189). Singh not only tries to rediscover the truth by himself, he invites the reader to join the quest. He uses words like "Consider", "See then", "Understand", "See how" and "Imagine" repeatedly to lead the readers to follow his search of the essential truth about the political movement in Isabella. He reveals that Browne and he see truth where they wish it to exist. With the necessary distance, when he is writing this memoir he realizes that what Browne and he have been doing "has happened in twenty places, twenty countries, islands, colonies, territories," where truth is evaded in "borrowed phrases," and where people are led to believe that the choice of a "particular" word "alters the truth", where a leader like Singh appears to "have been suddenly given a glimpse of the truth" (ibid: 192).

The "truth" about the revolution now obtained through the act of writing is that the political movement in the colonies in general is nothing but mimicry, and even the languages of revolution are derived from the West. The "borrowed phrases" and "jargons" become the resource of their power, which is, as Singh later realizes, "a matter of words" (ibid: 207). At a turning point in *The Mimic Men*, Ralph Singh discloses the circumstances of mimic men in the colony: "We, here on our island, handling books printed in this world, and using its goods, had been abandoned and forgotten. We pretended to be real, to be learning, to be preparing ourselves for life, we mimic men of the New World" (ibid: 146). This sense of inauthenticity and mimicry further leads to the colonial's realization of his precarious condition. Singh expresses this sentiment in his feelings about his house—for a time in his childhood he is obsessed with the fear that the family's old timber house is unsafe. From this we can see that for Naipaul, the empire, or the emblem of the empire, provokes colonials to reflect on their own situation, and realize that what they have been learning and doing to "prepare themselves for life" is not authentic and that they are but mimic men of the New World. Such mimicry, as is described in the novel, is the reason for the hollowness of the revolution and its failure. If we go a step further, we may ask why Singh and his fellow islanders have to "pretend" to be "real" and to be "learning". The answer lies in the novel and Naipaul's other works of Third World countries: they lack a greater past, what they have is nothing but "slavery, indentured servitude, colonial brutality, and colonial neglect" (Greenburg 2000: 228). With no sublime past to hold onto, the colonial people has to look up to the metropolis for a more respectable identity. Also, it shows that they are ashamed of their colonial identity, and their learning symbolizes their effort to get rid of it.

Naipaul's attitude toward the colonial people's mimicry is sympathetically satirical. In many places, Naipaul appears satirical to Third World countries for their lack of history, especially those in

Chapter Two An Exile between Islands: *The Mimic Men*

the Caribbean area: "The history of the island can never be satisfactorily told, brutality is not the only difficulty. History is built around achievement and creation; and nothing was created in the West Indies" (MP 1985: 29). Lack of history, partial modernization, and habits of dependent idleness all lead to the fundamental insecurity of colonial societies. To achieve security, they mimic the metropolitan "material values, political languages, and social institutions, all of which are appropriated in incongruous, denatured, and therefore damaging forms" (Nixon 1992: 132). According to Nixon, Naipaul employs "mimicry" to characterize a condition of insecurity that he considers endemic to Third World societies (ibid: 131). With Mustafa, Naipaul applies "mimicry" as a trope to characterize a particular moment of alienation in the novel (Mustafa 1995: 106). Before we come to the analysis of Naipaul's attitude toward mimicry, let's first look at the concept of mimicry.

In Bhabha's "Of Mimicry and Men", he conceives of mimicry as a facet of both colonial domination and colonial resistance. On the one hand, he sees the colonizer as a snake in the grass who speaks in "a tongue that is forked", and produces a mimetic representation that "... emerges as one of the most elusive and effective strategies of colonial power and knowledge" (Bhabha 1994: 85). Bhabha then recognizes that colonial power carefully establishes highly-sophisticated strategies of control and domination, but it is also anxious to create means to guarantee its economic, political, and cultural endurance. Macaulay describes in his "Minute on Indian Education" that the goal was to create a "class of interpreters who are between us and the millions who we govern—a class of persons Indian in blood and colour but English in taste, in opinions, in morals and in intellect" (ibid: 85). On the other hand, Bhabha notes that as an authorized version of otherness, as a reformed and recognizable other, these people produce a partial vision of the colonizer's presence, de-stabilize colonial subjectivity, unsettle its authoritative centrality, and corrupt its discursive purity. Actually, Bhabha adds, mimicry repeats rather than re-presents, and in that very act of repetition, originality is lost, and centrality de-centered. What is left, according to Bhabha, is the trace, the impure, the artificial, and the second-hand. "The desire to emerge as 'authentic' through mimicry—through a process of writing and repetition—is the final irony of partial representation" (ibid: 88). This reformed Other is almost the same, but not quite the same as the colonizer, he is an utterly alien "other", beyond the reach of recognition and comparison, and more threatening to the colonizer than one who has been brought up within the ambit of colonial values and measured by them. That is to say, in Bhabha's analysis, mimicry is an ambiguous process, it is a mark of subjugation but also, paradoxically, of potential empowerment, for while seeking to emulate the colonizers, the colonized can translate mimicry into a mockery of the colonizer, and by decentring and de-purifying the colonizers' construction, it may become a subversive force.

However, in addressing the mimicry of colonial people, Naipaul is more satirical and critical. As we have seen, when recalling his political days, Singh believes that they use "borrowed phrases" in their movement, and that the choice of a particular word can alter the truth. For Naipaul, the former colonies, exemplified in the case of Isabella, derive their language of resistance from the West, which becomes their source of power. To use Nixon's words, In the eyes of Naipaul, the "resistance" of the colonial people is merely "mimicry" (Nixon 1992: 153). Unlike Fanon, who insists that "the very forms of organization of the struggle will suggest a different vocabulary" (Fanon 1967a: 47), Naipaul thinks that the colonial's revolutionary movement offers only "drama" and is merely playacting. In an essay on Grenada entitled "An Island Betrayed", Naipaul demonstrates an ironic tension between the revolutionary's perception of their actions as alleviating the island's dependency, and his own understanding of these actions as mimic measures that leave the Grenadian more dependent. In Naipaul's eyes:

The revolution depended on language. At one level it used big blurring words; at another, it misused the language of the people [...] The revolution was a revolution of words. The words had appeared as an illumination, a short-cut to dignity, to newly educated men who had nothing in the community to measure themselves against and who, finally, valued little in their own community. But the words were mimicry. They were too big; they didn't fit; they remained words. (Naipaul 1984: 73)

This may imply that Naipaul is more concerned with "mimicry" in the colonial's psychology rather than in economy. "He conceives of mimicry as a function of geographical psychology—how people behave when they feel marginalized—rather than addressing psychological questions in tandem with economic ones" (Nixon 1992: 142). The difference between Bhabha and Naipaul's understandings of mimicry is now clear. First of all, Bhabha's discourse of mimicry is based on the heyday of colonialism while Naipaul is more concerned with the postcolonial situation in the newly independent ex-colonies. Secondly, whereas for Naipaul mimicry is more of an accusation against the colonials, it is an ambiguous process for Bhabha. It is a mark of subjugation as well as, paradoxically, an empowerment. In seeking to model themselves on the colonizers, the colonized can translate mimicry into a style of subversive mockery. Moreover, in Bhabha's conceptualization, it is the colonizer's desire to produce the mimic men who are like the colonizers, but not quite. With Naipaul, however, mimicry is the fate of the colonized people in their journey for identity. Beyond that, it is also a stage that must be surpassed.

In *The Mimic Men*, as we have seen, Singh deems his political actions nothing but a farce, and what he and his partners are doing simply offers "drama" to the island people. Instead of doing anything substantial, they only use "borrowed phrases" to carry out the movement. Singh realizes that his and his companion's efforts have been pointless and that "success changes nothing" (MM 1984: 203). After the failure of his political career, he decides to leave the island permanently because he feels:

I was too far sunk in the taint of fantasy. I wished to make a fresh, clean start. And it was now that I resolved to abandon the shipwreck island and all on it, and seek my chieftain-ship in that real world from which, like my father, I had been cut off. The decision brought its solace. Everything about me became temporary and unimportant; I was consciously holding myself back for the reality which lay elsewhere. (MM 1984: 118)

To long for the "reality" that lies elsewhere, is to regard the mimicked life in his colonial island as unreal, unimportant, and therefore not worth living. The wish to go elsewhere is also the wish to overcome the stage of mimicry en route to identification. It implies the abjuration of one's own homeland, and the embracing of a reality other than one's own. To long for a life elsewhere is therefore indicative of a wish for a more meaningful identity. In addition, as Iain Chambers insightfully explicates: "To live 'elsewhere' means to continually find yourself involved in a conversation in which different identities are recognized, exchanged and mixed, but do not vanish. Here differences function not necessarily as barriers but rather as signals of complexity" (Chambers 1994: 18). In other words, to long for the "reality" which lies elsewhere is to assume the fragmented and contradictory identities, or to be engaged in identification with a multiplicity of cultures.

Conflicting Identities

Interweaving memories and mutations, *The Mimic Men* masterfully evokes a colonial's inquiry of conflicting identification, from his homeland to the motherland as represented by England, resorting to flesh indulgence with women, political involvement and finally the act of writing a memoir. The very crucible Singh has lived through speaks against his search for roots. This route is open-ended and the destination is not a terminal point. The route may zigzag and the tentative destination may even change midway because the colonial's relationship to, and his understanding of, the ancestral and host cultural heritage remains unsettled. While most readings of this novel are limited to the theme of colonial mimicry, I think that as a profound novel of cultural displacement, the question of cultural identity is also at the centre of the novel's concern. Ralph

Singh seeks to understand what it means to be a colonial subject in a post-colonial society, in which no relationship is certain, be it between father and son, husband and wife, and even among friends. Like Mr. Biswas and the earlier generation of East Indians, most characters in this novel are represented as people with fragmented identities, who are uncertain of their position in society. The problematic concept of cultural identity, authenticity, as well as how the postcolonial subject constructs his cultural identity in the course of cultural displacement, are examined much more comprehensively in *The Mimic Men* than in Naipaul's earlier works.

The trajectory of Naipaul's identification, reflected in his protagonists' quest for identification, is similar to what Hall discussed in "The Question of Cultural Identity":

Identity becomes a "moveable feast": formed and transformed continuously in relation to the ways we are represented or addressed in the cultural systems which surround us. It is historically, not biologically, defined. The subject assumes different identities at different times, identities which are not unified around a coherent "self". Within us are contradictory identities, pulling in different directions, so that our identifications are continuously being shifted about. (Hall 1992: 277)

Singh has also experienced contradictory identities that pulled him in different directions. In his childhood, Singh tries to find refuge in the illusive identity of an ancient Aryan because he was not satisfied with his identity as an Isabellian, and felt only shipwrecked on the island, admitting in his memoir that "to be descended from generations of idlers and failures, an unbroken line of unimaginative, unenterprising, and oppressed, had always seemed to me to be a cause for deep, silent shame" (MM 1984: 83). He then goes to London to seek the "god of the city" and finds that London does not welcome him. He is not in his rightful place and cannot integrate into Western culture, to which he longs to belong. Faced with the dilemma of such conflicting identities, he is shifted about and "pulled in different directions", resulting in a crisis of identity that he never really recovers from. When Naipaul writes *The Mimic Men*, he is still attempting to hold onto one unified identity based on a coherent "self". It takes time and more writing for Naipaul to accept what Hall argues: "as the system of meaning and cultural representation multiply, we are confronted by a bewildering, fleeting multiplicity of possible identities, any one of which we could identify with—at least temporarily" (Hall 1992: 277).

Naipaul's understanding of postcolonial identity develops along with his writing career. In his early works, the problem of identity is more related to an existential situation in colonial society, exemplified by the case of Mr. Biswas, whose identity quest is closely connected to his longing for a house and a career. But in *The Mimic Men*, the identity quest is located not only in colonial society but in the metropolitan centre. In addition to characters like those in Naipaul's earlier works who barely leave colonial society in their lifetime, there is a new group of characters who, like Singh, have "all studied abroad and married abroad". As such they are "a group to whom the island was a setting" and for whom "the past had been cut away" (MM 1984: 55). That is to say, Naipaul's opinion of identity formation for a colonial when he wrote *The Mimic Men* is that neither drifting in the host country nor engagement in a decolonization movement could allow the colonial an independent identity. But Singh's final choice to reside in an anonymous suburban London hotel, like the characters in his early novels who either choose to escape from their island or to put their hope in the metropolitan centre, points to his unconscious hope of entering into the host culture and assuming an English identity. By the time Naipaul writes *The Enigma of Arrival*, it seems that he finally realizes his dream of becoming an English man through the sheer act of writing, and is at last able to enjoy an English identity, yet this interpretation oversimplifies the text. I will return to this point in detail in the next chapter.

Difficulty in identification invariably leads to a sense of homelessness, rootlessness, and a crisis of identity. In *A House for Mr. Biswas*, Mr. Biswas suffers from the agony of homelessness, and a crisis of identity because he lacks what he considers proof of independent identity: a house. Till the time in *The Mimic Men*, in the postcolonial milieu, homelessness and identity crisis become more acute, and universal a problem. Not only the colonial, but also the former colonizers, symbolized in Singh's English wife, Sandra, encounter the problem of homelessness and identity crisis. As we know, before writing *The Mimic Men*, Naipaul had traveled in the West Indies, India, and East Africa. Thus the scope of Naipaul's concerns by then had grown both in time and space, enabling him to see homelessness as a universal feature of the modern world, afflicting all races, including the former colonial rulers.

Like Naipaul himself, most of his characters resort to writing as a means to freeing themselves from their sense of homelessness, and help them construct and understand their identities. B. Wordsworth in *Miguel Street* claims to be writing a great poem; in *The Mystic Masseur*, Ganesh writes his autobiography *The Years of Guilt* before entering into politics; Mr. Biswas tries to write a story of "escape" to flee the forlornness of his actual life; likewise, Singh tries to better understand his identity quest by way of memoir writing. Writing becomes an escape: when they cannot leave physically, at least in their imagination they are able to free themselves from the "disorder" inherent to the half-made colonial society. From time to time, Singh reminds the reader of the process of his writing. In his writing, Singh connects himself self-reflexively to an imaginary ancestral land, his homeland of Isabella and to metropolitan London. For Singh, writing is a method to exorcise the profound and complex pain of dislocation, which he believes is his colonial inheritance. It also serves as a way to define his position in the world, to "give back the past", and to "impose order" on his chaotic history. Singh is different from the characters in Naipaul's earlier works who have never been to the metropolitan centre, and therefore still think of it with hope. *A House for Mr. Biswas*, for example, though a deeply ironic book, abounding in paradoxical statements, assumes explicitly that Mr. Biswas always believes that his real life will be elsewhere. This disorder is a peculiarity of colonial society in Trinidad, along with the delusion that the metropolis is a place of hope where everyone is entitled to dignity and identity. However, as Landeg White insightfully posits "if the order of London is genuine and if escape to London is easy, there is no need to take colonial problems seriously; [...] but if London is an illusion and the possibility of escape just another colonial myth, what and where then" (White 1975: 154)? Naipaul, of course, despite diatribes by some critics that he has become completely Anglicized, is far from being taken in by metropolitan values. The imperial myth that London is the centre of the world, and the home for colonials is precisely what is questioned in *The Mimic Men*, as we have seen from Singh's experience in London in the earlier section of this chapter.

As a legacy of colonialism, and an Indian descendent in Isabella, Singh is a "translated" man. He bears the traces of his ancestral culture, tradition, language, belief, and history, all of which have shaped his identity in one way or another. Translated men, as Hall cogently argues, are also "obliged to come to terms with and to make something new of the cultures they inhabit, without simply assimilating to them" (Hall 1992: 362). As products of several interlocking histories and cultures, belonging at the same time to several "homes"—and thus to no one particular home, such translated people are not, and will never be, unified culturally in the old sense.

Yet Singh fails to realize this, and has always tried to maintain a coherent self and a unified identity, which, since impossible, can only cause him more agony. In childhood, he secretly fantasized about a heroic India, yet deserted the name that was indicative of his ancestral culture, and gave himself a new Western name. Uprooted from his ancestral land, Singh carries with him illusions of a pure and real cultural origin. With this illusion shattered, he travels to England and tries to claim an English identity by marrying an English woman. Yet his short-lived marriage marks the fragmentation of the fantasy. After returning to Isabella, in the subsequent immersion in the roiling political movement of a newly self-governed nation, Singh ultimately discovers the crux of his disillusionment:

he has always tried to attach his identity to a given place, and to hold firm to the myth of a unified identity.

Additionally, Singh finds that his view of his own actions alters in the course of his writing. He begins with the feeling that his character has all along been molded by the vision of others, later, at the end of the novel, he changes his view and thinks that "the personality hangs together. It is one and indivisible" (MM 1984: 183). The evolution of his views about himself is essential in our understanding of Singh's quest for identity. At the beginning he allows himself to be subjected to other people's ideas about him and changes himself to conform to their views. Particularly in childhood when he romanticizes his Aryan origins, and in London when he loses himself in the city, he maintains an essentialist view of identity. When he develops doubts about whether personality is manufactured by the vision of others, and believes personality to be a complex thing that hangs together, he comes to a more elastic view of identity:

I no longer yearn for an ideal landscape and no longer wish to know the god of the city. This does not strike me as loss. I feel, instead, I have lived through attachment and freed myself from one cycle of events. It gives me joy to find that in so doing I have also fulfilled the fourfold division of life prescribed by our Aryan ancestors. I have been student, householder and man of affairs, recluse. (MM 1984: 250-251)

Residing in a transient location, a hotel that James Clifford specifically refers to in his essay as "the setting for Naipaul's *The Mimic Men*, a different place of inauthenticity, exile, transience, rootlessness" (Clifford 1997: 96), Singh accepts his position as an "exile" as he addresses himself and gives up his desire to binding his identity with an ideal landscape, as well as his wish to assimilate into metropolitan city life, to "know the god of the city". But the celebration of this freedom depends on having fulfilled what the Aryan legend holds about the fourfold division of life. According to Hindu religion, an ideal life is described as having four stages, or *ashramas*: (1) brahmacharya, the stage of the student; (2) grihastha, the stage of the householder; (3) vanaprastha, the stage of indulgence in sensual desires; (4) sannyasa, the stage of the wandering mendicant (Kinsle 1993: 94). Singh has experienced all these four stages in his life. The paradox here is that his freedom from tradition is based on fulfilling its requirements. Furthermore, it is the acceptance of this condition of exile that helps him fulfil the last: recluse. Maybe it is in this sense that when speculating on his present position in London, he thinks that "so this present residence in London, which I suppose can be called exile, has turned out to be the most fruitful" (MM 1984: 248). The fruit Singh has harvested is that he finally realizes that he has fulfilled the fourfold division of life in the Aryan legend, and has "lived through attachment and freed [himself] from one cycle of events" (ibid: 249).

He is now prepared for a fresh start, yet he does not "wish to be re-engaged in that cycle of events" from which he has just freed himself (ibid: 251). The new actions he wants to take are not dependent upon the binary logic of "departure" or "arrival", a repetition of the same cycle as before, but on the basis of a new diasporic vision. As a diasporic subject, who sees things both in terms of what has been left behind and what is actual here and now, he has a double perspective. This double perspective provides him, to quote Said, a "plurality of vision [which] gives rise to an awareness of simultaneous dimensions, an awareness—to borrow a term from music—that is contrapuntal" (Said 1993: 55). Through the contrapuntal reading of his past experience, Singh is able to see, from his repeated failure in his search for identity, that his quest, based on reclaiming his cultural heritage, has shifted from "an essence" to "a positioning" (Hall 1990: 236). In Singh's experience, he has actually unconsciously undergone this route from "essence" to "positioning", yet it is only in his writing that he achieves a conscious understanding. His search for cultural heritage is eventually situated in the flexibility of identification.

Chapter Two An Exile between Islands: *The Mimic Men*

Another important factor in the colonial's identification, as the title of the novel suggests, is mimicry.³ For Naipaul, the stage of mimicry is inevitable in the course of the colonial's identification. He believes that the process of mimicry requires that part of his colonial's past be sacrificed. This is exactly where he differs from

---

3 | In his explanation of mimicry in the West Indies, Naipaul distinguishes between the African Americans of Northern America, and blacks in the Caribbean. The former seek to differentiate themselves from white culture by asserting their blackness, in accordance with what Hall writes about "the new postcolonial subject" who celebrate their "blackness". The latter group, however, grow up in a white culture and tend to accept it.. For Naipaul, Caribbean culture is rooted in Western culture, and Caribbean values are those of the Christian-Hellenic tradition. Naipaul equates this Christian-Hellenic tradition with whiteness, and says that in order to pursue this tradition, "the past has to be denied, the self despised" (MP 1985: 67). The West Indian therefore accepts his blackness as his guilt, and looks upon it with contempt. He inherits from this "borrowed culture" (ibid: 65) the prejudices as well as the privileges. This is why Naipaul says that racism in the West Indians is different from that in Northern America or Europe because it is not between white and non-white, but among the non-whites. In the West Indies, people as a whole cannot relate to each other because they are from such different origins and racial backgrounds. According to Naipaul, "...there was no community. We were of various races, religions, sets and cliques; and we had somehow found ourselves on the same island. Nothing bound us together except this common residence. There was no nationalist feeling; there could be none. There was no profound anti-imperial feeling; indeed it was only our Britishness, our belonging to the British Empire, which gave us an identity" (ibid: 43). As he later finds, the colonial cannot even claim this Britishness. What Naipaul actually means is that people in Trinidad are victims of colonization, which makes them mimic men of Western culture. In Martinique, he finds that the Martiniquans are more French than the French themselves. This is because when all cannot be white, "all can aspire to Frenchness, and in Frenchness, all are equal" (ibid: 198). Mimicry therefore becomes a way to assert identity.

Bhabha. Bhabha holds that mimicry is almost the same but *not quite*, thus turning the colonial into a difference that is almost total but not quite. This, Bhabha says, is a menace to colonial discourse but an agency to the colonial (Bhabha 1994: 90). Naipaul, however, is satirical of mimicry, and believes that some elements of original ethnicity are lost through the colonial's transformation into another culture. He believes this because he has yet to accept the concept of a hybrid identity. At this stage in his writing, as has been stressed, Naipaul persists in holding on to the idea of a single, unified identity. Reflected in his concept of mimicry, he maintains that to mimic white culture means to completely negate one's ancestral culture and become a pure English man. This is also what Singh's final residence in a London hotel suggests to us. But abiding in a hotel also reveals the author's doubts about whether he will ever attain an English identity.

***

Intended to "impose order on the chaotic past", *The Mimic Men* actually seems to be disorderly unchronological and capricious. Various explanations are offered here and there in the memories, with the focus of the novel shifting from section to section. The complex movement back and forth in time suggests Singh's internal disorder as he struggles to exorcize his vision of chaos. This type of writing is also in accordance with the postcolonial subjects' displacement, and the very theme of the novel, that is, to seek order out of disorder, and to find a way to construct an identity. At the same time, the self-reflexive tone of the narrator constantly draws the reader's attention to the act of the writing of the memoirs. At one time in his active life, Singh considers writers as "incomplete people" and writing a "substitute for life" (MM 1984: 292). He finds "writing, for all its initial distortion, clarifies, and even becomes a process of life" (ibid: 301). Writing clarifies and wards off the fear of extinction; it becomes a vital way through which both Naipaul and Singh build their identity. Besides the act of writing, he also resorts to sex and political movement to claim his own identity, both of which, he feels, require self-violation and mingling to become the hinder block of identification. As Singh tells us at the beginning of his memoirs, ideally an extension of the self, a moving out of the self, sex is intended to discover "the larger erotic dream, the god", yet such intention is never realized in his seductions and visits to prostitutes. Instead, they bring him close to breakdown. Politics leads him into withdrawal. When Browne imposes an awareness of racial distress, Singh's reaction is to withdraw: "Now I felt the need only to get away, to a place unknown, among people whose lives and even languages I need never enter" (ibid: 145). Both sexual and political involvement end in failure, and Singh has to end his search for an authentic past, and to abandon the notion of a fixed identity with an authentic culture as its root.

Perusal of *The Mimic Men* enables us, as Roger Celestin comments, "to retrace the change from colonial to postcolonial and post-modern world, to observe a shift from "essence" to "processes"; that is, to outline a "shift from essence—a world in which cultural definitions are ruled by a static (imperial) point of reference—to process—a world in which so-called objective or natural or given points of reference are questioned and undermined" (ibid: 180-181). Singh has been student, picturesque Asiatic, householder, politician, extravagant colonial, dandy, intruder, exile, and writer. Such proliferating identities rest on positioning determined, to borrow Stuart Hall's words, by:

the continuous "play" of history, culture and power, because Cultural identities come from somewhere, have histories. But, like everything which is historical, they undergo constant transformation. Far from being eternally fixed in some essentialized past, they are subject to the continuous "play" of history, culture and power. Far from being grounded in a mere "recovery" of the past, [...] identities are the names we give to the different ways we are positioned. (Hall 1990: 223)

The Mimic Men concludes on a note of optimism. Though at the beginning of the memoirs Singh presents the reader with a bleak vision of his life in London, he does not give up hope. As we can see, he is writing his memoirs in a suburban London hotel, apparently suggesting that it is his drifting in the postcolonial urban space that has ultimately enlightened him with the necessary perspicacity to pursue cultural identity. The very form of the novel, its shifting between Isabella island and London, thereby, constitutes the route of Singh's identification, and this is exactly what Naipaul and Singh achieve through writing: identity cannot be fixed onto authentic cultural roots, rather, it is in constant evolution. Identity is identification, indeed and is always in conflict with itself.

Chapter Three An Enigmatic Identity
The Enigma of Arrival

> The diaspora experiences as I intend it here is defined, not by essence or purity, but by the recognition of a necessary heterogeneity and diversity; by a conception of "identity" which lives with and through, not despite, difference; by hybridity. Diaspora identities are those which are constantly producing and reproducing themselves anew, through transformation and difference. (Hall 1990: 235)

Beginning with *Finding the Centre* and *The Enigma of Arrival*, followed by *A Turn in the South* and *India: A Million Mutinies Now*, Naipaul's works shows signs of his attempt to reconcile himself with the three cultures that have contributed most to his identity formation—England, Trinidad, and India. Even Nixon, who strongly disapproves of Naipaul's works, finds in his works a recovery of "generosity not seen since *A House for Mr. Biswas*" (Nixon 1992: 167). We feel in these works an emotion that borders on hope. Indeed, this stage opens a new phase in Naipaul's work, which, since *A House for Mr. Biswas*, becomes progressively gloomier, i.e., *The Mimic Men, In a Free State, Guerrillas*, and *A Bend in the River*. *The Enigma of Arrival* is thus crucial in our reading of Naipaul's identification process.

In contrast to *A House for Mr. Biswas*, which is generally a story of pain and small victories, *The Enigma of Arrival* is more of a celebration of how "we had made ourselves anew" (EA 1988: 317).

Also, the narrator of *The Enigma of Arrival* inhabits in, and writes from, the pastoral to which Singh in his standard and characterless London hotel room can escape only through his imagination. Residing at Waldenshaw, a manor and village near Salisbury, England, where he has rented a cottage for ten years, the narrator has found "a safe house in the woods" and experienced a sense of "a second childhood", seeing in the landscape and its inhabitants an actuality commensurate with his school-boy fantasy of the England of Shakespeare, Gray, Wordsworth, Hardy and other literary masters. The narrator confidently feels that his "presence in that old valley was part of something like an upheaval, a change in the course of the history of the country" (EA 1988: 15). The former colonial, who lived at the margins of the empire, now arrives at the centre. In some sense, the present work represents the author's endeavour to trace how this arrival is made and how it becomes "an upheaval" and "a change" in the history of the country. In *The Enigma of Arrival*, the experience of displacement and change—which in Naipaul's earlier works is tied to homelessness, depression, and despair—is convincingly blended into a new mood of reflective calmness, as Richard Kelly reviews:

> the novel recapitulates and offers a tentative resolution of many of the major themes of Naipaul's previous work [...]. Within the space of ten years Naipaul gradually subdues the panic and fear that drove such characters as Mr. Biswas. [...] In facing his own mortality and the decay of his dreams and ambitions, Naipaul has achieved a measure of fulfilment [...]. Despite the grief that decay inevitable brings, he has come to accept the paradoxical nature of change. Change may destroy the perfect landscape but it also offers the possibility of new landscape. (Kelly 1989: 162-163)

However, *The Enigma of Arrival* is "another of Naipaul's controversial novels" (King 1993: 138). The controversy mainly centres on the tendency toward identification Naipaul reveals in the book. Derek Walcott and Rob Nixon hold that this book is a celebration of Naipaul's transformation into an Englishman, and that the book shows Nai-

Chapter Three An Enigmatic Identity: *The Enigma of Arrival*

paul's undue deference toward English culture. Bruce King, however, differs slightly, proposing instead that what Naipaul celebrates is his final entrance or intrusion into English literature. Other critics, such as Weiss, read the novel as an expression of Naipaul's condition of permanent exile in the world. Contrary to these reviewers, Helen Tiffen interprets *The Enigma of Arrival* as a confrontational work, like George Lamming's *The Pleasures of Exile* and Jean Rhys's *The Wide Sargasso Sea*. For Tiffen, *The Enigma of Arrival* challenges the colonial concept of England by emphasizing that England's pastoral heartland is subject to decay, and by exploring the relativistic and socially-constructed character of perception. Similarly, Suleri suggests that the relationship between the narrator and the ailing landlord, on whose grounds the narrator's cottage stands, is an impression of inverted imperial images. According to Suleri:

Each time the narrative focuses on the physical helplessness of the landlord as a synecdoche for imperial devolution, the narrator is somehow able to situate his own body as a racial presence in the text. This presence becomes increasingly strong in a directly oppositional relation to the landlord's disablement, and the postimperial narrator learns to acknowledge that his imperial counterpart is a secret sharer in his own progress toward bodily stability. (Suleri 1988: 29)

In this chapter, I will analyse the text from the perspective of Naipaul's identity development, and show that a binary division between English/non-English identity is not adequate to studying Naipaul, whose mixed background—a Caribbean of Indian descent living in England—determines that the problem of his identity cannot be judged using the either/or logic. Instead, a more inclusive reading is necessary if we are to obtain an objective understanding of his identity. What's more, Naipaul and his narrator arrived in England during the 1950's a time just after the Second World War, when many people swarmed into England and began to question the very notion of Englishness or Britishness as a unified and homogeneous entity. People made the discovery that there actually exist many different ways of being "British". According to Hall, Britain was at the centre of the largest *imperium* of modern times, governing a variety of different cultures. "The imperial experience profoundly shaped British national identity [...] this more-or-less continuous intercourse with 'difference', which was at the heart of colonization, has framed the 'other' as a constitutive element of British identity" (Hall 2000). When British identity itself has become a question, to say Naipaul has become British is too hasty a claim. A better way to approach this question may be found in what Naipaul's narrator at the very beginning of the book reflects: his presence in the heart of England is more of a change, and an upheaval in the course of the history of the country. In this way, the narrator not only puts himself at an equal stance with the colonizer, but also actively asserts his own subjectivity so that the previous inferiority of identity is obscured.

At the same time, for a typical colonial man like Naipaul, to claim any single identity is not an easy choice. Trinidad is a place he obviously abhors, yet it is the place of his birth and he spends his first 18 years of life there. It remains a central component in the subject matter of his works. India is his ancestral home, and exists in his mind mainly in the rituals he witnessed in childhood, and his two journeys (by the writing of *The Enigma of Arrival*) there prove to be more disheartening than encouraging. England is the place he has longed for, a place he experiences a sense of "second childhood" (EA 1988: 88). However, as we have already seen in *The Mimic Men*, his experience in London is not as encouraging as what he imagined from his colonial education. London, which he thought he knew very well, was strange and unknown to him on his first arrival. Actually, Naipaul's history of the world begins in a primordial sense of loss and estrangement. As he says, "The history I carried with me, together with the self-awareness that had come with my education and ambition, had sent me into the world with a sense of the glory dead; and in England had given me the rawest stranger's nerves" (EA 1988: 52). Colonial people like Naipaul are taught to be ashamed of their ethnic identity and to long for an English one, yet when they finally get to London they find that it betrays their ambitions and dreams, that they remain the colonial Others, or the strangers once there. Accordingly, this "second childhood" in England is too ambiguous a manifesto to be read as a sign of Naipaul's becoming an Englishman.

Homi Bhabha's articulation of the hybrid or "in-between" identity helps us to see more clearly what Naipaul wants to say about his identities, and the identities of postcolonial subject. Bhabha makes senses out of the "confused" and mixed identities of the colonial, and holds that with the emergence of the marginalized people to the fore, the identification of the colonial is neither that of the colonist Self nor the colonised Other but "the disturbing distance in-between that constitutes the figure of colonial otherness" (Bhabha 1994: 45). The other no longer feels alienated because there are so many like him. Bhabha's argument provides a useful theoretical basis to explain the resolution of the colonial's identity revealed in *The Enigma of Arrival*. To reach such a resolution, however, the colonial undergoes a common stage of mimicry, an imitation of or an attempt to conform to the norms and beliefs of the host country, as we have already discussed in the previous chapter.

In most of his writings since *The Mimic Men*, Naipaul has been writing his personal experiences into the history of a larger changing world, seeing global interactions in the "paradigms" of displacement, deracination, and disorientation. In his earlier novels, the protagonist always lives in hostile relation with his homeland, and is at the mercy of diasporic changes and cultural displacement. In *The Enigma of Arrival*, by contrast, diasporic changes, the ultimate sense of placelessness that plague the protagonists of his earlier novels, are accepted, and the fear of losing Indian tradition is no longer implied, but overcome and replaced by cultural syncretism. Naipaul's desire "to arrive in a book, at a synthesis of the worlds and cultures that had made me" suggests above all that what the writer "arrives" at in the novel is essentially a syncretic construct of identity (EA 1988: 157).

In his "The Game of Critical Arrival", Jose Piedra recapitulates some discerning observations about *The Enigma of Arrival*:

In his part-autobiography, part-revisionary journey, part-tourist travelogue, part-cultural critique, *The Enigma of Arrival*, Naipaul exposes the mutual discovery of Self and Other as a game of arrival. This game of arrival plays by rules that are retrospectively colonial. It is difficult to discern in Naipaul's case who is the Self and who is the Other on both sides of the colonial divide. He not only is the author of both characters, the colonizer and the colonized, but also insists on playing both parts and rejoices in the double-impersonation. (Piedra 1989: 36-37)

Being the author of both the colonial Self and the colonized Other, Naipaul situates himself in the in-between place or "the third space", where he "challenges our sense of the historical identity of culture as a homogenizing, unifying force, authenticated by the originary past" (Bhabha 1994: 37). Bhabha's "third space" is a possibility opened up to those living in the colonized position, that is to say, the "third space" is a way in which the subordinate undoes and unsettles the logic of the colonizer. It is in this "third space" that Naipaul endeavours to construct his identity through the act of writing.

Articulation of Identity

Although the dust-jacket of the book names *The Enigma of Arrival* "A Novel" and the title page refines it to "A novel in five sections", some reviewers are not persuaded. One critic argues that the novel is a complicated contraption, "a triumph or failure of artifice", and "there is nothing of artifice about Naipaul's new book" (Hughs 1988: 97). Likewise, Frank Kermode, Bruce King, Selwyn R. Cudjoe and Rob Nixon also tend to read it more as a piece of autobiographical work. In his famous article "In the Garden of the Oppressor", Kermode posits that "described as a novel, but [it] virtually [is] a slice of autobiography" (Kermode 1987: 11). With Nixon, "despite being marketed as fiction, *The Enigma of Arrival* comes closer to the autobiography" (Nixon 1992: 161). Even if it is not an autobiography in the strict sense, *The Enigma of Arrival* combines elements of fiction and non-fiction, and blends material not directly concerned with the personality of the author with autobiography. Speaking of *The Enigma of Arrival*, Naipaul himself proclaims that the writer, the observer, is scrupulously himself. In an interview he admits:

> I had to identify my narrator, my seeing eye, my feeling person. I didn't want to invent a character and give him a bogus adventure to set him there. I thought I should make the writer be myself—let that be true and within that set the fictional composite picture because you can't use real people to hang philosophical ideas about flux and change. That's where creation comes in. So there were the two aspects. To me I didn't do it out of any sense of being experimental. It just seemed natural. (Jussawalla 1997: 163)

It is at least safe to say, accordingly, that there is a very strong sense of autobiographical elements in the present work. It makes, naturally, a typical case for the study of Naipaul's identification because, as Susan Hafen postulates, "one's identity is created by stories that one tells of oneself (and others, sometimes retrospectively, making sense of past events), and their narrative logic into a coherent biography" (Hafen 2004: 184). Giddens holds similar opinions: "the existential question of self-identity is bound up with the fragile nature of the biography which the individual supplies about himself" (Giddens 1991: 54) . According to Giddens, self-identity is both "robust and fragile": fragile because the individual selects only one of many potential stories to tell, and robust because that story is held tightly "to weather major tensions or transitions in the social environments within which the person moves" (ibid: 55).

Autobiographical writing first appeared in most European countries in the late eighteenth century. The rise of autobiographical writing, similar to that of pre-Romanticism, is closely related to the change of the concept of man. During that period, people began to realize the value and uniqueness of the individual person's life experience. Understanding of man had also changed during that time. People began to view man as a historical being. Man creates history, but on the condition of history which is not of his own making, Marx claims. Besides its ability to explore the rich and colourful inner life of a person, autobiography transforms the individual life experience from something at the margin of society, into something worthy of social value, by externalizing one's inner self and showing it to others. Autobiographical writing is shaped by the interplay between the desire to assert a connection between a past and present self—to establish continuity over time which could be thought to define the very notion of identity—and an opposing sense of distance from the earlier self (Hayward 2002: 39). The purpose of an autobiographical work is to express a profound unity of life. It should convey meaningfulness, observing the often contradictory requirements of faithfulness and coherence. Autobiographical writing, therefore, is a mode of self-representation. Through the unfolding drama of consciousness, by reflecting on his past life, the author constructs in autobiography the image of his self for the reader. Accordingly, autobiographical writing must face the problem of how to represent the self and the identity of the author. In a sense, the writing of autobiographical work is a practice of self-definition and self-construction.

Obviously, it is impossible to record every detail one has experienced in life in an autobiography. To write an autobiography means to engage in an act of choice, which involves the reworking of a life experience, the editing out of unsuitable materials, and a tidying up of the confusions of experience according to some ordering principles. The writer must make choices in the reservoir of his memory, which are already the choices of the mind, and to decide what to include and what to leave out in his autobiography. Accordingly, in the organization of the narration, between the unification of meaning and the emotional representation of the experiences, between interpretation and recollection of the past, the autobiographer must try to attain a balance.

Naipaul used autobiographical materials earlier in *A House for Mr. Biswas, The Mimic Men,* and in his travel narratives as reminiscence or association, and has written a more organised survey of important events of his early life in "Prologue to an Autobiography." In *The Enigma of Arrival,* Naipaul reviews his personal history from a new vantage point, recreating it within the context of the history of Wiltshire, a site in England's ancient past, where he lived in a rented cottage on a decaying estate, a place that serves as the convergence of many elements: his childhood in Trinidad, which fed his panic and ambition, the other places he has lived, his travels, the books he has written and the one he is writing, and the Hindu tradition. In this book, his dreams and illusions are all linked with his life in Wiltshire. The fact that Naipaul looks at himself and the world around him from the perspective of Wiltshire may account for critic's diatribe about his having become completely Anglicised. However, as we are going to see in the next section of this chapter, Naipaul's residing in Wiltshire, as well as people like Jack, challenge the very idea of British identity and serves as a deconstruction of Englishness. Moreover, his writing at the centre of the empire redefines his place in both the Empire itself and its literary domain.

The very form of the work, therefore, invites meditation on the path to identification Naipual has been through. Actually, the most important theme of this novel is "change", as the narrator reflects at the end of the work, "I had lived with the idea of change, had seen it as a constant, had seen a world in flux, had seen human life as a series of cycles run together" (EA 1988: 301). At the beginning of the book, close to the beginning of "Jack's Garden", surveying the driveway nearby his cottage, he makes the following observation:

But already I had grown to live with the idea that things changed; already I lived with the idea of decay. (I had always lived with this idea. It was like my curse: the idea, which I had even as a child in Trinidad, that I had come into a world past its peak.) Already I lived with the idea of death, the idea, impossible for a young person to possess, to hold in his heart, that one's time on earth, one's life was a short thing. These ideas, of a world in decay, a world subject to constant change, and of the shortness of human life, made many things bearable. (ibid: 23)

While "decay" indicates a feeling of regret at having missed something, "change" assuages disappointment with the knowledge that what he sought never existed. From "decay" to "change", the narrator has gone through a shift from the mentality of a colonial other, to a postcolonial subject capable of evaluating from the perspectives of both, the colonizer and the colonized. It is in the active interplay between the past and the present that the shift from "decay" to "change" happens. In the author's foreword to *Finding the Centre*, a book about Naipaul's process of writing, he remarks that "A writer after a time carries his world with him, his own burden of experience, human experience and literary experience (one deepening the other); and I do believe—especially after writing 'Prologue to an Autobiography'—that I would have found equivalent connections with my past and myself wherever I had gone" (FC 1985: ix). What *The Enigma of Arrival* intends to show is the connections of the author's past and his present as a famous writer[1] who has enjoyed great fame and has resided in the metropolitan centre for almost thirty years, and who has got rid of the sense of inferiority of being a colonial other.

At the outset of the novel, the authorial I is eloquently staged to reiterate the reality of his presence: "For the first four days it rained. I could hardly *see* where I was. Then it stopped raining and beyond the lawn and outbuilding in front of my cottage I *saw* fields with

---

1 | By the time Naipaul writes *The Enigma of Arrival*, he is already the author of 20 books and has won numerous literary prizes: John Llewellyn Rhys Memorial Prize for *The Mystic Masseur* in 1958; Somerset Maugham Award for *Miguel Street* in 1961; Hawthornden Prize for *Mr. Stone and the Knights Companion* in 1964, W.H. Smith prize for *The Mimic Men* in 1968; Booker Prize for *In a Free State* in 1971; the Bennet Award in 1980; the Jerusalem Award in 1983; and T.S. Eliot Award in 1986. During this time, he bought his first house in Stockwell, South London; in 1968 he sold his house and travelled in West Indies, Central and North America, and briefly settled in Canada; he returned to England and lived in the Wiltshire cottage described in *The Enigma of Arrival*; after much travelling in places like India and some Islamic countries, he moved into the cottage near Salisbury in the English country of Wiltshire.

stripped trees on the boundaries of each field" (EA 1988: 5, italics mine). The work proceeds to depict what it is that the narrator fails to see, and the process of his learning to interpret it:

I saw what I saw very clearly. But I didn't know what I was looking at. I had nothing to fit it into. I was still in a kind of limbo. (ibid: 7)
I saw things slowly: they emerge slowly. (ibid: 16)
So much of this I saw with the literal eye, or with the aid of literature. A stranger here, with the nerves of the stranger, and yet with a knowledge of the language and the history of the language and the writing, I could find a special kind of past in what I saw; with a part of my mind I could admit fantasy. (ibid: 18)
I saw with the eyes of pleasure. But knowledge came slowly to me. It was not like the almost instinctive knowledge that had come to me as a child of the plants and flowers of Trinidad; it was like learning a second language. If I knew then what I know now I would be able to reconstruct the seasons of Jack's garden or gardens. (ibid: 30)

The recurrent appearance of the phrase "I saw" signifies the subjectivity and confidence of the narrator we seldom find in Naipaul's earlier works. Gradually, during the "seeing" process, the narrator masters this "second language". While doing so, he incessantly revises what he sees before and repeatedly retraces his steps to reconsider the same events and places from a fresh perspective. We have to be patient to follow the author's journey of perception, understanding and arrival because it comes at its readers "in repeating waves, depositing bits of information, and then receding, only to surge forward again, a little father this time, depositing a little bit more" (Jussawalla 1997: 147). The repeating and revising method deployed by the author is in accordance with its thematic concerns. Arriving in England, the narrator tries to understand things he has long ago learned from the colonial school at home in a gradual process. What is significant is that the narrator is trying to "see" here. It is in this active "seeing" practice that the narrator finds his presence, and together with other immigrants, decentres the centre of the colonial world: London.

The *Enigma of Arrival* comprises five chapters: "Jack's Garden", "The Journey", "Ivy", "Rooks", and "The Ceremony of Farewell", which are woven together through a slow unfolding of layered narrative with space and time compressed.² Different from Naipaul's earlier novels—which tend to end in escape and illusion—each section of this book concludes on a note of celebration: of Jack who created his own life and world; of the author's departure from the past both "intellectually and imaginatively"; of Pitton's growing out of what he had been and becoming a "new man"; of Bray the servant's masterly help of the solitary woman; and of the author's laying aside hesitations and writing fluidly about Jack and his garden. The work begins and ends with Jack's garden, thus a cycle of creation is constructed, which echoes the author's understanding of "human life as a series of cycles run together" (EA 1988: 301). But why does the author name the book "The Enigma of Arrival"? Where does he want to arrive at and where has he departed from? And before the arrival is arrived at, what type of journey has he lived?

The title of the book, as the narrator tells us in the section of "Journey", is inspired by the photography of a painting *The Enigma of Arrival* by Giorgio de Chirico. He is attracted by the title "The Enigma of Arrival" because he feels that it refers to something in his own experience in an indirect and poetic way. The painting depicts a wharf, a mast, a voyager, and "muffled" figures in a deserted street of an ancient Mediterranean city. The painting is a classical scene of "desolation and mystery", speaking of the mystery of arrival (ibid: 98). Inspired by this painting, the narrator makes up a fable,

---

2 | In the interview with Schiff, Naipaul tells him that to get the fullest out of the book a slow pace of reading is required because "Everything is here for a purpose. Please don't hurry through it. If you race through it, of course you can't get it, because it was written so slowly. It requires another kind of reading. You must read it at that rate, perhaps, at which the writer himself likes to read books. Twenty, thirty pages a day, because you can't cope with more. You have got to rest after reading twenty good pages. You've got to stop and think" (Jussawalla 1997: 149).

imagining a traveller who arrives on the quay of a foreign city and is drawn into the city's intrigues, yet he is gradually overwhelmed by a sense of aimlessness, hopelessness, and an awareness of betrayal and danger (EA 1988: 98). The narrator imagines that the traveller would walk past the muffled figure on the quayside and that "He would move from that silence and desolation, that blankness, to a gateway and door. He would enter there and be swallowed by the life and noise of a crowded city" (ibid: 98). The title of the painting, nevertheless, is not given by the painter himself, but by the surrealist poet Apollinaire. "The Enigma of Arrival," the title of a European painting that had not even been named by the painter himself, is thus appropriated, personalized, and attached with thematic significance. Over the years, memory of the painting keeps changing in the narrator's mind. The narrator says he has plotted two other stories about the painting prior to the writing of the present one. When he first sees the picture, he contrives it to be "a classical scene, Mediterranean, Roman"; later it becomes the story of how a traveller lived out his life in a strange land and has no way to return; and finally, the book under our discussion. What is common in the three versions is that they are all about the experience of leaving home and proceeding into the unknown. In addition, the provocation of this enigmatic painting implies that cultural heritages receive renewed bearings when perceived from different perspectives.

An analysis of the trope of arrival is necessary to better understand the book. The arrival may have a threefold tropical meaning: the geographical arrival, referring to the narrator's arrival at the centre from the margin; the cultural arrival, referring to the narrator's writing at the centre about his experience; and the psychological arrival, referring to his feeling at home in England. It is also an allegory that refers simultaneously to the departure from home, and to the arrival at a cultural other. Between the departure and arrival is a voyage to an adopted culture, in which cultural collision is inevitable. Yet there are different ways to deal with cultural collision. By the time Naipaul writes *The Enigma of Arrival*, the shock brought about by cultural collision is not as serious as when he wrote his earlier works. Cultural collision, up to then, had gone through a stage of cultural negotiation, and become more of a hybrid rather than a bone of contention between the mother and adoptive cultures. In a more metaphorical sense, therefore, the arrival in the title of the novel suggests Naipaul's proclamation of arrival at a state of hybridity in the postcolonial metropolis. He is now comfortable with his "in-betweenness", with existing in a "third space".

Naipaul doesn't arrive at this state suddenly. Throughout the novel, Naipaul seeks to re-imagine and relive the experience of a colonial's "arrival". The shock of arrival at "nowhere" in the beginning—the panic of entering and being "swallowed by the life and noise of the crowded city" (ibid: 98,99)—is substantially addressed in his London episode, in which the postcolonial scenario of metropolitan London is fleetingly registered but profoundly enunciated. Arrival is thereby a process indeed. In retrospect, his arrival in England in 1950 seems like that of the "earliest Spanish traveller to the New World, medieval men with high faith" who quickly took for granted the "wonders" of God's world they had ostensibly travelled for. Like the Spaniards, "having arrived after so much effort" and being interested only in what he expected to find, he had little to record (EA 132). However, his response to such an allegorized arrival is ambiguous because he both rejects and recognizes the impossibility of return: there is no return and no escape from the complexities of postcolonial arrival in an adopted culture. The anticipation of any path of escape can only be elusive and destined to impasse. Accordingly, the use of the trope of arrival in the novel carries with it a significant thematic concern. Arrival, as suggested in the meditation of the surreal painting and its ensuing conjectured fable, articulates the metaphysical moment of the confluence of cultural differences. It signifies in this novel a deliberate intervening act—writing when surrounded by a culture other than one's own. And as a successful deployment of the postcolonial engagement with the metropolitan-centred culture, *The Enigma of Arrival* secures the postcolonial' writer's access to the centre. Meanwhile, the heatedly discussed or debated novel ensures Naipaul's textually (re)invented arrival.

Autobiographical writing is usually embedded in the author's effort of self-understanding and self-definition. As Naipaul's autobiographical work demonstrates, his self-understanding is neither simple nor univocal. We cannot, therefore, conclude that his arrival in England is simply a symbol of his arrival at the heart of English literature and that he has become an Englishman at the expense of his ethnicity. It is not as Nixon argues that *The Enigma of Arrival* stages Naipaul's transformation into an English writer (Nixon 1992: 161). Even if it is true that Naipaul has become an ENGLISH writer, and that he has won himself a place in the great pastoral tradition of English literature, there exists another way to approach this question: Naipaul's racial presence in English literature ensures that he both continues and disrupts the lineage. As Helen Tiffin holds: *The Enigma of Arrival* dismantles the English tradition, unmasking the constructed nature of Englishness, and destabilizing the cultural authority represented by the heliocentric idea of England (qtd. in Jussawalla 1997: 147).

DECONSTRUCTING ENGLISHNESS

Most of Naipaul's works describe what happens in Third World countries, for example, India, Africa, Latin America, and the Middle East. *The Enigma of Arrival* is his second book set in London. In 1963 Naipaul published his first book with London as the setting, *Mr. Stone and the Knights Companion*, which was written during his first trip back to India. The book is about the routine life of a librarian-office worker, and the passively cruel metropolitan world as a place of alienation and exile. The opening pages of *The Mimic Men* allude to the themes of *Mr. Stone and the Knights companion*: "The pacific society has its cruelties," Singh says, "Once a man is stripped of his dignities he is required, not to die or to run away, but to find his level" (MM 1967: 8). Whereas *The Mimic Men* laments the absence of a New World order, *Mr. Stone and the Knights companion* deplores a numbing Old World orderliness. In *The Mimic Men*,

Singh goes to London with great expectations, hoping to find the "flowering" of his self. Mr. Stone, however, the product of the great city that Singh has sought, is transformed into stones by the stifling order of London.

More than twenty years later, Naipaul chooses England as his subject once again. What is significant this time is that the narrator of *The Enigma of Arrival* is actively engaged in learning about England, like "learning a second language". Rather than disillusioned or lost passively in England, as in the case of Mr. Stone and Ralph Singh, the narrator in this book is able to obtain the necessary distance between the person who experienced the disillusionment and the person who is looking at all this with a clearer sight and a sober mind. He has now spent his second childhood here and has learned enough about the country to accept as well as to reject it. Here he is about to assimilate what his experience has made him, thus decentring the very notion of Englishness with his "intrusion" into the heart of England, along with many others just like him, who emigrated to London while he was there. Naipaul gets to London at a time of great displacement because there is a rush of immigrants from the New World to the Old World. The torrid events have thrown millions into motion, bringing them to rest in unfamiliar places among people who are strange and, frequently, unwelcoming. It is a time when one's life, from birth to death, is no longer bounded by a few short miles. In the old days, people were raised to belong to the social and physical world in which they would live as adults. Opportunities for bettering the self were meager; ambition could produce little more than frustration and bitterness, but at least people felt at home among those to whom they belonged. Since the late twentieth century, however, especially during the post 1945 period, the lure of places where one could better oneself or the dangers that threatened if one stayed put, have set large numbers of people in motion. Naipaul arrives in London against this historical background.

In *The Enigma of Arrival,* Naipaul delineates a subtle and complicated documentation of such a passage, including a review of the personal and social conditions in Trinidad, an account of the uprooting and passage to the new land, a reminiscence of the unexpectedly harsh conditions found and endured on arrival in London, and a tale of triumph and success in the construction of a new life. Recollecting on that period of his life, Naipaul realizes:

In 1950 in London I was at the beginning of that great movement of people that was to take place in the second half of the twentieth century—a movement and a cultural mixing greater than the peopling of the United States, which was essentially a movement of European to the New World. This was a movement between all the continents [...] Cities like London were to change. They were to cease being more or less national cities; they were to become cities of the world, modern-day Romes, establishing the pattern of what great cities should be, in the eyes of islanders like myself, and people even more remote in language and culture. They were to be cities visited for learning and elegant goods and manners and freedom by all the barbarian peoples of the globe, people of forest and desert, Arab, Africans, Malays. (EA 1988: 141-142)

Indeed, London, the imperial city, which can justifiably claim to be the real metropolis at the centre of centre, is inevitably changing and decentring against this backdrop. More significantly, with the great movement of people and the convergence of former colonials, imperialism is reversed. In the past, London reached out expansively into "the world", but now "the world" shrinks in upon London. As we can see from the narration, London is not so much a city of homogeneity, as a space of dislocated culture. It has become a site of global heterogeneity. The phenomenon of migration Naipaul experienced and witnessed when he went to London makes a striking example. After World War II, the decolonizing European powers thought they could pull out of their colonial spheres of influence, leaving the consequences of imperialism behind them. But global interdependence now works both ways. The influence of Western styles, images, commodities and consumer ideologies outwards has been matched by a momentous movement of peoples from the peripheries to the centre, which is one of the largest and most sustained periods of "unplanned" migration in recent history. As Hall insightfully points out, "in the era of global communications, the West is only a one-way airline charter ticket away [...] Ethni-minority 'enclaves' are formed within nation-states of the West, leading to a 'pluralisation' of national cultures and national identities" (Hall 1992: 306-307). The settled contour of British identity is problematized and new identities are now emerging.

Mike Featherstone argues that the movement of people in the post-war era results in the borderless culture of globalization. More people are living between cultures, or on the borderlines. European and other nation-states, which formerly sought to construct a strong exclusive sense of national identity have to deal with the fact that they are multicultural societies as "the rest" have returned to the West in the post-1945 era (Featherstone 1995: 10). This is exactly the case with the narrator of the book and many other immigrants like him. They moved into London and felt that their departure from the host country uprooted them from their mother culture. Living between cultures, with no fixed identity to claim, these people felt out of place in the context of the new culture. The narrator's first impression of the London house he lodged in is as follows:

I felt the house was no longer being used as the builder or first owner had intended. I felt that at one time, perhaps before the war, it had been a private house. [...] I felt, as I saw more and more of my fellow lodgers—Europeans from the Continent and North Africa, Asiatics, some English people from the provinces, simple people in cheap lodgings—that we were all in a way campers in the big house. (EA 1988: 129)

The houses that were intended as private places had become camps for people from all over the world; they were now no one's home in particular. People from outside London, who came with the dream of finding a home, becoming instead mere campers, now populate London. The presence of these people, on the one hand, renders London a global city, and on the other, decentres it. Significantly, however, Naipaul's attitude toward London is ambiguous. London is no doubt a place he has long dreamed of. Talking about her despairing experience and unfulfilled expectations with London, Jean Rhys, who also came from the West Indians, grieves:

I would never be part of anything. I would never really belong anywhere, and I knew it, all my life would be the same, trying to belong, and failing. Always something would go wrong. I am a stranger and I always will be, and after all I didn't really care. [...] it was Jack, who is a writer, who told me that my hatred of England was thwarted love. I said disappointed love, maybe. (Rhys 1979: 124, 168)

Jean's description of the feeling of being a stranger in London is typical of the colonial's experience there. "Disappointed love" may be the right word to express the colonial's feelings toward London when they first arrive. Likewise, the narrator of *The Enigma of Arrival* repeatedly claims that he feels he has come to London at the wrong time: "so I grew to feel that the grandeur belonged to the past; that I had come to England at the wrong time; that I had come too late to find the England, the heart of Empire, which (like a provincial, from a far corner of the empire) I had created in my fantasy" (EA 1988: 120). Reflecting on his experience of London, the narrator found the city "strange and unknown". In *An Area of Darkness*, Naipaul recorded this disjunction between expectation and experience: "I came to London. It had become the centre of my world and I had worked hard to come to it. And I was lost. London was not the centre of my world" (AD 1981: 45). In spite of this disillusionment, he remains in London anyway.

Back at home, the narrator was equally dislocated and lost. The world he was brought up with is one among advertisements for things that were no longer made. It was a world where signs were without meaning, or without the meaning intended by their makers (EA 1988: 130-131). This double dislocation suffered by colonial people reminds us of DuBois's notion of the double consciousness of Black people. DuBois argues that Blackness and Black consciousness were and are significant components of Black reality—they were and are being Black in America. With DuBois, double consciousness is the myopia of a dual or bipolar consciousness of identity that produces a fundamental alienation in Black people; double consciousness causes Black people and, one could claim, members of any "minority" group, to view themselves through both their own eyes and the eyes of people from the dominant culture. The result is a self in search of its own identity and fulfillment through the presence of the other. (DuBois 1982: 5) Double consciousness does more than account for the double bind and ethnic identity of African Americans, it can also be extended to other minority groups. In the case of Naipaul, and other immigrants in London from the periphery of the world, this double consciousness is also inscribed in their identity. Back in their homeland, the colonials tend to view themselves through the paradigm of the colonizer's standard, the result of which is a sense of inferiority about themselves and the home country, and a longing to leave. Colonial education changes them into intellectuals with English tastes. For example, C.L.R. James, another writer from the West Indies, sees himself as a product of the colonial education system. In *Beyond a Boundary*, he recollects that he thought of himself as a British intellectual, even before he was ten, already an alien in his own environment among his own people, even his own family (James 1963: 28). When the colonial people finally arrive in London and experience traumatic disillusionment, they begin to view themselves from the consciousness of their own and come to the realization that they are only "campers" in London, and that London is but a "fantasy". To sum up, it is this double consciousness of viewing himself as a colonial and from the perspective of the colonizers that constitutes his ambivalent attitude toward England.

Paradoxically, however, this double consciousness serves as a necessary preparation for the deconstruction of the notion of Englishness. At the very beginning of the book, at Wiltshire, the heart of England, the narrator feels he "could hardly see where he was" (EA 1988: 1). This consciousness of being lost in England drives the narrator to look at his environment more intensely, leading to a consciousness of the active cultivation of the narrator's subjectivity. He is to look and find out what England really is, and to understand his own place in it. Before coming to England, the narrator believed he knew the country well enough through reading about it in literary works. After living there for almost twenty years, however, he still feels himself to be in another man's country, somewhat like a solitary stranger. The sense of "out-of-placeness" in the country leads to the narrator's consciousness that his presence in that old valley of Salisbury is like an "upheaval" and a "change" in the course of the history of the country. It is this "upheaval" and "change" that serves to deconstruct the concept of Englishness.

Scholars in postcolonial studies have done significant research to detect and deconstruct the former homogenous concept of Englishness. People begin to understand that Britain is not just a political unit but also an imagined community. Like all national discourses, Britishness is deeply embedded in the dense integument of a complex tissue of cultural meanings, symbols and images, selectively woven together in a dominant national narrative. Hall holds that the dominant version of the national story has systemically overplayed the unity and homogeneity of the nation, while the deep differences of nation, region, locality, class, and gender and language, which have persisted throughout, is underrepresented (Hall 2000). Instead of reflecting a unity that is already there, national discourses constitute a sort of unity built out of the many differences with which it is confronted. There exists a distinction between the old and today's notion of Englishness: "Englishness of the past is often represented in terms of fixity, of certainty, centerness, homogeneity, as something unproblematically identical with itself", but Englishness today is "a heterogeneous, conflictual composite of contrary elements, an identity not identical with itself" (Hall 1995: 2-3). Simon Gikandi has made similar discoveries: "[...] Englishness was itself a product of the colonial culture that it seemed to have created elsewhere. [We began] to read Englishness as a cultural and literary phenomenon produced in the ambivalent space that separated, but also conjoined, metropole and colony" (qtd in Hall 1996: XII).

In Naipaul's heavily autobiographical work, while trying to construct his own identity at the centre of former Empire, he simultaneously deconstructs the fixed, unified and homogenous concept of Englishness or Britishness. "Change" or "mutability" as the theme of the book conforms to his changed understanding of the country he has longed for, and to the acceptance of his identity. This change, however, stems from the narrator's sense of "decay" as is expressed at the beginning of *Jack's Garden*, "But already I had grown to live with the idea that things changed; already I lived with the idea of decay" (EA 1988: 10). Almost 200 pages later, the narrator comes to a new understanding: "I lived not with the idea of decay—that idea I quickly shed—so much as with the idea of change. I lived with the idea of change, of flux, and learned, profoundly, not to grieve for it. I learned to dismiss this easy cause of so much human grief. Decay implied an ideal, a perfection in the past" (ibid: 210).

From "decay" to "change", the myth of the British imperial past is demystified. What colonial discourse teaches the colonials about the British Empire are its power, progressiveness, intellectual potentiality, and everything that is superior. Britain's colonization of its colonies is not only geographical intrusion and political hegemony, but covers almost every sphere of colonial life, imbuing the colonial with various Euro-centric and Euro-superior concepts. It is by way of culture, education, religion, media etc. that the colonizers colonize the mind of the colonial people. Indeed, the colonizers' aim is to establish a "hegemonic" culture so that the colonials will unconsciously identify with the culture of the colonizers, because, to quote John Storey, "to share a culture is to interpret the world—make it meaningful and experience it—in recognisably similar ways" (Storey 2004: 69). Many postcolonial critics recognize the importance of cultural colonization. While studying some English novels written during the heyday of British colonization, Said found that novels, as an aesthetic and cultural form, played a significant role in the colonization movement. Because culture is an important source of identity, it is naturally a highly competitive place where colonial and anti-colonial discourse would wrestle with each other heatedly.

Chapter Three An Enigmatic Identity: *The Enigma of Arrival*

To put it in Storey's words, "cultures are never simply shifting networks of shared meanings. On the contrary, cultures are always both shared and contested networks of meaning. That is, culture is where we share and contest meanings of ourselves, of each other and of the social worlds in which we live" (ibid: 68-69).

Naipaul's experience may be taken as the epitome of such cultural colonization. In Trinidad, Naipaul received a completely English education: the language taught at school, the curriculum at school and the ambiance of the school, are all English. Reflecting on Trinidadian colonial education, Naipaul quotes from C.L.R. James' *Beyond a Boundary* with regard to the public-school code of the Queen's Royal College:

Our masters, our curriculum, our code of morals, everything began from the basis that Britain was the source of all light and learning, and our business was to admire, wonder, imitate, learn... If the masters were so successful in instilling and maintaining their British principles as the ideal and norm it was because within the school, and particularly on the playing field, they practiced themselves... They were correct in the letter and in the spirit. Under such educational system, James educated himself into a member of the British middle class. (OB 1987: 22-23)

With Naipaul, besides the colonial education he receives at school, the vast amount of literary works he read in childhood under the guidance of his father help shape his understanding of the glory of the Empire, and his admiration of it, which may account for why in his earlier works, almost all the protagonists choose to leave their colonial motherland with the belief that hope is only possible in London. Before *The Enigma of Arrival*, we can see that both Naipaul and his protagonists identify more with a British identity. This is why when he arrived in London in the 1950s, precisely the period when the empire was collapsing, he would experience a feeling of decay, which, as he himself explains, implies an ideal, and a perfection of the past. From the feeling of "decay" to "change", therefore, Naipaul undergoes an important transformation in his identification.

Critics differ in their opinions as regards Naipaul's identification tendencies in *The Enigma of Arrival*. For instance, Bruce King holds that this work shows the author's sense of "homelessness", and Nixon claims that what Naipaul demonstrates in the present work is that he has proudly fulfilled his dream of becoming an English man. In my opinion, however, what Naipaul has achieved is more of a hybrid identity. To construct this hybrid identity, the narrator first establishes the fictionality of Englishness. Out of the five sections of the book, three of them can be legitimately read as the deconstruction of Englishness. Entitled "Jack's Garden", the first section recounts the inevitability of vicissitude, the inventory decay and regression, and the factuality of the flux and change that are taking place in the heart of England. Near the end of the first section, the narrator realizes Waldenshaw, the name of the village where he lives, has long been absorbed into other languages and speaks of "invaders from across the sea and of ancient wars and dispossessions" (EA 1988: 92). In a rented cottage in Wiltshire where he is to stay for ten years, the narrator gradually redirects himself. The slowed-down rhythm of his writing reflects the process of his understanding of what he sees. What he notices most sharply is the historicity of the village. the traces of the former activities of old cultivation, outdated customs, and objects of ruins.

The narrator's understanding of Jack is of significant importance in the book. At the beginning, the narrator admires Jack's heartiness and dedication to the land. Together with the Wiltshire countryside scenery, Jack has become the central image of the narrator's romance with Old England. In the narrator's eyes, Jack is "rooted to the earth", and thus stands for English tradition, and perhaps part of the English world of Chaucer and Shakespeare. Critics who deem Naipaul has become totally Anglicized draw their conclusion on the basis of the narrator's identification with, and his admiration for, Jack's rootedness. The narrator's view of Jack changes later, however. He finally becomes aware that Jack might well be a foreigner of sorts, that he lived "in the middle of junk, among the ruins [...] that the past around his cottage might not have been his past; that he might at some stage have been a newcomer to the valley; that his style of life might have been a matter of choice" (ibid: 15). Jack managed to come to terms with the decay of the once flourishing farms, with abandoned homes, and with change in renewal by creating himself a garden at the heart of England. What is most moving about Jack is his death. Knowing that he is dying, he still goes to a pub to celebrate Christmas Eve, embracing the last pleasure life offers him. In face of inevitable annihilation, with his heroic effort to taste life, Jack demonstrates the "primacy" of life. Although a foreigner in this land, Jack lives his life to the fullest. Jack's death helps the narrator cast a different look at Waldenshaw: it is not so much a remnant of old England as part of a fragile and constantly changing world. He finally comprehends that the perfection of England is but a construct of both the colonizers and the colonized. As change is the essence of all things, the narrator's presence and change at the heart of England is inevitable in the course of history and therefore, he can also create his own garden. Section one concludes with a celebration of Jack:

He was not exactly a remnant; he had created his own life, his own world, almost his own continent. [...] he had created a garden on the edge of a swamp and a ruined farmyard: had responded to and found glory in the seasons. All around him was ruin; and all around, in a deeper way, was change, and a reminder of the brevity of the cycles of growth and creation. But he had sensed that life and man were the true mysteries; and he had asserted the primacy of these with something like religion. The bravest and most religious thing about his life was his way of dying: the way he had asserted, at the very end, the primacy not of what was beyond life, but life itself. (ibid: 93)

As an outsider to England, Jack makes himself at home right at the heart of it.

Images of decay and death pervade the third chapter "Ivy". At the beginning of this section, the narrator presents us with a "ragged, half-rotted-away carcass of a hare" (ibid: 185). It seems that the manor is in total decay: the beech trees are now like "a natural—wasting—monument" of the landlord's father's grandeur; part of the estates are only "bush and forest debris" and rotted bridges; and the boathouse is like "a spectacular ruin" (ibid: 187). The most dramatic image of decay is the ivy that is smothering the trees on the manor, yet the landlord forbids people to cut it down. The narrator speculates that the reason the landlord "cherishes" the ivy might be that it serves as "a comforting reflection" of his persistent depression. But the narrator never meets the landlord. He only catches glimpses of him. His knowledge comes from what others have said about him, and from the landlord's writings and drawings. The landlord sends the narrator poems he wrote decades before about an "Indian romance" of Krishna and Shiva and "the days of imperial glory" (ibid: 212). He also sends a mischievous novel, illustrated with drawings reminiscent of Beardsley, about a young woman who gets tired of the English social world, and decides to become a missionary in Africa. However, the woman is captured by the native Africans and is eaten by cannibals. Before being eaten, the woman has fantasies of sexual assault by the African chief to whose compound she is taken.

 We are not told whether the landlord has ever been to India or Africa. But his writings about those places are thematically important. Living on the deteriorating manor, suffering from acedia, in the post-War period when the British Empire is already a historical term, the landlord still immerses himself in the colonial imagination of the former colonies of the Empire. This Indian romance of the landlord stems not from any contemporary fashion. Rather, it is something he inherited from the days of imperial glory, like his manor. It was rooted in England, the empire, with wealth, the idea of glory, material satiety, and a high level of security. With his ground-breaking work, *Orientalism*, Said makes the ingenious contention that the discursive construction of Orientalism was self-generating, and bore little, if any, relation to its putative object, "the Orient". Western knowledge about the Other can, therefore, be perceived as a construction out of the whole system of Orientalist discourse, which can "create not only knowledge but also the very reality that they appear to describe" (Said 1978: 94). The lascivious Krishna and the drug-taking Shiva described in the landlord's poems are his own conceptualizations of India. As such, the narrator feels that "his Indian romance had very little to do with me, my past, my life or my ambitions" (EA 1988: 212). It is common knowledge now, in postcolonial study, that literature as an aesthetic form plays an important role in the establishment and solidification of the empire. The landlord's writing about the Indian romances in his days of depression reflects his effort to hold on to the past glory of the empire.

The story about the missionary woman eaten by the African cannibals carries with it similar references to the colonizer's conceptualization of colonial people. We are told that the English woman has fantasies of the Africans' sexual aggressiveness, which, together with the cannibals' eating people alive, represent the colonials' stereotypical knowledge of Africans. The landlord wrote this story in the 1920s, when he was a young man of eighteen. Things were still good for the landlord at that time when he had wealth, good health and fame. The narrator speculates that the landlord's knowledge about Africa is based on his manor and grounds (ibid: 282). That is to say, it is the wealth of the empire that enables colonizers like the landlord to "create" knowledge about the peripheral places of the world according to their bias toward colonial society. Yet the narrator dismisses the landlord's writing as nothing but "joke knowledge" (ibid: 282). Paradoxically, though, it is the type of fantasy held by the colonisers about a barbarian Africa that takes the life of the English lady, who intended to "save" the Africans with her religion. This story, on the one hand, represents the ugly and backward prototype of African people in the Westerner's eye, and on the other, it describes the ambivalence in colonial discourse.

Ambivalence is a psychological term introduced to the field of postcolonial study by Homi Bhabha, and refers to "a continual fluctuation between wanting one thing and its opposite" (Young 2004: 161). A complex mixture of attraction and repulsion characterizes the relationship between the colonizer and the colonized. Ambivalence disrupts a clear-cut authority of colonial domination because it disturbs the simple relationship between the colonizers and colonized. The aim of colonial discourse is to produce compliant subjects, mimic men who reproduce the assumptions, habits and values of the colonizer. "Ambivalence describes this fluctuating relationship between mimicry and mockery, an ambivalence that is fundamentally unsettling to colonial dominance" (Aschroft et al. 1995: 13). Bhabha's argument is that colonial discourse is compelled to be ambivalent because it never really wants colonial subjects to be exact replicas of the colonizers, which would be threatening. Since the colonial relationship is always ambivalent, it generates the seeds of its own destruction. In the story of the landlord, what seemingly kills the English woman seems to be the African, but actually what takes her life is also her colonial fantasy. Thus we can read the story as a revelation of the barbarity of the African, as well as the curse of a lady who tries to colonize Africans culturally. Furthermore, the English lady's motivation for doing missionary work in Africa is not unproblematic. She goes to Africa mainly because she is tired of English social life. This embodies the colonizer's idealization of Third World countries as places of fantasy where they can kill the dullness of life at home.

The landlord and the narrator are at "opposite ends of wealth, privilege, and in the hearts of different cultures" (EA 1988: 191). Since the landlord's fortune was accumulated during the expansion of the empire in the nineteenth century, the narrator thinks that it is the empire that "lay between them" (ibid: 191) At the same time, however, the narrator admits that the empire also links them, because the empire explained his birth in the New World, the language he used, the vocation and ambition he had, and his presence in the landlord's manor. Arriving at Waldenshaw "at a time of disappointment and wounding" in his life, the narrator empathizes with the landlord who out of a malady of the spirit—an acedia—has ceased to be a doer and wishes to "hide" from the world (ibid: 192). Initially the narrator sees Waldenshaw as a safe island, an almost perfect world, but later he begins to spot its fragility: "One morning's work with a chain saw" could destroy it (ibid: 178). What's more, the landlord prefers to let his manor go to ruin, as he does not allow the ivy to be cut down though he knows it is smothering the tress on his manor. The symbol of the empire's glory is therefore deteriorating from both within and without.

The title of the section "Rook" is from an "old wise tale" which tells that the rooks' nesting announces the arrival of death or money (ibid: 297). Mr. Philips told the narrator that these rooks lost their nests when the elms on the manor died. Yet the rooks didn't just die with the elms, instead, they began to build their nests in the beeches. Wiltshire and Hampshire, two places where used not be any rooks, are now being colonized by these big squawking birds. "If you think they're birds of death you can't stand the noise. If you think it's money, you don't mind" (ibid: 297), Mr. Philips tells the narrator. Yet this is a section about deaths: the death of Alan, a literary figure; the death of Mr. Philips, the caretaker; the death of Mr. Philips' cousin; and the death of the elms. After the death of Mr. Philips, who is the caretaker of the landlord as well as the "human force behind the landlord's stable condition" (Weiss 1992: 200), the narrator feels it is time for him to leave Waldenshw. The scenery that used to be so attractive in the valley now appears bleak:

The elms had finally died in the valley. Many, before they had finally died, had been felled, cut up; others had died standing up, remaining bare, going grayer against the summer green. And the valley road became suddenly open. Curves once overhung with green, mysterious and full of depth, showed plain; tilled downs, without a border of elms and wild growth between the elms, sloped down simply to the asphalt road. House plots showed plain, and houses and their ancillary little corrugated sheds looked naked. The shallow river and its wet banks remained enchanting; but the land on either side became ordinary. (EA 1988: 299)

Initially, the narrator is greatly attracted by the manor and is keen to make discoveries. He feels that he can understand his landlord and sympathize with him. In "Rooks", however, the narrator undergoes further changes in his understanding of the manor. As was already discussed, he used to live with the idea of decay, but later the notion of change and flux replaces the sad feeling of decay. It is his new discovery that almost everyone living and working on the manor was once a new comer like himself, and none of them but the landlord really belongs to the manor. After witnessing the deaths that occur one after another on the manor, the narrator begins to feel himself an intruder from another hemisphere who has destroyed the past of an old woman, as his own past has been destroyed. That is to say, in a world where the flux of people is common, the binary distinction between the centre and the periphery is now overthrown. Naturally, the centrality of Englishness is deconstructed.

While writing about people who live and work on the manor, the narrator actually demystifies the purity of Englishness, or the English identity. According to Robert Young, in the nineteenth century, the very notion of a fixed English identity was doubtless a product of, and a reaction to, the rapid change and transformation of both metropolitan and colonial societies which meant that, as with nationalism, such identities needed to be constructed to counter schisms, friction and dissent (Young 1995: 4). Therefore, the Englishness of the past was often represented as fixed, certain and homogeneous. According to Hall, the assumption that Britain had a unified and homogenous culture until the post-war migrations from the Caribbean and the Asian sub-continent is a highly simplistic version of a complex history. Britain has existed as a nation state only since the eighteenth century, and it has associated significantly different cultures—Scotland and Wales—with England. The so-called homogeneity of "Britishness" as a national culture has been considerably exaggerated (Hall 2000). Englishness as an identity became strongest during the colonial period when the central government incorporated all the differences of regions, people, classes, and gender, in order to form the national culture as a homogenous entity. The fixity of English identity, namely English people as benevolent, progressive, and superior in everyway to colonial people, seen as typically vicious, lazy, and inferior to the colonizers, is in fact what the English national discourse tries to instil into the minds of the colonized in particular. The narrator of *The Enigma of Arrival* holds this kind of understanding of English identity when he first arrives in Wiltshire. He contributes everything beautiful on the manor to the English. He admires Jack and thinks him to be rooted in the manor. Even Jack's father-in-law is thought of as a literary figure from the works of Wordsworth. He later finds that Jack, the same as himself and workers on the manor, comes from somewhere else rather than being a native resident. That is to say, before the post-war wave of immigration of people from the former colonies, Britain already had a culture of mixture. The purity and superiority of English identity is mere fantasy. Had the narrator not had the experience of living on the manor at Wiltshire for almost ten years, and got to know both about the country and the people's lives there, it would have been impossible for him to reach this conclusion.

With the emergence of marginalized people to the fore, Homi Bhabha posits that the identification of the colonial is neither that of the colonist Self nor the colonized Other but "the disturbing distance in-between that constitutes the figure of colonial otherness" (Bhabha 1994: 45). The Other no longer feels alienated because there are so many people who are just like him. What Bhabha broaches here opens a new space of identification for the colonized people where they can strike a strategic balance between the Self and Other, and the Self and Other can constantly re-negotiate and re-define their relationship in a way in which both the traditional values, and those of the adopted culture, are taken into account to form a hybrid identity. In Bhabha's views, hybridity is not "a third term that resolves the tension between two cultures [...] in a dialectical play of 'recognition'" (ibid: 113-114), but a strategy to overcome the exclusivity of the dominant discourse whereby migrants are "free to negotiate and translate their cultural identities" (ibid: 38). In this sense, hybridity becomes a form of constant identification rather than identity in itself. These processes of negotiating and translating of identities take place in the "third space" of the "in-between", a space that is a temporal construction which, due to the mingling of the migrant's ethnic background and cultural presence, is characterized by a cultural heterogeneity that enables the migrant writer to develop his double vision whereby the migrant's experience of his past and present may interact and contribute toward a new kind of creativity.

Naipaul's deconstruction of Englishness does not result in his total denial of it, of course. What appears to be a demystification about the British imperial past, therefore, does not cancel its influence on his writing career. Instead, the "change" and "flux" of Britain's dismantled empire is what allows for his current right of abode. If it is the empire that uprooted his ancestors from India to Trinidad, it is also the empire that brings him from the New world to the Old, and allows his presence at Waldenshaw, where he can have his "second childhood" and a "safe house", unlike that of Mr. Biswas' on Sikkim Street. Naturally, the deconstruction of Englishness leads to Naipaul's reconciliation with his past and to the construction of a hybrid identity.

TOWARD A HYBRID IDENTITY

The deconstruction of Englishness is of great importance to Naipaul and to postcolonial subjects in general, because it enables them to face their multicultural background positively and cherish the complexity of their cultural heritage. In the previous chapters, we have proposed that Naipaul's identity formation begins from the negation of his homeland, and a longing for a place in the metropolitan centre. To overcome the sense of alienation, he undergoes the stage of mimicry. After much travelling and writing, Naipaul comes to realize that it is necessary for the colonial to reconstruct an identity out of the multiple cultures of his background. Instead of clinging to a single identity, he now begins to move toward a hybrid identity.

In post-colonial theory, hybridity identifies the potential for identities to shift and/or merge, suggesting that encounters between different cultural identities can produce a new way of being. According to Bhabha, all cultural narratives and systems are constructed in a space of what he calls the "third space of enunciation" (Bhabha 1994: 37), which is a contradictory and ambivalent space. It is in this space that cultural identity always emerges, making the "purity" of cultural identity untenable. Hybridity, Bhabha argues, subverts the narratives of colonial power and dominant cultures. The logic of inclusion and exclusion on which a dominant culture is premised is deconstructed by the very entry of the formerly excluded subjects into mainstream discourse. The migration of yesterday's "savages" from their peripheral spaces to the homes of their "masters" creates "fissures" within the very structures that sustain it by "Third-Worlding" the centre. Hybridity thus "makes differences into sameness, and sameness into difference, but in a way that makes the same no longer the same, the different no longer simply different" (Young 1995: 26).

While demystifying the purity of Englishness, Naipaul shows a tendency toward reconciliation with his colonial background. As we can see from the above section, by the time Naipaul writes *The Enigma of Arrival*, he has realized that change is inevitable in the world, and that the concept of pure Englishness is only a construction conspired by both the colonizers and the colonized. Early in the book he says, "Change was constant" (EA 1988: 32). What has changed is not only the outer world of the narrator, of course, but the narrator himself. In the middle part of "Ivy", once again he tells the reader, "The world had changed; [...] my ideas had changed" (ibid: 191). Both the world and the narrator's way of looking at the world have changed and the change inside him helps overcome "his biggest handicap of being born in Trinidad" (Cudjoe 1988: 217), making him far more willing to accept his colonial heritage. This acceptance is the basis of a hybrid identity.

In the second section of the book, the narrator gives the reader an account of his career, between his departure from Trinidad as a scholarship student bound for England in the early 1950s, and the publication of *Among the Believers* in the early 1980s. To a certain degree, this section is a continuation of "Prologue to an Autobiography" in *Finding the Centre*, in which he returns to the Trinidad he had escaped from with the intent of becoming a writer after seeing his father's dream of being a writer dashed by the bleak environment there. If "Prologue to an Autobiography" is a desperate search for roots, *The Enigma of Arrival* is an attempt at reconciliation with reality and a quest for a new beginning. Without an honest confrontation with the past, there could be no meaningful future. Written three years after "Prologue to an Autobiography", *The Enigma of Arrival* mulls over journey as metaphor and event. "Journey" is the theme of this section as well as of the whole book: the narrator's journey from Trinidad to England at the age of eighteen; his journey back to the West Indies and to Central and South America, Asia, and Africa as a writer; the journey of his writing career; and his own life as a journey. Journey may also be read as the key to unlocking the "enigma" of arrival: the arrival is enigmatic because it is the arrival at a "journey" and suggests an open process pointing to the future. To arrive somewhere is the aim of the journey but arrival at a place means a new journey is to begin. Arrival and journey are interdependent here. One cannot exist without reference to the other. It, then, is the tension between the journey and the arrival that constitutes the enigma.

In the section "Journey", Naipaul also returns to the time of his first arrival in London, recounting his solitude, loneliness, and disillusionment. Strangers from other countries, the "flotsam of Europe" after World War II, populated the city. He regrets now having missed the opportunity to observe more closely those immigrants who like himself, comprised the fractured and immigrant world of London. He muses that they would have made the best materials for writing— something he only realizes years later when he begins to work at the BBC radio room. At the time, he assumed that only "sensibility"—the ideas of the aesthetic movement of the end of the nineteenth century and the ideas of Bloomsbury, ideas bred essentially out of empire, wealth and imperial security—could make suitable subject matter for a writer. After much pain and chagrin, he finally understands that what he and many other immigrants were experiencing, along with the collision of incongruous worlds, would have made perfect subject matter for him. He should not have pretended to be what he was not, falsifying his experience and hiding from his identity. The narrator reflects that at the time, he tried to mask his cultural identity as a Trinidad Indian and attempted to be an "English" writer—like Maugham, Huxley, or Waugh, and he wrote stories like "Gala Night", the very title of which suggested the distance between the story and the reality of the immigrants' life (ibid: 120, 135). The writer and the man were separated by a gap then. Had he not focused on his identity as a Trinidad Indian in England, he would not have been able to find his subject matter and fill the gap between the writer and the man. It was only five years later that he learned to face his identity as a colonial in the metropolitan centre, and to make his own experience the sources of his writing.

Earlier in "Prologue to an Autobiography", Naipaul makes clear his discovery: "To become a writer, that noble thing, I had thought it necessary to leave. Actually, to write, it was necessary to go back. It was the beginning of self-knowledge" (FC 1985: 34). As is shown in the previous chapters, the earlier works of Naipaul are characterised by the characters' sense of marginality, exile, and insecurity. In his works before *The Enigma of Arrival,* Trinidad is not a place pleasing to his protagonists, and almost all of them want to leave their home island and have a place in the metropolitan centre of London. *The Enigma of Arrival* differs from those earlier works in that it signifies an important transformation in the author's viewpoints of both England and his homeland. While decentring England, he begins to come to terms with his own history and his "Trinidadian-Indian" background. Earlier in *Finding the Centre,* he says,

A writer after a time carries his world with him, his own burden of experience, human experience and literary experience (one deepening the other); and I do believe—especially after writing "Prologue to an Autobiography"—that I would have found equivalent connections with my past and myself wherever I had gone. (ibid: 10)

Writing helps Naipaul build the connections between his past and present. More importantly, writing gives him a sense of security. After publishing *A House for Mr. Biswas*, which he felt to be important to him (ibid: 151), he returned home "with a security that was entirely new, the security of a man who had at last made himself what he had wanted to be, that I went back to the island" (ibid: 151). The following passage about his experience in Trinidad after the publication of *A House for Mr. Biswas* is worth our attention:

And everything I saw and felt and experienced then was tinged with celebration: the hills, the spreading shacks, the heat, the radio programs, the radio commercials, the noise, the route taxis. That landscape—with all its colonial or holiday motifs: beaches, market women, coconut trees, banana trees, sun, big-leaved trees—had always, since I had known it, been the landscape of anxiety, even panic and sacrifice. The education that had made me had always been like a competition, a race, in which the fear of failure was like the fear of extinction. I had never, as a child, felt free. [...]
If there was a place, at this stage of my career, where I could fittingly celebrate my freedom, the fact that I had made myself a writer and could now live as a writer, it was here, on this island which had fed my panic and my ambition, and nurtured my earliest fantasies. And just as, in 1956, at that first return, I had moved from place to place, to see it shrink from the place I had known in my childhood and adolescence, so now I moved from place to place to touch it with my mood of celebration, to remove from it the terror I had felt in these places for various reasons at different times. Far away, in England, I had created this landscape in my books. The landscape of the books was not as accurate or full as I had pretended it was; but now I cherished the original, because of that act of creation. (ibid: 151-152)

The childhood panic is still there, but the narrator is now able to acknowledge his debt to the island of his birth, which has fed his ambition and nurtured his earliest fantasies. It is the island that has prepared for him the materials for writing and the themes important in the twentieth century. And it is the marginality of the island that has made him a metropolitan, not only in the sense that he enjoys permanent residence in London and that he writes about those living there, but in the sense that he writes as a global and international writer. With success in writing, Naipaul becomes more accommodating and milder in his attitude toward both Trinidad and India. In his first travelogue, *The Middle Passage*, he quotes from Froude that in the West Indies there are no people in the true sense, and that they are "like monkeys pleading for evolution" (MP 1985: 87). Now he admits that at that time he was seeing with the eyes of an English man (EA 1988: 153). This new attitude by Naipaul results from the success of his writing, and leads to the coming together of the man and writer. He is now able to face his identity as a whole.

This gap between the writer and man stems from the two paths to history that colonial people must face. One is imperial history with its glory, sovereignty, nobility, etc., and the other is of the dateless darkness and barbarity of native history. Naipaul explains in *The Enigma of Arrival* the tearing apart and the coming together of the man and the writer, the gradual development of his curiosity about the world and its many histories. In the section of "Journey" Naipaul records that almost thirty years ago, on his first journey from Trinidad to London, there appeared "a gap between the writer and man" in him (EA 1988: 110), which resulted from two ways of thinking about himself: the writer as closely linked to colonial education and the ideal of the nobility in the calling to be a writer, for which he travels, and the man close to the village ways of his Asian-Indian community. Naipaul's narrator initially believes that he arrives in England by learning to "see", which, for the young writer, means finding "metropolitan" writing material. Yet he feels inferior and lost in London, a metropolis with its "imperial history and culture", which runs contrary to the half-made societies of former colonies. The writer rejects the man's past in the "half-made place" of Trinidad, and regards his present place, England, as the only place where he can become a writer. However, the solitude and anxiety he experiences during the journey makes the bridging of the "gap between man and writer" possible:

I witness this change in my personality; but, not even aware of it as a theme, wrote nothing of it in my diary. So that between the man writing the diary and the traveller there was already a gap, already a gap between the man and the writer. Man and writer were the same person. But that is a writer's greatest discovery. It took time—and how much writing—to arrive at that synthesis. (ibid: 110)

Like a Bildungsroman, *The Enigma of Arrival* uses the autobiographical form as a means of self-discovery and self-examination, through which the narrator's double vision of himself is unified and the man and the writer is able to become one at last. The merging of the writer and the man into one indicates that the writer is now able to overcome the alienated part in his identity, and allow a new identity to bear fruit. It is actually from within the gap that Naipaul's narrator begins to "see" and realize that his personality is "distorted", which, paradoxically, is the prerequisite to closing of the gap. The gap between the writer and the man can be taken as a personal "third space" for the narrator, where he negotiates and translates between English culture and his home culture. The gap between the writer and the man is a translational terrain where "the creolisations and assimilations and syncretisms were negotiated" (Hall 1990: 234). Bhabha's illustration of the "third space" illuminates our understanding:

[...] if, as I was saying, the act of cultural translation (both as representation and as reproduction) denies the essentialism of a prior given originary culture, then we see that all forms of culture are continually in a process of hybridity. But for me the importance of hybridity is not to be able to trace two original moments from which the third emerges, rather hybridity to me is the "third space" which enables other positions to emerge." (Bhabha 1990: 211)

With Naipaul and his narrator, the other position that emerges in the "third space" is a position of "in-between", which translates between the present and the past. Writing initiates this gap between the writer and the man, and also closes it. Naipaul went to London to become a writer, yet he could not find suitable materials for his writing. Therefore the writer has to go back to a place the man is familiar with and write about the world that has been left behind by him. Through writing the writer and the man comes together and the narrator also begins to come to terms with his homeland. The narrator's deconstruction of Englishness, and his reconciliation with his past ensures the possibility of the "synthesis" of the writer and the man, which leads to the hybrid identity of the narrator.

***

Autobiographical writing faces the problem of how to represent the self and the identity of the author. In a sense, the writing of an autobiography is an act of self-definition and self-construction. It is true that many of Naipaul's works before *The Enigma of Arrival* are dominated by the negation of his homeland, and a longing for London. But in *The Enigma of Arrival,* Naipaul deconstructs and reconciles his Trinidad and Hindu origins. It is therefore intended as a resolution to important factors affecting Naipaul's identities, as neither completely Anglicized, nor a rootless traveller, as critics generally hold. Instead, what Naipaul reaches is a hybrid identity, which is neither cut off from his cultural roots nor a floating one. Rather, this identity operates in what Homi Bhabha calls the "intersticies" of the different cultures of England, Trinidad, and India.

In *The Enigma of Arrival*, we have seen a milder Naipaul who has recovered from the agony of his early "homelessness", and shows reconciliation with his past and has come to accept his identity as one of hybridity. This enigmatic book fraught with the author's self-reflective rumination of his experience is the symbol of Naipaul's arriving at an understanding of his identity. In a most subjective form, Naipaul delineates the route of his identification toward a hybrid identity, which is not only his route, but what most of us are experiencing in this era of globalization. This new form of hybrid identity signifies the fluidity of identity and an acceptance of the otherness in our identity. The hybrid identity has surpassed the passiveness and inferiority of the Oriental prototype under the "gaze" of the West. It is also distinct from what Fanon described as people with "black skin" wearing "white masks", meaning that the black soul is a product of the white man's power, or a tragic identity in being the other. Bhabha's hybrid identity has in itself the forces of subversion and liberation. This is true of Naipaul who, with his new hybrid identity, is liberated now from the agony of being an other in the colonial system, and at the same time, has gained new strength to reflect on his colonial past.

The hybrid identity that the narrator achieves is not only a strategic one for the colonial people, it also provides a new way for us to adjust in today's globally dislocated world, because in the global context, the tension between "local" and "global" is far from being finally resolved. The hybrid identity inspires us to approach this question in a new way: the relationship between the "global" and "local" should not be taken as a binary division, instead, it should be a "weave" of similarities and differences that refuse to separate into fixed binary oppositions (Hall 2000). The struggle between the "global" and "local" is similar to that of the gap between the writer and the man in the narrator, whose identity is not fixed but "positional". Because of the gap, neither the writer nor the man, together with what they adhere to, can keep their older, traditional ways of life intact. This gap can become potential sites of resistance, intervention and translation, and the bridging of which leads to a hybrid identity.

Chapter Four The Historical Perspective
A Way in the World

> Modern cultural contacts need not be romanticized, erasing the violence of empire and continuing forms of neo-colonial domination. The Caribbean history from which Cesaire derives an inventive and tactical "negritude" is a history of degradation, mimicry, violence, and blocked possibilities. It is also rebellious, syncretic, and creative. This kind of ambiguity keeps the planet's local futures uncertain and open. There is no master narrative that can reconcile the tragic and comic plots of global cultural history. (Clifford 1988: 15)

Anyone attempting to study Naipaul's quest for identity without exploring his concept of history is prone to misread him given that history plays a significant role in the construction of his colonial self. By probing the histories of the people from the many places that he visits, Naipaul learns about the repetitive features of history—the rise and fall of power, the continued occupation of the same place by different people, and men as victims of historical forces—a realization that leads him to write about history, and to try to find a past that differs from other postcolonial writers or nationalists, who tend to glorify their cultural heritage and use history as a collective past in order to unite people. Rather than examine what history means for a particular group of people, Naipaul endeavours to explore what history does to individuals, what it says about the self and how it helps shape identity.

The past, no matter how painful and humiliating, must be rediscovered as it helps people to understand the present and those who control the present have a say in the future. This fact may explain why colonials have been robbed of their legitimate past by the master narrative of the imperial ruler. Colonial education transforms people in the colonies into "children" by not allowing them to take any responsibility for themselves: they are denied access to their own cultural heritage and have to learn the culture, including language and history, of the colonizers. The colonizers instruct them to look at their own history from an Orientalist perspective, and to become an Other in their own eyes. In *The Mimic Men*, for example, Singh finds in a book—*The Missionary Martyr of Isabella*—many photographs which

> [...] contrived to make Isabella look exceedingly wild. [...] Isabella became almost a Biblical land, full of symbols and portents and marks of God's glory, a land of stoic journeys through scoffing crowds, encounters with khaki-clad officials hostile to the work, and disputations with devious Brahmins hostile robes seeking to undermine the work. It was not an island I recognized. (MM 1984: 87)

Obviously, the book is written to glorify the "benevolence" of a Western God. The wilder the island is, the more powerful the saving God will appear. Reading such a book, Singh gets the impression that the book is focused on missionary work: "everything led outwards from this and led back to this" (ibid: 87). Depicted as a converter and an "enlightened" assistant to the religious work, Singh's father in the book is represented as a "saved" local person who has been transformed into a harbinger of the Gospel. In the photographs he appears "in a badly-fitting old-fashioned costume, which appeared to force his neck and chin out and up, [...] faintly aboriginal and lost, at the end of the world, in a clearing in the forest" (ibid: 87)—clearly an Orientalist portrait. Singh is astounded to see his father portrayed in this way, but then remembers that his father never speaks of that book, "I never saw him reading it. Perhaps he too felt it described another man" (ibid: 88). Even people like Singh's father, who is involved in the colonizer's work, is aware of the distortion and irony in the historical record kept by the colonizers.

Like most postcolonial writers, Naipaul attributes the impossibility of recognizing one's history to colonization, and to the master narratives written by the colonizers. In "Passage to the West Indies," he tells Nina King:

> [...]the idea of a background—and what it contained: order and values and the possibility of striving: perfectibility—made sense only when people were more truly responsible for themselves. We weren't responsible in that way. Much had been taken out of our hands. We didn't have backgrounds. We didn't have a past. For most of us the past stopped with our grandparents; beyond that was a blank. If you could look down at us from the sky you could see us living in our little houses between the sea and the bush; and that was a kind of truth about us, who had been transported to that place. We were just there. Floating. (King 1994: 1)

Master narratives in the West Indies simply neglect colonial people and their past. In *A Way in the World,* Naipaul comments on travel books about the West Indies written at the beginning of the twentieth century, and finds that they "descended in form from Victorian travel journals" (WW 1995: 74). He calls them "cruise books" which, "though very much about travel in the colonies, were about a part of the world that had, as it were, been cleansed of its past" because "the local people were far away, figures in the background" (ibid: 74), and "as for Indians of the countryside, they were a people apart; very little was known about their language or religion. And it was felt by the writer and his guide that this kind of knowledge didn't matter" (ibid: 75).

By the time he writes *The Mimic Men,* Naipaul's attitude toward the history of his homeland has undergone some changes. As we have already seen, in Naipaul's works written at his early period, there exists a clear tendency toward negation of his homeland, and only till he writes *The Enigma of Arrival* does he begin to reconcile with it and to develop a hybrid identity that incorporates otherness into his subject. Early on, to become rid of the otherness in his personality caused by a colonial discourse specifying a binary division between master and slave, centre and periphery, Naipaul attempts to deny his homeland, and instead embrace London wholeheartedly, seeking to become an Englishman. Paradoxically, during his process of mimicry, he learns to accept the otherness implicit to his identity. By being different from what makes him different he can surpass the stage of mimicry, and enter an important new stage in his journey of identification.

Similarly, Naipaul's attitude toward the history of his birthplace changes during the course of his writing. In his first travelogue, *The Middle Passage*, Naipaul writes satirically, "How can the history of this West Indian futility be written? What tone shall the historian adopt? [...] The history of the islands can never be satisfactorily told. Brutality is not the only difficulty. History is built around achievement and creation; and nothing was created in the West Indies" (ibid: 29). During this period, Naipaul views his homeland from a Eurocentric perspective. This is also obvious in the first book of his Indian trilogy: *An Area of Darkness*. It is not until Naipaul writes his historical work, *The Loss of EL Dorado*, "made up of two forgotten stories" (LED 1982: 17) representatively central to Trinidadian history, that he begins to change his views and comes to realize that:

Port of Spain was a place where things had happened and nothing showed. Only people remained, and their past had dropped out of all the historical books [...] History was a fairy tale about Columbus and a fairy tale about the strange customs of the aboriginal Caribs and Arawaks; it was impossible to set them in the landscape. [...] History was also a fairy tale not so much about slavery as about its abolition, the good defeating the bad. It was the only way the tale could be told. Any other version would have ended in ambiguity and alarm. (WW 1995: 375)

Through writing the history of Trinidad, Naipaul comes to understand that colonial people's misery, and their actual lives are denied in the master narratives of European history. When he writes *The Enigma of Arrival*, Naipaul seems to have become gentler and kinder, and begins to consider more calmly the importance of history to men: "Men need history; it helps them to have an idea of who they are" (EA 1988: 353). In *A Way in the World*, once again, Naipaul tries to write the history of his homeland, only that his version of history is one of tension and mutation, one of "ambiguity and alarm", one that is clearly different from the version of history recorded by European historians, and one that is intended to help colonial people understand who they are and how they have come to the present situation. We are told about how the New World has been converted into a colony, an unimportant agricultural colony of slave labour and indentured labour. Yet that part of the world was once thought to be a magical one, i.e. for Columbus in 1498, the freshness of the waters of the Gulf of Paria indicated the nearness of the Garden of Eden, while a hundred years later that same Gulf was thought to stand at the entrance to the land of El Dorado. This is the history, then, of a lost or degraded romance. Europe in this book is far away; great events only send echoes over the ocean.

To a certain degree, *A Way in the World* is a rewriting of *The Loss of El Dorado* in that both works take the history of Trinidad as the centre of narrative, although their approaches are different. In an interview for the BBC with Bryden in 1973, Naipaul said that *The Loss of El Dorado* "symbolizes the whole imperial process, what had been done to places by having the imperial idea imposed on them from outside" (Bryden 1973: 10). In the present version of the history of Trinidad, Naipaul puts this tiny island in a greater context, looking at what has happened to it in connection with other parts of the globe. Reflecting on *The Loss of El Dorado* after the publication of *A Way in the World*, Naipaul told Mel Gussow in an interview, "I borrowed the form of the history and damaged the work" (Gussow). *A Way in the World* is intended to be a corrective. It is made up of nine narratives, including autobiography, fiction, history, and imagined versions of actual lives, in which Naipaul has written a new kind of nonlinear and non-progressive history, which he thinks closer to the historical truth. Asked to comment on the unique form of the text, Naipaul asked the reporter to call it "A Naipaul" (Gussow). With this Naipaulian form, Naipaul integrates his own experience with that of his characters. When all the plots are put together, we obtain a complete picture of the history of Trinidad as well as that of Naipaul. In the Minerva edition of *A Way in the World*, the text is subtitled "A Sequence".[1] To categorize the fragmented narratives as "a sequence", Naipaul blurs the established divisions between "history", "novel", and "autobiography". This subtitle also suggests Naipaul's effort to create internal coherence from a number of separate anecdotes. Meanwhile, a sequence also points to a kind of structural tension between the integrity of each story, and the interpretative function of the story's position within the text. As Stephanie Jones insightfully points out:

> The resolution of this structural tension is tied to the text's concern with the relative and shifting violability and inviolability of history-telling and fictional narration. [...] The relativity and open construction of the narratives within the text may be investigated in terms of Paul Gilroy's negotiation and ultimately implicit collapsing of the (closed, teleological, liner) politics of diasporic "identity" as construed in opposition to the (open, anti-teleological, spatially networked) politics of diasporic "identification." (Jones 2000: 88)

In what follows, I will explore Naipaul's unique way of writing history, and its function in exposing to us the complexity of a colonial's identity.

---

1 | The North American version (New York: Alfred A. Knopf, 1994) defines the text as "a novel" on the title.

UNCERTAIN HISTORY

Beneath the challenge of the old way of writing history is Naipaul's search for selfhood, for an understanding of the effects of inheritance, and for the way in which individual identity is shaped by historical forces. *A Way in the World* is therefore also a highly personal narrative in which Naipaul looks back at his earlier books[2] and relives the creative process in a new form. In his interview with Mel Gussow, Naipaul says that *A Way in the World* is "a settling of accounts for me with myself" (Gussow). In the same interview, Naipaul talked about his impetus for writing *A Way in the World*. Three years prior, upon completion of *India: A Million Mutinies Now*, the last of his trilogy about India, his ancestral country, he made many returns, summing-up journeys—for the emotion and for the feeling of completeness (Gussow), in essence, seeking closure. As a reworking of experience, *A Way in the World* covers the expanse of the author's life, running from his boyhood in Trinidad, to his apprenticeship in England and on through his travels and literary life. This book is therefore of great importance to understanding Naipaul's identity.

Traumatized by the deprivation of a history of their own, postcolonial writers often engage in re-conceptualizing the past, which inevitably results in the re-de-construction of their consciousness of history. It is common knowledge in postcolonial studies that the colonized are economically and culturally colonized and represented as an Other. Western representations of Third World countries serve the political interests of colonizers in general. The result of "cultural colonization" is subjects "burdened by double consciousness and divided loyalties" (Leitch et al. 2001: 25). Colonial people, on the one hand, look at themselves from their own position, but it is not uncommon that they also use western eyes to evaluate themselves.

---

2 | *A Way in the World* is a complicated reversionary work which alludes to quite a few of Naipaul's earlier works such as *The Middle Passage* (1962), *The Loss of El Dorado: A History* (1969), *In a Free State* (1973), *A Bend in the River* (1979), and *Finding the Centre: Two Narratives* (1984).

Thus they suffer from divided loyalties to both Western and vernacular norms and systems. Postcolonial writers' attempt to rewrite their own history must confront several fundamental assumptions underlying European perceptions and interpretations of the region's past because they serve as a vital channel for the reconstruction of the colonial's identity or subjectivity. As Nana Wilson-Tagoe has observed, "Active self-formation or 'subjectification', a major concern of modern critical theory, is thus a necessary and frequent discourse in Caribbean writing" (Wilson-Tagoe 1998: 2).

Caribbean writers' attempt to redefine and re-conceptualize the regions' history coincides with a new scepticism about the discipline of history itself, and the homogenizing categories of critical discourse. "The idea of history as a construction is indeed a fundamental aspect of the West Indian writer's relation to the past and is the inevitable outcome of the tension between a one-dimensional linear perception of history and commitment to a future which seeks transformative meanings instead of progression." (ibid: 90) Criticising history's inherent conspiracy with Eurocentric institutional enterprise, Hayden White notes:

Continental European thinkers—from Valery and Heidegger to Sartre, Levi-Strauss and Michel Foucault—have cast serious doubts on the value of a specifically "historical" consciousness, stressed the fictive character of historical reconstructions, and challenged history's claim to a place among the sciences [...] It is possible to view historical consciousness as a specifically western prejudice, by which the presumed superiority of modern, industrial society can retroactively substantiate. (White 1973: 1-2)

What White argues is that the presumed scientific concept of history has been carried out by the West in the pursuit of its own interests. The reflections on historical consciousness by continental European thinkers testify to the fact that the stasis of historical truth that Westerners endeavour to establish is counterfeit. In other words, representations of history are never as pure, detached and objective as historians claim because the past can only be available to us in a form of representation that is written to serve the ideological and institutional interests of history writers. As a mode of discourse, "pure" history of the past is thus forever untenable.

It is White's contention that the literary dimension of history should not be dismissed as mere decoration because historians deploy narrative devices to make sense of raw data, to organize and give meaning to their accounts of the past. According to White, historical narratives are verbal fictions with invented contexts. The historian explicates his story by executing three types of explanation: by plotting, by argument, and by ideological implication. "Plotting" is the process through which stories take their shape and in which the facts contained in "chronicles" are encoded as components of plots. The explanation by argument is consonant to common/universal law, which explains the process of development of the events. The explanation by ideological implication consists of conservatism, liberalism, radicalism, and anarchism. (White 1973: 9-24)

The object of meta-history is to present human history as a unified whole with a mode of interpretation, to endow history with meaning and to demonstrate a direction of historical development. Histories written under the guidance of such theories have the appearance of continuity and progressiveness. Such histories tend to institutionalize historical events and reject individual historical actions and memories. Real historical events, however, are fragmented and coincidental. The history we can access now is in actuality the narration of historical events, an interpreted and encoded history consonant with the interests of the dominant ideology. They are presented as history by plotting, argument, and ideological implication. Written in the guise of meta-history, and from the perspective of the colonizer gazing at the colonized, the history of the colonized is naturally twice removed from its true past. Differences between the true past and historical records should be excavated. Naipaul's *A Way in the World* is a different version of the history of Trinidad in which the differences in history voice themselves. More significantly, as most of the stories in the book are new versions of stories Naipaul has written before, the form of the book presents history as a "constant remaking and renaming of the world and of individual lives through simultaneous processes of displacement and accumulation" (Gourevitch 1996: 29). Different from the master narrative of Western history, Naipaul focuses on the history of the colonial individual, through whose stories he demonstrates the repetitive nature of history and the individual's vulnerability in face of historical forces and their own nature. The text is about the struggle of men—there are scarcely any women—to enter and alter the history into which they are born.

By focusing on the lives of the individuals living on the island, and those whose lives have been formed and transformed by their encounters with Trinidad, Naipaul gives us a sequence of "composite, tentative, self-questioning narratives" of the history of the place (Barnouw 2003: 133). Beneath the uncertain narratives of histories is the individual's quest for identity. To understand one's identity, a question asked frequently is "who am I and where do I come from?" History, as we understand it, plays an important role in people's identity, because to know about one's identity one needs to first make clear where one comes from.

With the intention of excavating origins, Naipaul opens *A Way in the World* with a brief "Prelude" (subtitled "An Inheritance"), in which he describes the constant "shifting about of reality" he experiences whenever he returns home to the island of Trinidad (WW 1995: 1). Reencountering familiar places and people, he finds "everything strange and not strange", and the dance of his perceptions gives him a feeling of "half-dream, knowing and not knowing (ibid: 2). The journey of return is a journey of finding and missing the once familiar. It is always like this when we try to look into the past: what we are familiar with is both present and absent because we are looking at it from a time and a perspective that is not identical to what we originally experienced. Reflecting on this state, Naipaul recalls the story of Leonard Side, a florist who also works as a dresser of bodies in a Trinidad funeral home, and as a maker and decorator of pastries. Although a Muslim, he keeps an image of "Christ in Majesty" over his bed (ibid: 6). The woman who tells Naipaul about

Chapter Four The Historical Perspective: *A Way in the World* 167

Side confesses that she always runs away from Side's presence because Side's idea of beauty—"mixing roses and nice flowers and nice things to eat with the idea of making the dead human body beautiful – upsets her" (ibid: 7). It seems that Naipaul identifies with the woman regarding the idea of mixing. Naipaul, too, has often expressed dismay at the mixing of things. Even in his later works, such as *Half a Life* (2001) and *Magic Seeds* (2004), Naipaul is persistently gloomy about the prospect of the mixing of people, especially marriage between people from different cultural origins, as is seen in the failure of both William and his sister's interracial marriages.

Side is an Indian residing in Trinidad at the time Naipaul hears of his story. He is a Muslim, yet he doesn't reject the beauty of the image of Christ. Naipaul thinks that he has no idea of where his ancestors have come from (ibid: 8). Everything about him is only guessed at, because "the recorded history of the place is short, three centuries of depopulation followed by two centuries of resettlement" (ibid: 8). What is more, no one knows what has finally happened to Side. Naipaul guessed he might have "joined the great migration to England or the United States" (ibid: 8). In conclusion of this part, Naipaul writes: "We cannot understand all the traits we have inherited. Sometimes we can be strangers to ourselves" (ibid: 9). Side thus becomes a prototype of the floating and "rootless" man, who in his route of migration has lost knowledge of his roots and origin.

In his article "Bordering Naipaul: Indenture History and Diasporic Poetics", Vijay Mishara suggests that within Naipaul's work, "the diasporic experience, the life of the diasporic individual, is seen as a parenthesis, as a bracket, a series of incidents before and after which the substantive narrative of empires and peoples [...] gets written down" (Mishara 1996: 225). Stephen Jones, however, argues against Mishara in his article "The Politics and Poetics of Diaspora in V.S. Naipaul's *A Way in the World*" that what is bracketed and put in parenthesis in *A Way in the World* is "the big moments of Empire and the famous figures of exploration and revolution", which are "spun out of and complexly win back into the seemingly obscure, contingent figure and location of Leonard Side" (Jones 2000: 89).

Both commentators are right in their own way, despite starting from different perspectives. When Mishara says that the diasporic experience of the individual is seen as a parenthesis or a bracket, he refers to the fact that the minor history of the individual is ignored and removed from the grand narrative of imperial history, which is more true of Naipaul's works before *A Way in the World*, since as Naipaul later said about *The Loss of EL Dorando*, the "borrowed form" damaged the work. Jones, however, is specifically referring to *A Way in the World*, in which Naipaul focuses on the diasporic experience of the colonial individual. As a counterbalance to Mishara's bracketed experience of the diasporic individual, Naipaul brackets the experience of the empire, and writes about the diasporic individuals' "way" in the world.

Naipaul seems to assume that there should be some inheritance, but that it is beyond our reach: "We go back all of us to the very beginning; in our blood and bone and brain we carry the memories of thousands of beings" (WW 1995: 9), yet Side's way in the world is suspended. Both his origin and destination remain unresolved and it may remain unresolved. When asked about his identity, a person who knows him " had to think and then says "He work [sic] all his life in flowers" (ibid: 3), another person said that "he gave courses at the WAA, the Women's Auxiliary Association" (ibid: 3), yet when the teacher went to look for him he was found dressing a body. No one is sure of his identity. Different people each know only bits and pieces about him. He himself is elastic in identification: an Indian Mohammedan, yet he doesn't reject the beauty of the image of Christ. As a representative of two rival civilizations, Islam and Christianity don't seem to clash in Side, who has lost the memories of his inheritance during his diasporic experience. Behind the bizarre eclecticism of Leonard Side, is the acknowledgment of the loss of ethnicity. The story of the enigmatic Leonard Side is a "prelude to a narrative quest for forms of identification with which to circumnavigate the enigma of racial and cultural inheritance" (Paquet 2002: 198). Side also embodies all the principal figures in the subsequent parts who, at different times and in different situations, "emerge from the hybridity of their cultural compositions—be they historically constituted or the result of developments during their lifetimes" (Mustafa 1995: 203).

A Way in the World is also about the difficulties of writing history given that the past is the ultimate stranger, more unknown than the most distant and remote physical phenomenon. Following the history of the individual person Side is the history of the Port of Spain. "History: A Smell of Fish Glue" is the second part of *A Way in the World*. In this clearly autobiographical part, Naipaul focuses on the time prior to his first trip to England as a scholarship student, when he worked as a temporary second-class clerk in the Registrar-General's Department, as well as on his sporadic trips back during the subsequent years. The history and political movements of Port of Spain are charted within the narrator's lifetime. As such, the history we read here is meant to be a recognizable subjective recollection of the past. Here, Naipaul describes himself as a "country boy" who travelled to Port of Spain in his late teens, and "loved the town" as "only a country boy could" (WW 1995: 11). Naipaul's description of Port of Spain in this text is light and exceptionally pleasant. The tone is unfamiliarly affectionate. In *The Middle Passage*, Naipaul was angry with Trinidad: "I had never wanted to stay in Trinidad. When I was in the fourth form I wrote a vow on the endpaper of my Kennedy's Revised Latin Primer to leave within five years. I left after six; and for many years afterwards in England, falling asleep in bedsitters with the electric fire on, I had been awakened by the nightmare that I was back in tropical Trinidad" (MP 1985: 41). Compared with the satirical and hateful tone in *The Middle Passage*, how different the present work reads:

I loved everything about the town that was not like the country; I liked the paved cambered streets and even the open kerbside gutters; every morning, after they had done their sweeping and gathering, the street-cleaners opened the water hydrants and flooded the gutters with fresh, clear water [...] Port of Spain was small, really, with less than a hundred thousand people. But to me it was a big town, and quite complete. (WW 1995: 11)

In lieu of his usual dismissal of the half-made society, Naipaul now casts a nostalgic eye at his hometown with affection and appreciation; different from the previously always angry Naipaul, behind the narrative of history is now a more sympathetic tone, one that is more willing to delve into the truth about the place he "escaped" from—as he likes to say—when he was eighteen.

As a second-class clerk, young Naipaul's job was to make copies of birth, marriage, and death certificates for people who need them. While there, he learned that the records of the colony were stored in the vault, all the births, deaths, deeds, transfers of property and slaves, all the life of the island during the century and a half long colonial period. Those original documents were bound into large volumes with fish glue. "It was the colour of honey; it dried very hard, and every careless golden drip had the clarity of glass; but it never lost the smell of fish and rottenness" (ibid: 21). Colonial history—as Naipaul tells us here—appears incomplete in that it only kept the records of what happened during the colonial period. The history of the Port of Spain is thereby shown to be a fragmented narrative, obscuring the history of the island before colonization. Meanwhile, the terrible smell of recorded history also signifies the cruelty of colonial history, and how difficulty it was for colonial people to access his history.

However, the major part of this chapter is not about the cruel history of Port of Spain. Instead, Naipaul elaborates on the changes taking place there. Indeed, Naipaul actually writes to challenge the written history as recorded by the colonizers, and says that in addition to the history held together with fish glue and stored in the government vault, there exists another version of unrecorded history. Naipaul's version of the history of Port of Spain is written from the perspective of someone who "escaped" to establish his identity, and therefore is acutely aware of other people's efforts to construct their own identity. Consequently, here we read more about how people construct their identity.

In Leonard Side's story, we witnessed the life of a person who has lost his ethnicity, and whose identity is floating and strategic. The story concludes with Naipaul's realization that "sometimes we can be strangers to ourselves" (ibid: 9), thus opening a vast discursive space for other narratives. To excavate the roots of this strangeness, Naipaul also casts his observing eyes on others, looking for ways to be rid of it. The focus of Naipaul's version of history in the second section is on the questioning of black people's identity construction. In this part, Naipaul depicts for us the gradual political awakening of the black population, which is consistently described as a politics of "racial redemption" (ibid: 36). The first time the question of racial identity is mentioned is before he goes to work at the registrar-general's department in the Red House, when he is introduced to the lawyer father of one of his school friends. The lawyer is locally famous for being a self-made man, yet he mistakenly attributes his name to Homer rather than Virgil. The mis-rooting of his name substantially problematizes the meaning of racial redemption. What surprises Naipaul even more is that during one of their conversations, the lawyer suddenly declared himself, "The race! The race, man" (ibid: 16)! Yet the public conception of the lawyer is that of a self-made black man who only wants to be white, and wants to have nothing to do with black people (ibid: 15). Deep in the lawyer's heart, however, the question of race troubles him. When Naipaul was introduced to this secret, he found it sentimental. He declined the lawyer's gesture of invitation into his secret world because he wished to belong to himself: "I couldn't support the idea of being part of a group. I would have felt tied down by it, and I thought Evander's idea of a great racial movement forward too sentimental" (ibid: 16).

This brief encounter with the black lawyer happened when Naipaul was seventeen years old. It is recorded in the section of "History" because it prefigures two important factors affecting Naipaul's understanding of identity. One is Naipaul's belief in the independence of individual identity. In *A Way in the World*, there is another occasion when Naipaul feels that he is lured to join a group, but for fear of losing the independent spirit that he deems vital to a writer, he refuses. "No other group would ever again make me an invitation so wholehearted or so seductive. But to yield was to cease to be myself, to trust to the unknown" (ibid: 124). Though there have been many diatribes against Naipaul, criticising the snobbishness of the imperial values, Naipaul has always been an independent writer, and living only from his writing. If Leonard Side presents different identities, with each tied to a profession, Naipaul is a writer, and nothing else. Indeed, if we were to use a single word to describe Naipaul's, both those for and against him would agree that he is indisputably a writer.

Another factor raised by the encounter with the lawyer is far more complex and less easily grasped because it has to do with ethnicity, about which Naipaul seems to be confused and contradictory. A person's ethnicity constitutes a large part of his identity. In pre-modern times, identity was decided mainly by ethnicity. Identity in the contemporary world, however, derives from a multiplicity of sources such as nationality, ethnicity, social class, community, gender, and sexuality—sources that may conflict and lead to contradictory and fragmented identities. Each of us may experience struggles between conflicting identities based on our different positions in the world. As the offspring of an indentured labourer born in Trinidad, Naipaul would have had similar problems related to the loss of ethnicity as those of black people like the lawyer. Admittedly, however, as we have seen, from the beginning Naipaul is ashamed of his ethnicity and on his first return to India, he views that piece of his ancestral land with an Orientalist eye: India for him is as the title of his book suggests, "an area of darkness". But his attitude toward both India and Trinidad changes during the course of his writing. In his later travel writings and fictions, we witness a kinder and gentler Naipaul. Yet Naipaul seems to bear prejudices against black people's movement of racial redemption. This prejudice against another ethnicity actually stems from his concern for the East Indians who were persecuted by the blacks.

Moreover, Naipaul feels alienated from his native land due to black people's agitation for independence: "In such way every black or African person from my past altered. And I felt a double distance from what I had known". Witnessing the black movement of independence, he feels the island "had passed to other hands" (ibid: 32-33). The population of black people equals that of Indian people in Trinidad. There always has been an antagonism between the Blacks and Indians. During the movement of independence, the Blacks ruled, and they persecuted Indians. Although Naipaul's attitude toward his Indian inheritance is ambiguous, facing the challenge of black people, he stands by the Indian. Thereby we see the hold of ethnicity on people, especially when threatened by others. But Naipaul is not fully unaware of his prejudice, or "orientalist" view of black people. As he remembers, when he wrote about the black beauty contest, he concentrated on "the master of ceremonies, his formal clothes, his ungrammatical speech, his vanity" (ibid: 27). He recalls the black woman's comment on his writing: "if it was an Indian man, you wouldn't have written like that" (ibid: 27). Still, however, he was worried that the hostility from the black movement would be focused on the Indians in Trinidad.

Naipaul deems the spirit generated by the black movement more like that of religion. This type of movement, however, provides Black people with a means to construct their identity. Blair, a Trinidadian of African origin, is the narrator's contemporary, who endeavours to make his own way in the world through the black movement. He successively works as Trinidadian government minister, ambassador, and UN representative. They first met when the narrator worked at the government office in Trinidad. In the last section "Home Again" they met again unexpectedly in a newly independent African country. Blair's failure to indict Uganda's Asian community in accordance with the demand of the authorities led to his being murdered in a banana field. It is with "race" that Blair finds his way in the postcolonial world, yet it is also because of race that his life is taken away. In his description of the Black movement, Naipaul observes something inspirational: against the colonial background, every one was wounded, and their pains now flow into a common stream of emotion. The nationalist politicians mobilize the colonized and the oppressed by reminding them of their shared history, victimization, resentments, religion, culture and ethnicity or race.

Naipaul is surprised that it has taken so long for black people to realize this. Too often they had trusted their representation to whites or part-whites. Yet Naipaul feels threatened by the new black politics because "much of the hostile feeling released by the sacrament of the square would have focused on the Indians, who make up the other half of the population" (ibid: 32-33).

Naipaul finds that Trinidad is ruled by a Black political party, which has come to power by combining Black history with Marxist ideas, and that in the island "disaffection grew, feeding on an idea of an impossible racial righteousness; and there was always a threat of an insurrection within the insurrection" (ibid: 36). What is more worrying to Naipaul is that some Black Trinidadians began to dress like Arabs—men in long gowns with skullcaps, and women in black veils. These new Trinidadian Muslims were in contact with the Arabic world, and they even built a settlement and a mosque. Their children went to a school where they studied and read books in Arabic. These people attempted a revolution and attacked the government, and at least twenty-nine people died in the looting. It was a Black against Black affair (ibid: 39-40). The Indian countryside remained quiet, as usual, its political fate being determined by the Blacks of Port of Spain. Naipaul's version of Trinidad's history reveals his cultural unawareness of himself as an Indian. In spite of the fact that Naipaul often openly advocates Western values, such as those he discussed in his famous speech "Our Universal Civilization", he remains an Indian in his cultural unconscious. Seemingly, Naipaul believes in a universal civilization, yet his Indian inheritance creates in his identity tensions and contradictions on different occasions. Therefore, I think that the identities we choose are never singular and fixed but floating and strategic. Naipaul's writing course is also one of self-discovery and self-knowledge. We have already seen that Naipaul's attitude toward both India and Trinidad had become milder, yet with Black people, and their racial redemption movement, he seems constantly antagonistic. I believe this reflects the essentialist part fixed in one's identity: the role inheritance plays in identification. Besides the strategic identities we choose to identify, what is precipitated in our cultural unconscious, like our ethnicity, is fixed in our identity.

At the end of the "History" section, Naipaul recalls the cruelties of the history of Trinidad, from the moment the Spanish claimed the island and scalded the five native chiefs with hot bacon fat, forcing them to sign documents surrendering their lands. Therefore the theme for this section, the cruelty and humiliation that are central to Trinidad's history are reinforced. In this sense, it echoes the subtitle—a smell of fish glue. As a descendent of Indians in Trinidad, Naipaul often refers to the "shipwrecked" situation of Indians in the West Indies. Since they are grafted into the history of the region much later than other ethnic groups, around the turn of the eighteenth century, and with racial animosity directed towards them particularly from the Black population, Indians feel they are alienated from Trinidad's history. Naipaul himself feels "the special incompleteness of the Indian child, grandson of immigrants, whose past suddenly broke off, suddenly fell away into the chasm between the Antilles and India" (EA 1988: 157). Without a share in the island's history, Trinidad Indians have difficulty constructing their identity. History writing therefore is of great importance to Naipaul's identity quest. His rewriting of history reveals to him that the historical record can be inauthentic, and the progress of history non-linear, that is, history does not necessarily progress as claimed by Western historians. With this realization, Naipaul tries to draw a way in the world, not the way in the world. By revealing the essence of history as narration, as poststructuralist critics claim, Naipaul gives us a more vivid picture of how colonial people find their way.

REWRITING HISTORY

Poststructuralists believe history to be a mode of discourse written in pursuit of the interests of the West. They reason that representations of history can never be pure, detached, or objective, and that history is a mirror of our specified contemporary concerns. This reflection on historical consciousness speaks to the fact that the stasis of historical truth that Westerners endeavour to establish is altogether counterfeit. In fact, not only the act of constructing history in the hope of glorifying the past, but also the effort to negate history or historical consciousness, is deemed imperialist. According to Stephen Slemon the effort to rescue the few privileged monuments of achievement as well as the act to excise the authority of the "pretext" of the past are "part of the imperial myth of history" and a "flip side of the same coin" (Slemon 1998: 158). That is to say, we can only access the past via a form of representation that is already ideologically conditioned and culturally mediated. In other words, what is past is past. The history we get to know is the recorded and represented version of history, which cannot be pure, detached or objective.

And the discourse of modernity advocates only one type of progressive world history, in which there is only one type of civilization that develops from low to high. All that does not follow this trend is discarded or erased from the discourse of the history of modernity. Such way of addressing history is the foundation for the colonist or imperialist's sense that their own history and civilization are superior to that of others. Such superiorities authorize conquering and invasion of areas they believe inferior under the guise of the beautiful terms of liberation, civilization and enlightenment. The Others, in their eyes, are primitive, prehistoric, barbarian, and uncultured. Their representation of Oriental history, culture, and civilization, according to Edward Said, is in general a stereotypically misleading and prejudiced image of the Other. By establishing the Other as inferior, the superiority of the West is verified. Postcolonial rehabilitation of history is aimed at deconstructing this stereotypical image of the Orient as the Other, and at constructing the subjectivity and identity of the once conquered and colonized. In a manner akin to the poststructuralist critical position, interrogative modes of postcolonial writing often employ textual strategies and tropes to critically rethink the accepted concept of history. More importantly, different from poststructuralist critics, whose concerns focus more on theoretical thinking, postcolonial writers do not simply deconstruct the concept of "History", rather, they construct where they deconstructed a variant of "histories", so as to voice the silenced, and to acknowledge the unrecognized forces productive in shaping cultural identity.

Earlier in *The Mimic Men*, Ralph Singh realizes that the colonial's values seem to come from the outside world. One morning, while listening to his teacher describing Canada, he imagined that was the true pure world, and that they were but "mimic men of the New World" (MM 1984: 146). Colonial mimicry stands both as reminder of the violation of imperialism, and of its acceptance. It is a sign of servitude, partly resulting from the lack of historical consciousness, given that they have been "abandoned and forgotten". Confused by not knowing the kind of job he should take, and the kind of social position he should project for himself, Singh picks up Latin, again. He finds reading the dead language soothing because, unlike himself, it has a definite past (ibid: 187). In *A Bend in the River*, we are provided a bleaker world in central Africa, a place whose past has been burned away and distorted for everyone. When he first arrives at the bend in the river, Salim finds a ruined monument inscribed with a Latin tag: *Miscerique probat populos et foedera jungi* (BR 1989: 62). The ruins are those of a memorial the colonial steamship company erected to celebrate itself, and the words mean that the gods approve of the mixing of the continents and their people. At independence, the monument was knocked down in order to "wipe out the memory of the intruder" (ibid: 26). Later, however, Salim learns that the Latin quotation is drawn from Book four of *Aeneid*, and actually means that the gods don't approve of the mixing of people there. Salim was appalled by the way the colonial powers had bent the past in the service of their authority. In *The Enigma of Arrival*, Naipaul recounts an incident after he moves to another farmhouse not far away from the Wiltshire cottage. He has done some remodelling on the house, and one day an old woman stops by to take a look at this place because it was where she used to stay with her shepherd grandfather. Yet the house has been altered so much that the old woman doesn't recognize it. The narrator is "horribly embarrassed [...] to have destroyed or spoiled the past for the old lady, as the past had been destroyed for me in other places, in my old island" (EA 1988: 318). Naipaul's embarrassment is prompted by his understanding that history is a source of a person's identity, and at times it is crucial for a person to know that the past is still there and intact. Conversely, this incident also shows that the colonial's presence in the metropolis is changing the history of the ex-colonizers.

A Way in the World is Naipaul's effort at rewriting the history of his native land. Trinidad is naturally an important place Naipaul would look to when attempting to find his own history. Owing to Trinidad's multi-cultural background, its history cannot be easily drawn. More importantly, colonialism has distorted it, and robbed the natives of the knowledge of their own history: they are taught with the imperial history of the host country so that the inhabitants are generally unsure of their identity. The robbery of native history is in actuality the robbery of the natives' consciousness of identity and their way in the world. *A Way in the World*, on the one hand, reveals the uncertainty of history, and on the other, it ventures to rewrite the history of Trinidad in a Naipaulian way. Writing such a history is also a process of learning for Naipaul. According to Michael Gorra, *A Way in the World* in effect "announces Naipaul's belated recognition that other West Indian intellectuals have made journeys that match his own, an acknowledgment that he is not an isolated figure; as such it provides a corrective to his earlier autobiographical work" (Gorra 2004: 380). Through this corrective writing, Naipaul rewrites history and remaps the journey of his identification.

Preceding *A Way in the World*, Naipaul wrote a history book entitled *The Loss of El Dorado* to retrieve the history of Trinidad. In the book that was originally commissioned by an American publisher, Naipaul tried to reveal the true history of Trinidad because he felt that the existing history of Trinidad was distorted and centred on European settlers, with the natives barbarized and marginalized. The stories of the slaves were obscured and erased, "In the records the slave is faceless, silent, with an identification rather than a name. He has no story" (LED 1982: 375-376). *The Loss of El Dorado* is made up of two forgotten stories representatively central to Trinidadian history. One is the search for El Dorado, a Spanish delusion taken over by Sir Walter Raleigh and others. The second story concerns "the British-sponsored attempt, from the newly captured island of Trinidad, to set going a revolution of high principles in the Spanish Empire. There was complication. Trinidad, the base for revolution, was at the same time being established as a British slave colony" (ibid: 17). *The Loss of El Dorado* is "an anti-epic of Empire, of the folly of human ambition and illusions" (King 1993: 84). The two central stories provide a wider panorama of Trinidadian history than the usual story of slavery. In between and after these two episodes, the island "drops out of history" (LED 1982: 315), and becomes "an outpost, a backwater" (ibid: 316). *The Loss of El Dorado* marks a crucial point in Naipaul's quest for identity. After finishing this book, Naipaul decided to leave England, where he had lived for two decades, and return to Trinidad. He went as far as selling his house in England, and travelling back to the New World (EA 1988: 163). Speaking of that trip that lasted many weeks, he writes, "I continued to exist in its [*The Loss of El Dorado's*] aura and exaltation, finding confirmation of the world I had dreamed about and created from the documents. I had given myself a past" (ibid: 163-164). Yet, in the end, the book was rejected by the American publisher, and Naipaul had to return to England, to continue his nomad life. This experience showed Naipaul that the West was not interested in knowing the true past of a colonial place, and that it was not easy for colonial people to retrieve their own past.

In *A Way in the World*, three sections are subtitled "Unwritten Stories". These are actually not "unwritten" stories but "re-written" stories. By entitling them as such, Naipaul rewrites not only history but also his own previously written works, with which he is able to reflect on colonial peoples', as well as his own, detour to identification and understand that the journey to identification requires a constant rewriting of identity. The first unwritten story "New Clothes: An Unwritten Storey", is the third section in the "sequence" of the book. The beginning of this story reads like a meta-fiction, in which Naipaul shares with the reader how the idea of this story first emerged while he was travelling to write *The Middle Passage*, when he first visited an Amerindian village in South America: "The first impulse came to me in the first or second week of 1961" (WW 1995: 43). Later when he was writing *The Loss of El Dorado*, as he learned more about the history of the Amerindian village, a story about the village began to take shape in his mind. But the idea wasn't realized until he wrote *A Way in the World*: "A story shaped in my mind, over some years. [...] My idea remained an idea, and (partly working it out for the first time) I write it down here" (ibid: 44). "New Clothes" narrates how the story emerged from this experience. It begins with the question: "Who is the narrator? What can he be made to be" (ibid: 47)? Whether this story can be classified as a meta-fiction is not the purpose of my discussion. Yet we can be sure of at least one thing: Naipaul's sharing the writing process with the reader is not strictly a technical device, instead, he has a message to convey: the inventiveness of history. History is not the past as such, rather, it is "his-story" written after it is tossed once and again in the mind of the writer. The naming of the character as "narrator" clearly points to the essence of the history as narrative. Of the form of literary works, Naipaul wrote, "Literature, like all living art, is always on the move. It is part of its life that its dominant form should constantly change" (Jussawalla 1997: 4). Naipaul is admittedly not an experimenter in literary form. Yet his achievement in form is remarkable, and that is likely due to his unique experience. As he says in an interview, "experience must look for proper forms to represent it" (ibid: 4). As a post-colonial writer, Naipaul himself experiences the agony of a life with no past, and the perplexity of identity resulting from that absence. The American publisher's rejection of the book *The Loss of El Dorado*, further supports the claim that the truth of colonial history is not appreciated in the West. They are only interested in a history that is appealing to their interests, regardless of the facts.

In "New Clothes" Naipaul invites the reader into a revolutionary's —referred to as "the narrator"—encounter with the Amerindians. The story is not entirely an "unwritten story", but he says that he is "partly working it out for the first time" within the text (WW 1995:

45) in that history looks different if it is approached from a different time and perspective. Though an experience mentioned before in *The Middle Passage*, it is different in that "the narrator" in this piece leads us to looking deeper into the relationship between the colonizer and the colonized, and shows us how history repeats itself. Who the revolutionary is does not really matter, for he is but another intruder, a "carrier of mischief. A revolutionary of the 1970s" (ibid: 46). He is engaged in a project to enlist the help of Amerindians to overthrow the African government on the coast.[3] Hardly has the narrator arrived at his destination, when he resolves to flee because he is worried that the people will remember him as "the man who stayed long and wasn't straight with them, who promised many things and then went away" (ibid: 64). When the narrator is introduced to the chief of the village, he finds that people recall Raleigh's visit as a recent event, and still await his return: they produce a Tudor doublet, the "relic of an old betrayal" (ibid: 67). The key to this riddle can be found in *The Loss of El Dorado*, in which we find the origin of the new Tudor clothes: fourteen years after Raleigh's first expedition to Guiana, Robert Harcourt visited the area and encountered an Indian chief dressed in tattered English clothes. Harcourt made excuses for Raleigh's failure to return, and was later greeted by Raleigh's Indian interpreter, Leonard, who told him that the English promised to come and build houses for them. He showed Harcourt a site and said it was good for *houses*, and the English word in the South American jungle startled Harcourt (LED 1982: 69). What the revolutionary meets in the present book are people who have been cheated by Raleigh's idea of revolution. The Tudor doublet is what Raleigh mailed to the natives for the new houses he promised them when he

---

3 | Two centuries ago, African slaves who ran away from Dutch and British slave plantations on the coast, were hunted down for bounty by Amerindians. When the narrator goes to stir up a revolt among the indigenous people to overthrow the Black government, the descendents of these slaves have taken over the old colonial government, and are rapidly modernizing their society, while the Amerindians have stayed the same.

first returned to England. He didn't keep his promise, of course, and the new Tudor doublet now becomes "the relics of an old betrayal". The narrator's journey in "New Clothes" rehearses once more the plot of Raleigh's expedition to Guiana—history repeats itself across the ages. Helen Hayward finds that history repeats itself across Naipaul's works: the uprisings which occur in the background of *Guerrillas*, *A Bend in the River* and *In a Free State* are presented as hysterias that can't change the situation (Hayward 2002: 97). The cycle of history—the rise and fall of power, the continued occupation of the same land by different peoples—teaches Naipaul a universal truth, and unleashes him from his nostalgia for history, freeing him from his attachment to a particular place, and giving him an identity in a diasporic space that is not place-bound.

The vague revolution the narrator is involved in is described as an effort at finding an ideal cover for its agents in the Christian mission-agents of the hinterland. The narrator finds that "The disguise is almost perfect. Both groups have the same kind of dedications; both talk about racial brotherhood; both talk about the wastefulness of the rich and the exploitation of the poor; and both deal in the same stern idea of imminent punishment and justice" (WW 1995: 49-50). Indeed, this linking of religious and political fervour is insistently re-established throughout the text, for example, in the second section "History", where Naipaul compares the Black Movement to a religious movement. With this, Naipaul reveals something inherent to the colonial discourse, that is, it is carried out in the benevolent name of religious redemption, which is a form of subtle cultural colonization and serves as preparation for other forms of colonization. Naipaul's understanding is in line with the basic assumptions in post-colonial study. But he goes further. Very subtly he seems to feel that the intrusion of the colonizers functions as a reference for colonial people: "[...] when there is nothing from outside to compare, what idea can man have of the passing of time" (ibid: 54)? He also discusses how the natives takes advantage of religious groups to go abroad: "since few people on the coast have the means to travel, there are many numbers of Africans, among them the relatives and

Chapter Four The Historical Perspective: *A Way in the World* 183

friends of local politicians, who want to be volunteers and go abroad" (ibid: 49). It may be because of such lures that local people cling to their belief that English people are coming to build *houses* for them. Thus, Naipaul illustrates something controversial: the colonial depend on the colonizer for the construction of their identity because, instead of building their own houses, local people keep awaiting of the arrival of English to build the houses for them.

The (great-great) grandfather, a figure remembered by the tribe to have returned from England, may well be the Amerindian who accompanies Raleigh in 1618 on his last trip to England, as described in section six, "A Parcel of Papers, A Roll of Tobacco, a Tortoise", the second "unwritten story". This story is about Sir Walter Raleigh's desperate and disastrous journey across the Atlantic to Trinidad in search of gold and redemption. Raleigh's story first appeared in *The Loss of El Dorado*, where we are told that he was imprisoned in the Tower of London for thirteen years because it was suspected he sought to overthrow the king. He gained his freedom by persuading the avaricious king that he knew the location of a gold mine in Guiana. The story retold in Naipaul's words, is "a play or a screen play, or a mixture of both" (ibid: 157). Combining the written form and oral accounts, through its deliberately designed moving scenes and theatre-like conversations, Naipaul's interpretation transgresses the genre. This narrative takes the form of dialogues, dotted with sporadic comments by the writer. The prolonged dialogues are carried out from varied perspectives: Raleigh conversing with his surgeon, and with Don Jose, an Amerindian accompanying Raleigh on his last days, and also with "a priest, Fray Simon, who is writing a history of the Spanish New World" (ibid: 181). In his conversation with the surgeon, Raleigh is accused of deliberately lying about the search for gold in his long-titled book: *The Discovery of the Large, Rich, and Beautiful Empire of Guiana, with a Relation of the Great and Golden City of Manoa (which the Spaniards call El Dorado) and Other Countries, with their Rivers adjoining. Performed in the year 1595 by Sir Walter Raleigh Knight*. The surgeon tells Raleigh that the book is fraught with deliberate factual inaccuracies, gaps, inadvertent falsehoods or distortions, and memory lapses. The surgeon says to Raleigh,

> I think it is a deliberately difficult book. [...] It's a deliberate mixture of old-fashioned fantasy and modern truth. Everything you write about this side of the Gulf, the eastern side, the Trinidad side, everything is correct and very clear. [...] On the riverside, it is a different story. When you get down to the main Orinoco, you write about a strange land of diamond mountains and meadows and deer and birds. It's beautiful, but only like a painting. The book's like the work of two different men. (ibid: 169)

History here becomes not only an open text, but also an inter-text, written to serve the interest of the writer, as in the case of Raleigh's book. It does not constitute total lies, but is a mixture of truth and lies. And the truth within will cheat the reader into believing the lies. At the same time, from the dialoguers, we can see that different people approach history in different ways: some may serve a cause, like Raleigh and Fray, some may function as a reflexive voice, and some may just be the victims of history. History is an open text. Looked at from different perspectives, it yields different interpretations.

The third rewritten "unwritten story" is "In the Gulf of Desolation: An Unwritten Story". It tells of Francisco Miranda, a Venezuelan revolutionary, whose story the author thinks as fabulous as that of Columbus and Raleigh, although "Miranda is not as well known as Columbus or Raleigh" (ibid: 238). Naipaul's implicative inscription of historically unknown people alongside famous historical figures is thematically significant. It implies the importance of the islanders to the history of the Western Indies. In contrast to the master narratives, which only record Westerners as masters of history, with Miranda's story, a prototype of the diasporic figure without the shelter of a nation-state, Naipaul endeavours to reconstruct the history of a silenced native people. We have already read Miranda's story in *The Loss of El Dorado*, therefore, instead of an omniscient third-person narration, Naipaul tells us his story through the eyes of

Chapter Four The Historical Perspective: *A Way in the World*

several characters, for example Bernard, Hislop and Level de Goda. In this newly rewritten narrative, Miranda appears as a "very early colonial, someone with a feeling of incompleteness, with very little to fall back on, with an idea of a great world out there, someone who, when he was out in this world, had to reinvent himself" (ibid: 244). Through the narration of different characters, we are given an account of how Miranda reinvents himself from the son of a Venezuelan merchant to the most famous South American or Spanish American of his time (ibid: 240). Nevertheless, in spite of Miranda's effort to reinvent himself, he is but a pawn to the colonizers: "And now, to buy peace, or at any rate to buy time, some of the very men who had called Miranda out from London, to lead their revolution, decide to hand him to the Spaniards" (ibid: 242). Before the end of his life, Miranda realizes that "I had gambled nothing of myself, taken no risks, exercised no personal will. ... They had done it for me. I had done nothing. I was nothing" (ibid: 329). The history of Miranda is the failure of a "mimic man" trying to assert himself and construct his identity by following a Western moral code, "because of the way I have lived, always in other people's countries, I have always been able to hold two or more different ideas in my head about the same thing. Two ideas about my country, two or three or four ideas about myself. I have paid a heavy price for this" (ibid: 332). Although by equating Miranda to Columbus and Raleigh, Naipaul attempts to give voice to the history of the silenced native, Miranda's history is also the history of a colonial's failure to construct his own identity because he has forsaken his home culture, and functions only as an instrument for the imperial forces.

By entitling stories that were previously written as "unwritten stories", Naipaul negates the pre-given identities that history has given the native Amerdians, Raleigh and Miranda, and at the same time, re-de-constructs their identities by rewriting their history. In his ironic view of history, Naipaul projects his own ideas about history and its importance to his quest for identity. Like most writers and scholars in the West Indies, Naipaul thinks it most crucial for the colonial to know their past. And a past is necessary for these intellectuals to explain their situation in the postcolonial period, and to reconstruct their identities.

Diasporic Identification

The problem of location, dislocation and re-location is central to postcolonial writers and critics. At the beginning of *A Way in the World*, the narrator recalls his first journey back to the homeland, "I left home more than forty years ago, I was eighteen. When I went back, after six years [...] everything was strange and not strange" (ibid: 1). This sense of "strange and not strange" marks a diaspora's bewilderment of stranding in a state of in-betweeness, unable to embrace the acquired cultural identity or be rid of a cultural heritage. This feeling of both "strange and not strange" is typical of the experience of postcolonial "exiles", who experience more than one culture, one environment and one home. Their life is nomadic and decentred; they develop a kind of diasporic consciousness, being ever aware of a transnational, translational and hybrid identity. In Clifford's word, their identity is "local, but translatable" (Clifford 1994: 302). In her doctoral dissertation, Liu Yuyan observes that "Naipaul's writing is based on a sort of 'diasporic consciousness' in the sense that the term diaspora, politically and culturally, evokes a state of travelling, a forever shifting cultural placement, displacement and replacement" (Liu 2003: 9).

Diaspora in Greek is *diasperirein*, where the prefix "dia-" means "apart or across", the root "speirein" means "to sow or scatter". It originally referred to the exiled Jews, who was scattered around the world because they disobeyed the will of God and killed the son of God, Jesus. In the 6th century BC, after Jerusalem was destroyed by the Assyrians, the Jews were expelled from Jerusalem, and scattered around the world, suffering great agony before founding Israel in 1948. The term diaspora in this older sense, therefore, has the denotation of victimhood and a forced severing with the homeland. Critics like Clifford emphasize that since contemporary diaspora have different characteristics then diaspora in its old sense can be taken as the point of departure, but not as the norm for contemporary diasporic discourse (Clifford 1994: 303). Diaspora in its most general sense refers to people who move from their homelands into new regions, whether voluntarily or by force (Ashcroft et al. 1998: 68). Today, diaspora is increasingly used as "metaphoric designations for several categories of people—expatriates, expellees, political refugees, alien residents, immigrants, and ethnic and racial minorities *tout court*" (Safran 1999: 57). Colonialism is a radically diasporic movement. The fact that Naipaul was born in Trinidad is the very result of colonialism, which caused his ancestors to be removed from the Indian subcontinent and transported to work on the plantations in the Caribbean island as indentured labourers. Diaspora in this sense suggests the weight of the pain of displacement from a land or society, and of being an outsider in a new place. It is usually connected with a feeling of alienation, loss, and suffering. Yet diaspora in contemporary discourse is more than feeling the loss of one's homeland. According to Stuart Hall, for example, diaspora encompasses more than those scattered tribes whose identity can only be secured in relation to some sacred homeland to which they must return at all costs, even if it means pushing other people into the sea. Displacement compels the unpredictable and imaginative occupation of culture and identity, and generates vibrant and creative ways of expressing them in cultural production. Diaspora, therefore, suggests lack, excess of loss and separation, as well as the possibility of new adventures into identity, and the continued imagination of the unconquerable countries of the mind (Hall 1990: 228). Suffice it to say that diaspora means a sense of belonging to more than one history, to more than one time and place, and to more than one past and future. Diasporic experience is not necessarily a loss for the subjects since it means more possibilities in spite of the fact that it also leads to tension between originality and hybridity, homogeneity and heterogeneity.

Diaspora is an important concept in the study of postcolonial literature because it highlights the multiple standpoints borne of migration and exile. It illuminates an ambivalent politics of positioning and being positioned, of identification and being identified, a politics antithetical to ethnic and cultural essentialism, and open to future possibilities. Diasporic hybridity demonstrates that identity is not essentially located in ethnicity or culture but is the effect of history and culture forged through memory, fantasy, narrative, and myth. Identities cannot, therefore, be straightforwardly preserved or even lost in the processes of acculturation, assimilation, pluralism, and multiculturalism. Against definitions and projections of diaspora as being "grounded in a teleological mythologizing of, yearning back to and programme for accessing a lost homeland" (Jones 2000: 88), theorists like Paul Gilroy, Stuart Hall and James Clifford are more concerned with the positive consequences of diaspora. As such, they work against the "regressive and millenarian politics of geographical restoration and cultural compensation" (ibid: 88). Rejecting the notion of linear history, Gilroy offers the concept of "fragile communicative relationships across time and space that are the basis not of diaspora identities but of diaspora identifications" (Gilroy 1993: 276). Diasporic identification here is an open process that is able to produce and reproduce through difference. Other postcolonial critics have similarly opined that diasporic people develop their own distinctive cultures which both preserve and often extend and develop their originary cultures, cultivating a creolized version of their own practices, modifying and being modified by indigenous cultures (Ashcroft et al. 1998: 70). The concept of diasporic identification necessarily interrogates essentialist models of unified and ethno-centric identities, and is a positive affirmation of the hybridity in identity.

Naipaul's works are deeply influenced by his diasporic experience. In his Nobel Prize acceptance speech he says, "The world is always in movement. People everywhere at some time have been disposed" (Naipaul 2001). In most of his works, Naipaul sets his protagonists adrift in a world in flux, encountering the inevitability of migration. The narrator in *The Enigma of Arrival* sees "a world in flux, [...] human life as a series of cycles that sometimes ran together" (EA 1988: 335). In *A Bend in the River*, the narrator exclaims,

Chapter Four The Historical Perspective: *A Way in the World*

"Everywhere men are in movement, the world is in movement" (BR 1989: 141). Almost all the works we have discussed in the previous chapters involve characters on the move, even assumed Englishmen such as Jack and Byan in *The Enigma of Arrival*, are revealed to have moved from somewhere else.

In *A Way in the World*, many characters' quests for identities are typical of what Gilroy describes as a journey of "diasporic identification" as opposed to "diasporic identities". They are always somewhere between the native culture and the adopted culture, creating their identity by virtue of travelling between them. Most characters are found to be in a culture other than their native one. Yet instead of being hostile to that culture, they seem to be quite content with travelling between homeland and adopted country. In lieu of the exilic melancholy, the diasporic vision becomes the shaping power that overwhelms the obsession with homeland hunting. The relatively open construction of *A Way in the World* thus dictates the metamorphosis from exile to diaspora.

Different from Naipaul's earlier works, which usually centre on one major character, like Mr. Biswas, Ralph Singh, and Salim etc., *A Way in the World* does not have a centre. There are neither central characters nor central events. Consistently running through the nine seemingly fragmented narratives is the characters' diasporic experience and their diasporic identification resulting from such an experience. Naipaul's characters' diasporic identification is a double-way journey: from the indigenous to the diasporic, and from diasporic back to indigenous, this journey is ever open and refusing to be settled. To diasporas, unsettlement is the means to settled identities. Living at cultural boundaries, they manage to "construct homes away from home" (Clifford 1997: 244), and "turn boundaries and limits into the in-between spaces through which the meanings of cultural and political authority are negotiated" (Bhabha 1990: 4).

Trinidadian Indians' ancestors are not aboriginal Trinidadian. They left their homeland and came to this "strange" place during the colonial period. The place where they reside used to belong to aboriginal Indians:

> Once aboriginal Indians were masters of these waters. They no longer existed; and that knowledge of currents and tides had passed to their successors. On the south-westernmost point of the long Trinidad peninsula that almost ran into the river estuary there had been an aboriginal port or anchoring place [...] There was still a fishing village there [...] Many of the fishermen of Cedros were Asian Indians, descendants of agricultural people from the Gangetic plain. In less than a hundred years the geography of their new home had remade these Asian Indian people of Cedros, touched them with old aboriginal aptitudes, and given them sea skills which their landlocked ancestors never had. (WW 1995: 217)

From farmers to fishermen, the Asian Indians had adapted themselves to the culture of the new land. Between the lines of the above quotation is something slightly satirical. As a critic says, Naipaul "lends a subtle twisted paradoxical truth to the very unsubtle colonial naming of the indigenous people of the Americas as 'Indian'" (Weiss 1992: 92). The Asian Indians now take the place of the aboriginal Indians. And in a place culturally and geographically different from their own, they construct themselves new identities, making their new culture different and hybridized. What Asian Indians have gone through is a gradual shifting from the diasporic into the indigenous—a hybridizing of a diasporic sense of community with an indigenous relationship to land.

The story of Sorzano, a Trinidadian Asian Indian Venezuelan, is one typical example of someone who reconstructs his identity across boundaries between diasporic and nationalist dimensions. He is "a new man", as the title of this story about him suggests, who enacts an elastic shifting of identification by travelling across borders, both geographically and culturally. When the narrator first meets Sorzano at an airport, he thinks that he is an "out-and-out Venezuelan, a coastal mestizo, a product of a racial mixture that had started with the Spanish settlement, someone who, with limited language, had known only his own landscape and his own way of life, and was cut away from everything else" (WW 1995: 219). Yet the Trinidad Indian pickles Sorzano brought with him make the narrator doubt his

Chapter Four The Historical Perspective: *A Way in the World*

judgement: "Had I misread him, then? Was he, after all, an Asian Indian from Trinidad, with ideas and assumptions I could intuit—and not the Venezuelan stranger I had taken him for? ... He was unusual. He could be one thing or the other: it depended on what you thought he was" (ibid: 219). When asked, Sorzano answers firmly that he is Venezuelan and his passport also shows him to be a Venezuelan. He does go back to Trinidad, however, to buy some Hindi devotional songs because he is in fact an Indian from Trinidad. By frequently crossing borders he develops a sort of fluid identity, travelling or negotiating between diasporic and national identities. He gives all his children Venezuelan names and talks to them in Spanish at home, although his wife speaks only Hindi at home. The narrator has to re-evaluate Sorzano, "A new land, a new name, a new identity, a new kind of family life, new languages even—his life should have been full of stress, but he gave the impression of living as intuitively as he had always done, making his way, surviving, with no idea of being lost or in a void" (ibid: 223). Uprooted from his ancestral culture, Sorzano manages to root himself in the new culture by way of shifting his identities as he travels across borders. Shifting identification is his new identity. The fact that he is now living on a new land, with a new name and even speaks a new language doesn't seem to make him feel lost or suffer a sense of emptiness, instead, he finds his way and arrives at a new mode of diasporic hybrid identification.

Sorzano's story is typical of positive diasporic identification. Rather than adhering to the calcified identities that centre around one nationality and one culture, Sorzano "intuitively" creates a hybrid identity for himself in a "position of liminality, in that productive space of the construction of culture as difference" (Bhabha 1994: 209). The new hybrid identity Sorzano creates is part of a different culture constructed in the liminal space. To achieve this new identity, he begins by speaking a different language, in this case Spanish. Yet people don't simply choose another language, and thus free themselves from previous history. The previous language, identity and peculiar inheritance can't be simply got rid of. "What we have inherited—as culture, as history, as language, as tradition, as a sense of identity—is not destroyed but taken apart, opened up to questioning, rewriting, and re-routing" (Chambers 1994: 24). For Sorzano, leaving Trinidad doesn't mean that he is severed from his cultural inheritance. In times of need, he still returns to Trinidad, turning to the Indian religious songs to seek peace and comfort. When his son is in trouble, he comforts him by saying Indian prayers for him. He tells the narrator, "as soon as I say it, I see it was the right thing to say. He [His son] know that I have special prayers in mind. He don't know much about these prayers, but he knows they are very important to his mother, and I take them seriously too" (WW 1995: 234). Born in Venezuela, Sorzano's son is given a Venezuelan name and speaks Spanish, and he believes in the power of his ancestral religion. Instead of sticking to either his ancestral identity or to the Venezuelan one, both Sorzano and his son shift between them intuitively and are always in the path of a diasporic identification. In other words, identity flows into shifting identification: at any given time, Sorzano can choose to present himself as native Venezuelan, while at others he travels on the route between the Asian Trinidadian and the Venezuelan. Slemom finds that "the degrees of separation between the two have rapidly and oddly reduced over time; the differential is minimal, mellifluous and ultimately within a national paradigm, subversively erasable" (Slemom 1998: 92). The result will be, as the narrator comments, "there would be no ambiguities about [his children]; they would be the kind of Venezuelan I had in the beginning taken their father for" (WW 1995: 223). These demonstrate that the route of diasporic identification is at the beginning from the indigenous to the diasporic, and the diasporic experience will lead back to becoming indigenous, as in the case of Sorzano's children. With Naipaul, as he stated in his Nobel speech, the world is always on the move and our identities are bound to be identification.

The narrative about Sorzano is preceded by the story of Sir Walter Raleigh, who promised the English King that he would find gold in El Dorado, and ultimately beheaded for failing. Ironical enough,

Chapter Four The Historical Perspective: *A Way in the World*

the "new man", a common Trinidadian Venezuelan makes his fortune by finding a gold hoard in Venezuela. The gold coins Sorzano finds are Victorian sovereigns, which were "cast in 1824, intended to be historical, a statement of certainty, commemorating an event in 1818, the first Congress of the independent South American state that Simon Bolivar had tried to set up" (ibid: 223). History has its irony here: the "statement of certainty" now becomes the symbol of failure; more importantly, Sorzano's later diasporic experience in the end turns out to be rewarding. As the narrator writes:

And just as the buriers of treasure at the time of the break-up of the Roman empire could have no idea of the twists of history, the further great migrations, that would one day lead people unknown to them, people beyond their imagining, to turn up the treasure they had laid up for brighter days; so those people in old Caracas, at a time of darkness, amassing (almost certainly by plunder) a secret hoard of sovereigns and gold coins, could have had no idea of the twists of history that would lead Manuel Sorzano, whose ancestors in the 1860s had not yet left India, to come upon their gold. (ibid: 224)

Migration, therefore, has linked originally unrelated peoples together, and become a strong force behind diasporic identification.

"On the Run", the longest story in the "sequence" is focused on Lebrun, a character based largely on the life of the famous black Trinidadian intellectual, C.L.R. James, who is a Marxist writer and revolutionary. Lebrun is first indirectly introduced in the second section, when referencing the 1937 oil field strikes, regarded as the event that led Trinidad to modern political awareness. Mistrusted by established postcolonial rulers, Lebrun continues his role of "impresario of revolution" without a popular base of his own, attaching himself to leaders more in touch with the "simpler people who had given them power and with a simpler idea of that power" (ibid: 111). His most loyal followers are Western Intellectual admirers, and in more than one sense he has remained "on the run" because, like Miranda, he has never stopped to consider the consequences of his political activism for himself and others. Lebrun presents his "revolution" as a "re-interpretation of Marx, with special reference to the struggles of non-European peoples in the twentieth century" (ibid: 120), especially in the Caribbean. Lebrun, who tried to see racial oppression as part of the class struggle, and who proclaimed a universal humanism, becomes in old age, a race hero. He is "'discovered' as one of the prophets of black revolution, a man whose name doesn't appear in history books, but who for years had worked patiently, had been behind the liberation movements of Africa and the Caribbean" (ibid: 107). But Lebrun is embittered in his old age. His wealthy white mistress and patron deserts him for another man. He rants against interracial relationships although he is brown and his daughter light skinned. At the very end of his life, Lebrun turns against his revolutionary principles and lapses into a form of racial redemption. To his great disappointment, he finds in West Africa a country ruled by a revolutionary Marxist tyrant has come to ruin, while a neighbouring country that has retained its chiefs and rituals is now modernized and people there live a more comfortable life.

"The man of the true revolution" of his early days, has become "a man of true African or black redemption" in his old age (ibid: 134) Forsaking the revolutionary cause he had been actively engaged in, Lebrun in his old age appears to stand "against the whole life of revolution he had lived; against the "political resolution" he had come to years before, the universality in which he had shed the burdens of race and shame; against the admiration of his New York supporters; against, even, the inspiration to me, as to a fellow humanist, in the copy of *The Second Struggle*[4]" (ibid: 127). The narrator thinks

---

4 | Several pages earlier, the narrator provides information about the book: "In 1973 [Lebrun] sent me his last book, *The Second Struggle: Speeches and Writings 1962-1972*. It was printed in East Germany, and the cover carried the 1956 photograph of him in Woodford Square in Port of Spain, standing at a microphone on the bandstand, before the crowd. "He had inscribed the book to me as to 'a fellow humanist'. And he had added, 'To understand that is at any rate to make a beginning.' A touch of the old

that Lebrun's "betrayal" of his "principles" is an inevitable choice for him. His changed political character is described as opposing "the universality in which he had shed the burdens of race and shame" (ibid: 127). The narrator observes that "It was as though at the very end of his life he had found the role he had been working towards since the beginning" (ibid: 131). Such satirical remarks reveal Naipaul's distrust of the revolutionary's absolute narrative of racial vindication, of the promise of a renewed and renewing purity through the reclamation of a pristine ethnicity and homeland.

As "an impresario of revolution", with no base of his own, a revolutionary without revolution, the life of Lebrun is actually shaped by the brutalizing African dispersal experience. He belonged to the first generation of educated black people in the region. "For a number of them—men as old as the century—there was no honourable place at home in their colony or in the big countries, they were in-between people, [...] they tried to make their way. [...] They were shipwrecked men" (ibid: 119). The story of Lebrun therefore further explicates Naipaul's ideas of diasporic identification. As a diasporic figure himself, Lebrun's life is shaped by his diasporic experience, yet both his early revolutionary claims and his later policy of racial redemption fail to take into consideration the complicated influence the diasporic experience has on the identity of blacks. With Naipaul, neither revolutions nor the back-to-Africa movement can provide a real way out, because in both efforts, Lebrun clings to the idea of fixed identity.

In the same chapter, Naipaul also tells us the story of Phyllis, a French-speaking woman from Guadeloupe. She marries an African in Paris, but the marriage is broken almost as soon as she gets to Africa with her husband. After the failure of her marriage, she leaves that country and goes to live and work in former French West Africa. Naipaul mentions the "fluidity of her character" twice (ibid: 136, 155),

---

charm, the way with words. It didn't mean anything, but I was moved to see his shaky hand'" (WW 1995: 125).

with which she could be "many things" to many people, and with which she finds her way in the world, as the narrator realizes:

WE ALL(sic) inhabit 'constructs' of a world. Ancient peoples had their own. Our grandparents had their own; we cannot absolutely enter into their constructs. Every culture has its own: men are infinitely malleable. And perhaps Phyllis, with the fluidity of character [...] had established her own further construct of the world. Perhaps in that fluidity, in that shiftingness, she had found freedom. (ibid: 154-155)

The fluidity of Phyllis' character is what her diasporic experience bestowed upon her. Different from Lebrun, who privileges cultural roots over routes and holds onto cultural essentialism, Phyllis is malleable and shifts between different "constructs" of the world and finds her freedom.

Suggested in Phyllis's story is Naipaul's critique of Lebrun's policy of racial redemption. The failure of Phyllis' marriage with the son of an African tribal chief, and the riot that happened in the country, reflect the rashness of the policy of racial redemption. In the last section of the book, we can see that Naipaul is clearly against the narrowed provincialism of Africanness, as practiced by political players in Africa, which eventually results in racist attitudes, as the narrator finds, "The country was full of special hate [...] Expatriates dealt in it to show their own commitment to the country. Some political people saw it as part of the business of building socialism, and gave it a doctrinal gloss" (ibid: 348-389). Behind such passionate commitments is an inverted racism that prevails in the newly independent country. The racialized space of existence that offers meanings and direction to the newly established country therefore justifies a "licensed" hate. Yet Lebrun never has to "live with the consequences of his action. He is always free to move on" (ibid: 155), and "When the dictatorship collapsed and the desolate country was opened up, no one thought of calling him to account" (ibid: 155). The universal diasporic experience has already blurred the rigid category of race, and thus racial redemption is not only a movement against reality, it is also a force

Chapter Four The Historical Perspective: *A Way in the World* 197

to displace people from where they have been residing. As Slemom insightfully remarks, "the narrative of absolute reclamation against the dispersals of the movements of empire becomes a brutalizing hegemonic reality which in fact continues rather than ruptures the Empire's cycle of displacement" (Slemon 1998: 90). In critiquing Lebrun's diasporic metaphysics of a "pure" homeland, the text becomes a critique of the very brutal implications of a racialist government in national power.

The juxtaposition of Lebrun and Phyllis' stories implodes the narrative of purity, reclamation and redemption. It is an interrogation of the priority of "roots" to the legitimation of "routes". In *The Black Atlantic*, Gilroy reads diasporas insightfully through the metaphors of "roots" and "routes". Whereas the "roots" metaphor requires the subject to construct a pristine, uncontaminated homeland to which, ideally, one ought to return, and the essence of which is always a "racialized" version of the homeland, the "routes" metaphor insinuates the significance of the trajectory itself, and the suggestive power of the journey and the historical interactions (Gilroy 1993: 212). Positioning "identity" in opposition to "identification", Gilroy indicates that through spatial shifting, centreless networks of identification, a constant affirmative dynamic placement, displacement and replacement—formation and reformation—of diasporic identity occurs. The reality of cultural hybridity and spatial interconnections leads Gilroy, as well as Naipaul, to argue against linear temporality and unproblematic reclamation of the past. Diasporic cultural identity is therefore a matter of "becoming", that "are constantly producing and reproducing themselves anew" (Hall 1990: 230).

***

A Way in the World is a counter-history to the accepted notions of the past. It is neither history from the established European perspective nor history from the usual Left and black counter-perspectives. By blending fact and fiction, it presents a diasporic vision of history, which questions the efforts made for cultural origin and homeland reclaiming. It posits that cultural essentialism is unlocatable and problematic because all cultures are trans-culturalized, and because roots can always be traced back to routes. It is also a book about writing: how Naipaul learned to write and how the history of those formerly colonized should be rewritten in contrast to how it has been written. As Stephen Jones contends, "so in an odd twist, through this textual structuring of his characters without/across/against a linear sense of time, Naipaul denied his characters the millennial, epochal sense of history and historic identity" (Jones 2000: 89).

What Naipaul aims at is to disrupt the linear sense of temporality, deterring the possibility of yearning for a consecrated past or claiming an authentically historical sense. It is true that "we all need history because it tells us where we are" (EA 1988: 353). Without a sense of history it would be difficult for us to orient ourselves both in time and space. However, for the imaginative writer, history can be both a nightmare and a challenge: a nightmare if his or her relation to it remains imprisoned in the fixed relations and attitudes of the region's linear past; a challenge if he or she exploits the artist's freedom to endow history and experience with figurative meanings, and explores other areas of experience beyond the rational linear order. What Naipaul tries to present in *A Way in the World* is a challenge against the axiom of history as facts and data with internal consistency and coherence. The deconstruction of the fixed notion of a recoverable past enables Naipaul to rewrite the history of the colonized individual and arrive at a diasporic identification.

Studying the history of the West Indies, Wilson-Tagoe points out, "The discourse on history, while confronting fundamental assumptions behind European perceptions and interpretations of the region's history, is really inspired by the imperatives of redefinition and subjectification which are basically colonial impulses (Wilson-Tagoe 1998: 4). Traumatized by the deprivation of history, the West Indian writer is continually haunted by its specter and is perpetually engaged with redefining it. In his effort to retrieve a personal and collective history, Naipaul does not just stop at pointing out the inadequacies of historiography, but also endeavors to rewrite it.

As a "reworking of experience" (Gusson), *A Way in the World* is a blending of memoir and novel. It is not always clear when real life steps aside and imagination takes over. For the author, the work establishes its own form. It is not, he said, a "work of history or scholarship or fiction", although, as with most of his books, it has aspects of all three. Naipaul's path to identify himself is reflected in the hybrid of genres—"autobiography", "history", "novel"—which reveals what history is to Naipaul: a mixture of the writers' subjectivity, facts, and fiction. For Naipaul, the mixture of cultures of the present and those of the past constitutes the essence of history; it shows the causality of historical events, and helps explain what we have become at present. With such a concept of history, the text interrogates the idea of an ultimate cultural origin and racial purity that repulse the signification of fragmentations and trajectories. For Naipaul, then, history is a stepping stone to move beyond the land of one's birth, beyond ethnicity and nationalities, and to reach for spiritual and intellectual development, and to start afresh toward the positive embrace of the diasporic identification that privileges "routes" instead of "roots".

Conclusion

> They bear the traces of particular cultures, traditions, languages, systems of belief, texts and histories which have shaped them. But they are also obliged to come to terms with and to make something new of the cultures they inhabit, without simply assimilating to them. They are not and will never be unified culturally in the old sense, because they are inevitably the products of several interlocking histories and cultures, belonging at the same time to several homes—and thus to no one particular home. (Gilroy 1993: 362)

In *In a Free State*, a tramp says a sentence that illustrates Naipaul's self-defined stance: "What is nationality these days? I myself, I think of myself as a citizen of the world" (IFC 1981: 11). To be "a citizen of the world" is Naipaul's way of acknowledging the impossibility of recovering what is left behind, be it ethnic or national identities. It is also a pronouncement of the difficulties with identification because, in a way "a citizen of the world" is a tag for having no identity. More importantly, however, the statement is an active affirmation of an identity that is not place-bound. Yet "a citizen of the world" is a paradox because a citizen is surely a citizen of a certain place, while a citizen of the world signals the rejection of a fixed place, that is to say, the tension between local and global remains resolved. To be "a citizen of the world" is therefore to exists between home and homelessness, it is to exist in the form of identi/ties, referring to identity in the singular and plural, as well as the subject's futile attempt to unite the singular and plural identities. A citizen of the world is, in the words of Gilroy, "the product of several interlocking histories and cultures, belonging at the same time to several homes—and thus to no one particular home" (Gilroy 1993: 362). To put it differently, a citizen of the world is also a vernacular cosmopolitan who is faithful to his instinct for a home as well as ready to face the diasporic history and reality that has made him. An Indian by ancestry, a Trinidadian by birth, and an Englishman by citizenship, Naipaul's experience embodies the typical trajectory of a postcolonial subject's quest for identity: from negation of the colonial identity to positive diasporic hybrid identification. Through a close reading of Naipaul's major fictions in chronological order, this book has been an attempt to trace this trajectory.

In *A House for Mr. Biswas*, we read of Mr. Biswas's lifelong attempts to construct a house of his own, to which he attaches his independence, dignity, and identity. The jerry-built house he finally acquires symbolizes the success of his struggle, as well as the compromises he has had to make with his social and historical environment. The fact that he is born into the Symbolic order of the colonizer suggests a bleak future for his quest. As Lacan says, desire is structured by the discourse of the Other, Mr. Biswas's desire for a house to represent his independent identity is actually a desire that he acquires through a colonial education, the purpose of which is to produce people catering to the values and beliefs of the colonizers. Both Naipaul and Mr. Biswas fail to realize that they are taught to desire the desires of the oppressors in a society where such desires cannot be realized. The impossibility of independent identity in the New World results in postcolonial subjects' negation of their homeland, which then leads to an important stage in their identification: mimicry. A colonial does not want to affirm his pre-given identity, instead, he produces an image for himself and then transforms himself to assume that image. Yet the independent identity he envisions in the colonizer is but an image, which, the same as that viewed by an infant in a mirror, is only misrecognition. To be like the image, the colonial has to transform himself and mimic the colonizers.

In *The Mimic Men*, by looking at Singh's life between his home island and London, Naipaul explicates the key concept in the colonial's route to identification: mimicry. Although disillusioned by London, at this stage Naipaul seems to be quite eager to become an Englishman, as many leftist critics have accused him. At the end of the novel, Singh chooses to stay at a London hotel to write his memoir, acknowledging that he has realized that his position in London is a marginalized one yet he is not willing to give up his hope of London and strives to obtain an understanding of himself through his writing practice. He has left Isabella, yet London does not embrace him. Mimicry cannot be the final resolution of the colonial's identity perplexity.

We find the narrator in *The Enigma of Arrival* in a traditional English manor. After having resided in England for almost thirty years, Naipaul is finally able to reflect on his position between English culture and the culture of his homeland. In *The Enigma of Arrival*, we see a milder Naipaul who has recovered from the agony of his early "homelessness" and is beginning to reconcile with his past. He has come to accept his identity as one of hybridity. This enigmatic book fraught with the author's self-reflective rumination of his experience is a symbol of Naipaul's arriving at a positive acceptance of his colonial and metropolitan identity. In a most subjective form, Naipaul delineates for us the route of his identification toward a hybrid identity, which is not only his route, but also that of millions also experiencing the era of globalization.

Naipaul's view of history affects his identification. *A Way in the World* counter narrates the history written from the established Euro-centric perspective. By blending fact and fiction, it presents a diasporic vision of history, problematizing the quest for cultural origin and homeland reclaiming. In *A Way in the World*, identification for Naipaul is reflected in the hybridization of genres—"autobiography", "history" and "the novel"—thus revealing what history is to Naipaul: a mixture of the writers' subjectivity, facts and the inner logic required by a plot. As such, the text questions the notion of an ultimate cultural origin and racial purity that repulses the signification of fragmentations and trajectories. For Naipaul, then, history is a stepping-stone beyond the land of one's birth, beyond ethnicity and nationalities, to reach for spiritual and intellectual development, and to start afresh stepping toward the positive embrace of diasporic identification.

As a prototype of the postcolonial subject, Naipaul's path begins with the negation of his homeland as he finds that independent identity is impossible there. He then undergoes the stage of mimicry. Naipaul's view of mimicry is different from Bhabha's, who thinks of mimicry as a marker of subjugation as well as an empowerment. In seeking to model themselves on the colonizers, the colonized can translate mimicry into a style of subversive mockery. It can therefore become a means of resistance. With Naipaul, however, mimicry is the fate of colonial people on their way to identification. Moreover, Naipaul satirizes the colonial's mimicry of the colonizer. Mimicry produces people who are like the mimicked but not quite, leading to people with hybrid identities. And yet, that attainment is based on the condition that the colonial must have already enjoyed some type of position in the colonizers' place, and is able to look at his homeland with ease rather than shame. With a hybrid identity, the colonial is confident enough now to view his position from a historical perspective, and understand that colonial history is written to serve the interests of the West. The rewriting of history is therefore necessary to de-re-construct the identity of colonial people. This historical sense also helps the colonial to look at his diasporic experience and arrive at a diasporic hybrid identity. Of course, these four stages do not necessarily develop sequentially, like an evolution, but may interweave and overlap at different stages.

Broadly speaking, apart from Naipaul's view of history and his own writing career, the key factor affecting the identification of Naipaul and postcolonial subjects like him is colonization. It is colonization that takes Naipaul's ancestors away from the Indian continent, and turns them into indentured workers in the Caribbean. Once there, their descendants are taught with English instead of with their native language. Although the East Indians in the West Indies try to construct an enclave of Indian culture, they are encompassed by colonial discourse. Bit by bit, the colonized people internalize their image as an "other", in response to colonial discourses' stereotypes. This internalization of themselves as an "other" in the colonial's mind is the major cause of the colonial's identity crisis. A related line of inquiry in postcolonial theory explains how institutions of Western education function to spread imperialism. Historical documents such as Thomas Babington Macaulay's *Minute on Indian Education* show that education—including the study of English literature and the English language—plays a strategically significant part in ruling over colonized people. Because it includes Western Eurocentric values, literary education supports a kind of "cultural colonization", creating a class of colonial subjects burdened with double consciousness and divided loyalties. Thus Western colonizers can rule by consent rather than by violence.

In face of cultural colonization, colonial people can either mimic the colonizer, or the rebel, and try to win back what has been robbed of them by the colonizers. Mimicry of the colonizer is accompanied with shame and resentment of the self, because, to be "saved", he must deny his own history and tradition. Nevertheless, mimicry with the goal of becoming identical to the colonizer, cannot grant the colonized equal status. However, to reconstruct identity and subjectivity through rebellion is not without its problems. As we have analysed in *The Mimic Men*, the colonial's knowledge of revolution and identity is constructed on the basis of what the colonizers have revealed to them in colonial discourse. They draw on the colonizers' ideas, way of thinking and methods in their struggle for identity, which remains mimicry of the colonizer.

In the era of postcolonialism and multiculturalism, how the former colonized attempt to construct their identity remains a problem. With intellectuals like Naipaul and other postcolonial theorists, we find one common thread: many of them have left their colonial birthplace and successfully established themselves in the Western world. Consciously or unconsciously, what they deploy to defend and speak for themselves and those formerly oppressed by the colonizer and today's global capitalism is what they learned from the West. In the case of Naipaul, writing is the most important means to shedding his shameful identity as a colonial, and constructing his identity and subjectivity. "Writing is a form of therapy; sometimes I wonder how all those who do not write, compose or paint can manage to escape the madness, the melancholia, the panic fear which is inherent in the human condition" (Graham 1980: VII). Naipaul has followed no other profession in his life, and writing is how he explores, questions and asserts his identity. Writing enables Naipaul to manoeuvre through the predicament of colonial life, and how he comes to understanding who he is in relation to the rest of the world. With writing, he constructs a psychological defence against the world, imposes a sense of order upon the chaos of the colonial experience, and secures a safe house for himself in the world.

Naipaul's sense of placelessness, alienation, dereliction and isolation leads to his rediscovery of life, and is the driving force behind his writing. Writing matures Naipaul enough to face his colonial dilemma, and becomes a compass to find his place in the world. Naipaul's writings consciously survey a symptomatic response of the need to discover a house of one's own. Where in the world is his home? In his fluctuation between home and homelessness, Naipaul becomes open to the condition of in-between, and creates a free space for himself. Writing becomes a space in which his identity takes form. Through travelling and writing, Naipaul creates a space to belong between the colonizer and the colonized that surpasses the dichotomy between the periphery and the centre. In the meantime, the "in-between" space provides Naipaul with broader imaginative and creative spaces. The space of the "in-between" also gives the exile or the colonial more opportunities to choose among their multi-cultural backgrounds. In the space of "in-between" and through writing, Naipaul breaks the dichotomy of identity as "self" and "other", the colonizer and colonized, and is able to negotiate between his different identities. In *The Mimic Men*, Naipaul's characters still grope about for unified and fixed identities. As such, they have to deny some parts of themselves to pursue the one identity that they think fits them. Yet none of his early fictions have characters that are successful in finding that one fixed identity. What Naipaul shows in his early characters is the predicament of the colonial's identity, his struggles and defeats. In Naipaul's later fictions, he reconciles with his colonial background and accepts theories such as that expounded by Clifford and Hall that identity is multiple, mixed and changing. The path of Naipaul's writing parallels that of his own identity quest, during which he tries to move beyond the identity of a colonial by subverting his identity as an "other". He replaces identity as such with hybrid, diasporic identification. In the analysis of the previous chapters, we find a Naipaul who has been transformed from the initial shame of his colonial identity to one who can look at it with open-mindedness and construct himself a diasporic hybrid identity.

This diasporic hybrid identity not only allows him to concentrate on the process of becoming, but it also exemplifies the mingling of varied cultural experiences at work in the postcolonial milieu. Cultural difference, according to Bhabha, is grounded in the notion of "difference" operating in the space of translation and hybridity. The realization of the extent to which the cultures of colonizers and colonized interact has prompted reflections on the hybrid nature of culture. That no culture is ever pure is everywhere evident in our era of global and post-industrial capitalism: the nationalism that undergirds notions of pure culture is called into question daily by the international flow of commodities, money, information, technology, and workers. These dynamics of globalization and hybridization preoccupy scholars of postcolonial studies. According to Bhabha, what is theoretically innovative and politically crucial is the need to think beyond narratives of originality and initial subjectivities, and to instead focus on those moments or processes that are produced in the articulation of cultural difference. The social articulation of difference, from the minority perspective, is a complex, on-going negotiation that seeks to authorize cultural hybridities that emerge in moments of historical transformation (Bhabha 1994: 1-2). Against such a background, our sense of being, identity and language, is experienced and extrapolated from movement because "I" does not pre-exist this process and then go out into the world, but is constantly formed and reformed in such movements.

In view of what has been said, perhaps we can say that writing serves as both mimicry and revolution for Naipaul because, while he conforms to the language of the colonizer—English, his subject matter is that of the alien. And while he began with a Western novel, he has deviated during his writing and found a new form of his own. In other words, Naipaul tries to represent his alienation in the authorial norm by using the English language, and to be accepted by the English world. Yet by adopting the imperial form, he speaks for those living in the periphery, silently. He regains what was robbed from him, like a revolutionary in a decolonization movement. His writing journey is a journey from mimicry to revolution. As Bhabha explicates, within mimicry lies subversive power because the very mimicry of the colonized denies the relationship between the colonizer and the colonized as the binary between self and other, slave and master. Ironically, though Naipaul does not believe in the subversive power of mimicry, his own mimicry of writing becomes a revolution in the end. All in all, the trajectory of Naipaul's work shows a critical concern with issues involving the representation of the conflicting, calamitous and revealing experiences of colonial people through the constant negotiation between cultural divides.

Stories are the key tool colonial explorers and novelists deploy to talk about remote colonized places. They can also become important channels for colonial people to affirm their identities and historical existence. The study of Naipaul's journey of identification through the reading of his fictions seeks to reveal how an ex-colonial constructs an identity in this era of postcolonialism and multiculturalism. Naipaul's experience offers the best example of Hall's elaboration that cultural identities have histories and undergo constant transformation. They are "the names we give to different ways we are positioned by, and position ourselves within, the narratives of the past" (Hall 1990: 222). Reading Naipaul's fictions uncovers the transforming process of his identity. The more he writes, the more he comes to understand his own identity. Writing helps Naipaul free himself from otherness, and enables him to construct a subjectivity and identity.

Of course, taking into consideration Naipaul's multiple positions as a colonial, a border-crossing itinerant, a postcolonial traveller coming to terms with hybridizing world cultures, and a diasporic writer whose writings are set in the remapping of territory and in a scenario that calls for the perpetual re-examination of his homeland in relation to his circumnavigation in the world, we have to admit that Naipaul's works have complexities that confuse either-or distinctions. We must bear in our mind that the strength of writing often comes from its indulgence in contradictions and ambiguities. My reading of Naipaul from the perspective of his controversial position aims to provide a comprehensive picture of his identity quest. In so doing, this book refutes the simplistic view of Naipaul's anglicised identity, analyzes the route of postcolonial subjects' identification, and provides an alternative approach toward the study of Naipaul, and a channel to knowing the world and the self better.

As a conceptual tool, identity is not only theoretically important, but is pertinent to everyone's life. A reading of Naipaul's fictions thus is not only about the literariness of the texts, it is also practical in our daily life because theory is not always grey: it can be passionate as long as it is connected to life. Our identities allow us to become acting subjects and define who we are in the world, but at the same time, they subject us to the controlling power of external categorization. Identity is the sense of oneself belonging to a group, and can be something essential, tangible, real and inherent in the self as well as shifting, constructed, a matter of creating meaning from social categories. Identities are never final products but are always in process—open ended, expansive, responsive to new changes, and future-oriented. Therefore it is also the intention of this book to exemplify that the reading of literary works may provide a method for people to obtain a better understanding of the world, either directly or indirectly.

Works Cited

PRIMARY SOURCES

Naipaul, V.S. (1981 [1958]): The Suffrage of Elvira, Middlesex: Penguin.

Naipaul, V.S. (1981 [1963]): Mr. Stone and the Knights Companion, Middlesex: Penguin.

Naipaul, V.S. (1981 [1964]): An Area of Darkness, New York: Vintage.

Naipaul, V.S. (1981 [1971]): In a Free State, Middlesex: Penguin.

Naipaul, V.S. (1981 [1971]): The Overcrowded Barracoon, Middlesex: Penguin.

Naipaul, V.S. (1981 [1980]): The Return of Eva Person with the Killings in Trinidad, New York: Vintage.

Naipaul, V.S. (1982 [1969]): The Loss of El Dorado, Middlesex: Penguin.

Naipaul, V.S. (1984 [1961]): A House for Mr. Biswas, Middlesex: Penguin.

Naipaul, V.S. (1984 [1967]): The Mimic Men, Middlesex: Penguin.

Naipaul, V.S. (1984 [1975]): Guerrillas, Middlesex: Penguin.

Naipaul, V.S. (1985 [1962]): The Middle Passage, Middlesex: Penguin.

Naipaul, V.S. (1985 [1967]): A Flag on the Island, Middlesex: Penguin.

Naipaul, V.S. (1985 [1977]): India: A Wounded Civilization, Middlesex: Penguin.

Naipaul, V.S. (1985 [1981]): Among the Believers: An Islamic Journey, Middlesex: Penguin.

Naipaul, V.S. (1985 [1984]): Finding the Centre, Middlesex: Penguin.

Naipaul, V.S. (1986 [1957]): The Mystic Masseur, Middlesex: Penguin.
Naipaul, V.S. (1986 [1959]): Miguel Street, Middlesex: Penguin.
Naipaul, V.S. (1988 [1987]): The Enigma of Arrival, New York: Vintage.
Naipaul, V.S. (1989 [1979]): A Bend in the River, New York: Vintage.
Naipaul, V.S. (1990 [1989]): A Turn in the South, New York: Vintage.
Naipaul, V.S. (1991 [1990]): India: A Million Mutinies Now, New York: Viking.
Naipaul, V.S. (1995 [1994]): A Way in the World, England: Minerva.
Naipaul, V.S. (1998): Beyond Belief: Islamic Excursions Among the Converted Peoples, London: Little, Brown and Company.
Naipaul, V.S. (1998): Letters Between a Father and Son, London: Little, Brown and Company.
Naipaul, V.S. (2000): Reading and Writing: A Personal Account, New York: New York Review Books.
Naipaul, V.S. (2000): Half a Life, New York: Knopf.
Naipaul, V.S. (2001): "V.S. Naipaul: Two Worlds: Nobel Lecture on December 7, 2001". http://www.nobel.se/literature/laureats/2001/naipaul-lecture-e.html.
Naipaul, V.S. (2002): The Writer and the World, New York: Vintage.
Naipaul, V.S. (2003): Literary Occasions: Essays. New York: Knopf.
Naipaul, V.S. (2004): Magic Seeds. London: Picador.

SECONDARY SOURCES

Aschroft, Bill/ Griffiths, Gareth /Tiffin, Helen (1989): The Empire Writes Back: Theory and Practice in Post-colonial Literatures. New York: Routledge & Kegan Paul.
Aschroft, Bill/ Griffiths, Gareth /Tiffin, Helen (1995): The Post-colonial Studies Reader. London and New York: Routledge.
Aschroft, Bill/ Griffiths, Gareth /Tiffin, Helen (1998): Key Concepts in Post-colonial Studies. London and New York: Routledge.

Achebe, Chinua (1980): "Viewpoint." In: Times Literary Supplement, Feb. 1, pp. 21-27.

Ahmad, Aijaz (1992): "Jameson's Rhetoric of Otherness and the 'National Allegory'." In: Theory: Classes, Nations, Literatures, London: Verso.

Anderson, Linda R (1978): "Ideas of Identity and Freedom in V.S. Naipaul and Joseph Conrad." In: English Studies 59, pp. 510-517.

Angrosino, M.B. (1975): "V. S. Naipaul and the Colonial Image." In: Caribbean Quarterly 21/3, pp. 1-11.

Anonymous (1980): "V.S. Naipaul." In: New Yorker, May 19, pp. 12-17.

Barnouw, Dagmar (2003): Naipaul's Strangers. Indianapolis: Indiana State University Press.

Bald, S.R. (1995): "Negotiating Identity in the Metropolis: Generational Differences in South Asian British Fiction." In: R. King. J. Connell and P. White, (eds.), Writing Across Worlds: Literature and Migration, London: Routledge.

Belitt, Ben (1981). "The Heraldry of Accommodation: A House for Mr. Naipaul." In: Salmagundi 54, pp. 23-42.

Bennett, Tony/ Grossberg, Lawrence/Morris, Meaghan (2005): (ed.) New Keywords: A Revised Vocabulary of Culture and Society, Oxford: Blackwell.

Bhabha, Homi K (1990): Nation and Narration, New York and London: Routledge.

Bhabha, Homi K (1994): The Location of Culture, London and New York: Routledge.

Bhabha, Homi K (2001): "Vernacular Cosmopolitanism." In: The Chronicle of Higher Education. 48/9, pp. 34-37.

Bingham, Nigel (1972): "The Novelist V.S. Naipaul Talks to Nigel Bingham about his Childhood in Trinidad." In: Listener, 88, September 7, pp. 11-13.

Boehmer, Elleke (1995): Colonial and Postcolonial Literature, Oxford: Oxford University Press.

Bongie, Chris (1998): Islands and Exiles. California: Stanford University Press.

Booth, Wayne (1963): The Rhetoric of Fiction. Chicago: Chicago University Press.

Boxhill, Anthony (1976): "The Little Bastard Worlds of V.S. Naipaul's *The Mimic Men* and *A Flag on the Island*.", In: International Fiction Review 3, pp. 12-19.

Boxhill, Anthony (1976): "V.S. Naipaul's Starting Point." In: Journal of Commonwealth Literature 10/1, pp.1-9.

Brereton, Bridget (1981): A History of Modern Trinidad 1783-1962, Kingston: Heinemann.

Bryden, Ronald (1973): Interview for the BBC, transcript of broadcast of 29, January.

Celestin, Roger (1996): From Cannibals to Radicals: Figures and Limits of Exoticism, London and Minneapolis: Minneapolis University Press.

Chambers, Iain (1994): Migrancy, Culture, Identity, London: Routledge.

Childs, Peter (1999): (eds.) Post-colonial Theory and English Literature: A Reader, Edinburgh: Edinburgh University Press.

Ciompi, Fausto (2002): "The Politics of Fluidity in *A Bend in the River*", In: The Atlantic Literary Review, 3/1, pp. 22-36.

Clifford, James (1988): The Predicament of Culture: Twentieth Century Ethnography, Literature, and Art, Cambridge, Massachusetts: Harvard University Press.

Clifford, James (1994): "Diaspora", In: Cultural Anthropology, 9, pp. 302-338.

Clifford, James (1997): Routes: Travel and Translation in the Late Twentieth Century, Cambridge: Harvard University Press.

Cocks, Joan (2000): "A New Cosmopolitanist? V.S. Naipaul and Edward Said", In: Constellations: An International Journal of Critical and Democratic Theory 7/1, pp. 46-64.

Conrad, Joseph (1966): Heart of Darkness, New York: Airmont Publishing Company.

Cudjoe, Selwyn (1988): V.S. Naipaul: A Materialist Reading, Amherst: University of Massachusetts Press.

Culler, Jonathan (1997): Literary Theory: A Very Short Introduction, New York: Oxford University Press.
Dayan, Joan (1993): "Gothic Naipaul", In: Transition 59, pp. 158-170.
Dhareshwar, Vivek (1989): "Self-fashioning, Colonial Habitus, and Double Exclusion: V.S. Naipaul's The Mimic Men", In: Criticism, 31/1 pp. 75-102.
Docker, John (2001): 1492: The Poetics of Diaspora, London and New York: Continuum.
DuBois, W.E.B (1982): The Souls of Black Folk, New York: Dodd Mead.
Eagleton, Terry (1983): Literary Theory: An Introduction, Oxford: Basil Blackwell.
Epstein, Joseph (1987): "A cottage for Mr. Naipaul," In: New Criterion, Oct., pp. 23-29.
Fanon, Frantz (1967a[1963]): The Wretched of the Earth, (trans.) Farrington, Constance, New York: Grove Press.
Fanon, Frantz (1967b): Black Skins, White Masks, (trans.) Markmann, Charles Lam, New York: Grove Press.
Featherstone, Mike (1995): Undoing Culture: Globalization, Postmodernism and Identity, London: Sage.
Feder, Lillian (2001): Naipaul's Truth: The Making of a Writer, Lanham, Maryland: Rowman & Littlefied Publishers, Inc.
Foucault, Michel (1980): Power/Knowledge: Selected Interviews and Other Writings 1972-1977, New York: Pantheon Books.
Friedman, Jonathan (1994): Cultural Identity and Global Process, London: Sage.
Frosh, Stephen (1991): Identity Crisis, London: Mcmillan.
George, Rosemarry Marangoly (1996): The Politics of Home: Postcolonial Relocations and Twentieth-century Fiction, England: Cambridge University Press.
Giddens, Antony (1991): Modernity and Self-identity: Self and Society in the Late Modern Age, Cambridge: Polity Press.
Gikandi, Simon (1992): Writing in Limbo: Modernism and Caribbean Literature, Ithaca and London: Cornell University Press.

Gikandi, Simon (1996): Maps of Englishness: Writing Identity in the Culture of Colonialism, New York: Columbia University Press.

Gilroy, Paul (1993): The Black Atlantic: Modernity and Double Consciousness, London and New York: Verso.

Gilroy, Paul (1997): "Diaspora and Detours of Identity", In: Identity and Difference, (eds.) Woodwardd, Kathryn. London: Sage.

Gorra, Michael (2004): "V.S.Naipaul", In: World Writers in English Vol. I, (eds.) Farini, Jay. New York: Charles Scribner's Sons.

Gourevitch, Philip (1996): "Naipaul's World", In: Commentary, 98/2, pp. 27-31.

Graham, Greene (1980): Ways of Escape, New York: Washington Square Press.

Greenberg, Robert M (2000): "Anger and the Alchemy of Literary Method in V.S. Naipaul's Political Fiction: The Case of The Mimic Men." In: Twentieth Century Literature, 46/2, pp. 214-237.

Gussow, Mel . "V.S. Naipaul in Search of Himself: A Conversation", June,7,1998(http://www.nytimes.com/books/98/06/07/specials/naipaul-conversation.html)

Hafen, Susan (2004): "Lesbian history and politics of identities", In: Fong, Mary/Chuang, Rueyling (eds.), Communicating Ethnic and Cultural Identity, New York: Rowman and Littlefield Publishers, Inc.

Hall, Stuart (1990): "Cultural Identity and Diaspora", In: Jonathan Ruthereford (ed.), Identity, Community, Culture, Difference, London: Lawrence and Wilshart.

Hall, Stuart (1992): "The Question of Cultural Identity," In: Stuart Hall/ Tony Mcgrew (eds.), Modernity and Its Futures. Cambridge, England: Polity Press.

Hall, Stuart (1996): "New Ethnicities", In: David Morley/Kuan-Hsing Chen (eds.) Critical Dialogues in Cultural Studies, London and New York: Routledge.

Hall, Stuart (1997): "The Spectacle of the 'Other'", In: Stuart Hall (ed.) Representation: Cultural Representations and Signifying Practices, Book 2, London: Sage.

Hall, Stuart (2000): "The Multicultural Questions", In: Pavis Papers, Faculty of Social Sciences. Milton Keynes: The Open University, no. page.
Hall, Stuart (2005[1996])): "Who Needs Identity?" In: Stuart Hall/ Paul Du Gay (eds.), Questions of Cultural Identity, London: Sage.
Hayward, Helen (2002). The Enigma of V. S. Naipaul: Sources and Contexts, New York: Palgrave Macmillan.
Hawle, John C (2001): Encyclopedia of Postcolonial Studies, Westport: Greenwood Press.
Hudson, Robert/ Reno, Fred (eds.) (2000): Politics of Identity: Migrants and Minorities in Multicultural States, London: Macmillan.
Huggan, Graham (1994): "V. S. Naipaul and the Political Correctness Debate", In: College Literature, Oct., pp. 200-206.
Hughes, Peter (1988): V. S. Naipaul, London and New York: Routledge.
James, C.L.R (1963): Beyond a Boundary, London: Hutchinson.
Jameson, Fredric (1986): "Third World Literature in the Era of Multination Capitalism." In: Social Texts 15, pp. 56-88.
Jarvis, Kelvin (1989): V. S. Naipaul: A Selected Bibliography with Annotations 1957-1987. Metuchen, N.J.: Scarecrow.
Jin, Huimin (2007): "Redefining Global Knowledge" In: Mike Featherstone (ed.), New Encyclopedia Project: Problematizing Global Knowledge. Vol. 1, London: Sage.
Jones, Stephanie (2000): "The Politics and Poetics of Diaspora in V.S.Naipaul's *A Way in the World.*" In: Journal of Commonwealth Literature 35/1, pp. 87-97.
Joseph, John E (2004): Language and Identity: National, Ethnic, Religious, New York: Palgrave Macmiltan, 2004.Jussawalla, Feroza (ed.) (1997): Conversations with V. S. Naipaul. Mississippi: Mississippi University Press.
Kelly, Richard (1989): V.S. Naipaul. New York: Continuum.
Kermode, Frank (1987): "In the Garden of the Oppressor", In: New York Times Book Review, 22 Mar., pp. 12-13.
Kidd, Warren (2002): Culture and Identity, New York: Palgrave.

King, Bruce (1993): V.S. Naipaul. London: Macmillan.
King, Nina (1994): "Passage to the West Indies", In: Washington Post (Book World) XXIV, 20 May 15, pp. 17-21.
Kinsle, David R (1993): Hinduism: A Cultural Perspective, New Jersey: Prentice Hall.
Kirpal, Viney (1989): The Third World Novel of Expatriation: A Study of Émigré.
Fiction by Indian, West African and Caribbean Writers. New Delhi: Sterling Publishers Private Ltd.
Kristeva, Julia (1988): Estrangers à nous-mêmes, Paris: Fayard.
Kurmar, Amitava (ed.) (2002): The Humour and the Pity, New Delhi: Buffalo Books.
Laming, George (1991): The Pleasures of Exile, Michigan: University of Michigan Press.
Landry, Donna and Gerald Maclean (eds.) (1996): The Spivak Reader: Selected Works of Gayatri Chakravorty Spivak, New York: Routledge.
Lash, Scott/ Friedman, Jonathan (eds.) (1992): Modernity and Identity, Oxford: Blackwell, 1992.
Leitch, Vincent B/ Cain, E. / Finke, Laurie/ Johnson, Barbara/ McGowan, John/ Williams, Jeffrey J. (eds.) (2001): The Norton Anthology of Theory and Criticism. London & New York: Norton.
Liu, Yuyuan (2003): Metaphorizing Migrancy: Naipaul's Fiction and Diaspora Poetics, Diss. National Taiwan Normal University.
Mcsweeney, Kerry (1983): Four Contemporary Novelists: Angus Wilson, Brian Moore, John Fowles and V. S. Naipaul, London: Scholar Press.
McRobbie, Angela (2005): The Uses of Cultural Studies, London: Sage.
Mercer, Kobena (1990): "Welcome to the Jungle: Identity and Diversity in Postmodern Politics", In: Jonathan Rutherford (ed.), Identity, Community, Culture, Difference, London: Lawrence and Wishart.
Mishra, Vijay (1996): "(B)ordering Naipaul: Indenture History and Diasporic Poetics", In: Diaspora, 5, pp. 46-59.

Morris, Mervyn (2002): "Sir Vidia and the Prize", In: World Literature Today, Spring, pp. 12-30.
Moya, Paula M. L./Hames-García, Michael R. (eds.) (2000): Reclaiming Identity: Realist Theory and the Predicament of Postmodernism, Berkeley and Los Angeles: University of California Press.
Mustafa, Fawzia (1995): V. S. Naipaul, England: Cambridge University Press.
Neill, Michael (1982): "Guerrillas and the Gangs: Frantz Fanon and V.S. Naipaul", In: Ariel, 13/4, pp. 21-62.
Nightingale, Peggy (1987): Journey Through Darkness, Queensland: University of Queensland Press.
Nixon, Rob (1992): London Calling: V.S. Naipaul, Postcolonial Mandarin, New York: Oxford University Press.
Niven, Alastair (ed.)(1976): "World's End: V. S. Naipaul's *The Mimic Men*", In: The Common Wealth Writer Overseas, Brussels: Didier.
O'Reilly, Christopher (1998): *Post-Colonial Literature*. Cambridge: Cambridge University Press.
Paquet, Sandra Pouchet (2002): Caribbean Autobiography: Cultural Identity and Self-Representation. Wisconsin: The University of Wisconsin Press.
Phillips, Caryl (2000): "The Enigma of Denial", In: The New Republic 29 May, pp. 43-49
Piedra, Jose (1989): "The Game of Critical Arrival", In: Diacritics 19/1, pp. 34-61.
Pritchard, William H (1998): Talking Back to Emily Dickinson and Other Essays, Amherst: University of Massachusetts Press.
Quayson, Ato (2000): Postcolonialism: Theory, Practice or Process? Cambridge: Polity Press.
Ramraj, Victor (1972): "The All-Embracing Christlike Vision: Tone and Attitude in *The Mimic Men*", In: Anna Rutherford (ed.), Common Wealth, Aarhus: Akademisk Boghandel.
Rhys, Jean (1979): Smile Please: An Unfinished Autobiography, London: André Deutsch.

Rushidie, Salman (1992): Imaginary Homelands: Essays and Criticism 1981-991, London and New York: Granta Books & Penguin.
Said, Edward (1978): Orientalism, New York: Pantheon, 1978.
Said, Edward (1993): Culture and Imperialism, New York: Knopf.
Said, Edward (1994): Representations of the Intellectual, New York: Vintage.
Said, Edward (1998): "Ghost Writer", In: Progressive, 62/11, pp.40-42.
Said, Edward (2000): Reflections on Exile and Other Essays, Massachusetts: Harvard University Press.
Safran, William (1991): "Diasporas in modern societies: myths of homeland and return", In: Diaspora, 1/1, pp.230-256. .
Safran, William (1999): "Comparing Diasporas: A Review Essay", In: Diaspora, 8/3, pp. 255-291.
Sarkar, R.N (2004): India Related Naipaul. New Delhi: Sarup & Sons.
Seepersad, Naipaul (1976): The Adventures of Gurudeva. London: Andre Deutsch.
Simpson, Louis (1984): "Disorder and Escape in the Fiction of V.S. Naipaul", In: Hudson Review 37/4, pp. 571-577.
Singh, H.B. (1969): "V.S. Naipaul: A Spokesman for Neo-Colonialism," In: Literature and Ideology, Summer, pp. 71-85.
Slemom, Stephen (1998): "Post-Colonial Allegory and the Transformation of History", In: Journal of Commonwealth Literature 23, pp. 157-168.
Staples, Brent (1994): " 'Con Men and Conquerors,' A Review of *A Way in the World*," In: New York Times Books Review. May 22, pp. 65-79.
Storey, John (2004): Cultural Theory and Popular Culture: An Introduction, Beijing: Peking University Press.
Suleri, Sara (1988): "Naipaul's Arrival", In: The Yale Journal of Criticism, 2/1, pp. 25-50.
Swedish Academy (2001). "The Nobel Prize in Literature 2001 V.S. Naipaul", November 15, 2006, (http://www.nobelprize.org/nobelprizes/literature/laureates/2001/press.html)

Swinden, Patrick (1984): The English Novel of History and Society, 1940-80, London and Basingtoke: Macmillan.
Theroux, Paul (1998): Sir Vidia's Shadow, New York: Houghton Mifflin Company.
Thieme, John (1987): The Web of Tradition: Uses of Allusions in V. S. Naipaul's Fiction, London: Dangaroo Press.
Thorpe, Michael (1976): V. S. Naipaul, London: Longman.
Tiffen, Helen (1989): "Rites of Resistance: Counter Discourse and West Indian Biography", In: Journal of West Indian Literature, 3, Jan. pp. 28-46.
Tsomondo, Thorell (1989): "Metaphor, Metonymy and Houses: Figures of Construction in *A House for Mr. Biswas*", In: World Literature Written in English, 29/2 pp. 69-82.
Turner, Graeme (2003): British Cultural Studies: An Introduction, London and New York: Routledge.
Walder, Dennis (1998): Post-Colonial Literatures in English: History, Language, Theory, Massachusetts: Blackwell.
Weiss, Timothy F (1992): On the Margin: The Art of Exile in Niapaul, Amherst: The University of Massachusetts Press.
Wheeler, Charles (1977): "It's Every Man for Himself—V.S. Naipaul on India", In: Listener, 98 Oct. 27.
White, Hayden (1973): Metahistory: The Historical Imagination in Nineteenth-Century Europe, Baltimore: Johns Hopkins University Press.
White, Landerg (1975): V.S. Naipaul: A Critical Introduction, London and Baisingstoke: The Macmillan Press.
Whitley, David (1995): "Cultural Identities Under Pressure", In: Julia Swindells (ed.) The Uses of Autobiography, London: Taylor and Francis.
Williams, Eric (1984): From Columbus to Castro: The History of the Caribbean 1492-1969, New York: Vintage Books.
Wilson-Tagoe, Nana (1998): Historical Thought and Literary Representation in West Indian Literature, USA: Florida UP, UK: Oxford, & Caribbean: West Indies UP.

Winokur, Scott (1999): " The Unsparing Vision of V.S. Naipaul", In: Image, May 5. pp. 21-32.
Wood, James (2001): "Damage", In: The New Republic, Nov. 5, pp. 31-35.
Woodward, Kathryn (1997): Identity and Difference, London, Thousand Oaks and New Delhi: Sage.
Wyndham, Francis (1968): "An Interview with V.S. Naipaul", *Sunday Times*, Sep. 10.
Young, Robert J.C (1995): Colonial Desire: Hybridity in Theory, Culture and Race, New York: Routledge.
Young, Robert J.C (2004): Postcolonialism: An Historical Introduction, Oxford: Blackwell.

WORKS IN CHINESE

阿里夫·德里克:《跨国资本时代的后殖民批评》,王宁等译,北京:北京大学出版社,2004年。

爱德华·W·萨义德:《东方学》,王宇根译,北京:三联书店,1999年。

_____《赛义德自选集》,谢少波等译,北京:中国社会科学出版社,1999年。

_____《知识分子论》,单德兴译,陆建德校,北京:三联书店,2002年。

_____《文化与帝国主义》,李琨译,北京:三联书店,2003年。

_____《格格不入》,彭淮栋译,北京:三联书店,2004年。

艾勒克·博埃默:《殖民与后殖民文学》,盛宁,韩敏中译,沈阳:辽宁教育出版社,1998年。

埃里·凯杜里:《民族主义》,张明明译,北京:中央编译出版社,2002年。

安东尼·D·史密斯:《全球化时代的民族与民族主义》,龚维斌、良警宇译,北京:中央编译出版社,2002年。

本尼迪克特·安德森:《想象的共同体》,吴睿人译,上海:世纪出版集团,2003年。

巴特·穆尔—吉尔伯特等编:《后殖民批评》,杨乃乔等译,北京:北京大学出版社,2001年。

巴特·穆尔—吉尔伯特:《后殖民理论:语境 实践 政治》,陈仲丹译,南京:南京大学出版社,2004年。
保罗·利科:《历史与真理》,姜志辉译,上海:上海译文出版社,2004年。
曹文轩:《小说门》,北京:作家出版社,2002年。
查尔斯·泰勒:《自我的根源:现代认同的形成》,韩震等译,南京:译林出版社,2001年。
丹尼斯·托马森:《不幸与幸福》,京不特译,北京:华夏出版社,2004年。
方汉文:《后现代文化心理:拉康研究》,上海:上海三联书店,2000年。
方生:《后结构主义文论》,济南:山东教育出版社,2001年。
菲力浦·勒热讷:《自传契约》,杨国政译,北京:三联书店,2001年。
弗雷德里克·杰姆逊:《后现代主义与文化理论》,唐小兵译,北京:北京大学出版社,1997年。
_____《晚期资本主义的文化逻辑》,陈清侨等译,北京:三联书店,1997年。
_____《政治无意识》,王逢振、陈永国译,北京:中国社会科学出版社,1999年。
格非:《小说叙事研究》,北京:清华大学出版社,2002年。
海德格尔:《人,诗意地安居》,郜元宝译,桂林:广西师范大学出版社,2002年。
海登·怀特:《后现代历史叙事学》,陈永国、张万鹍译,北京:中国社会科学出版社,2003年。
胡全生:《英美后现代主义小说叙述结构研究》,上海:复旦大学出版社,2002年。
黄汉平:《拉康与后现代文化批评》,北京:中国社会科学出版社,2006年。
姜飞:《跨文化传播的后殖民语境》,北京:中国人民大学出版社,2005年。
克利福德·格尔茨:《文化的解释》,韩莉译,南京:译林出版社,1999年。
拉康:《拉康选集》,褚孝泉译,上海:上海三联书店,2001年。
李建军,《小说修辞研究》,北京:中国人民大学出版社,2003年。
李钧:《存在主义文论》,济南:山东教育出版社,2001年。
李欧梵:《现代性的追求》,北京:三联书店,2000年。

流心：《自我的他性》，常姝译，上海：世纪出版集团，2005年。
鲁道夫·奥伊肯：《生活的意义和价值》，上海：上海译文出版社，2005年。
陆建德：《思想背后的利益》，桂林：广西师范大学出版社，2005年。
陆扬：《精神分析文论》，济南：山东教育出版社，2001年。
罗刚：《叙事学导论》，昆明：云南人民出版社，1992年。
罗刚，刘象愚编：《文化研究读本》，北京：中国社会科学出版社，2000年。
———《后殖民主义文化理论》，北京：中国社会科学出版社，1999年。
马元龙：《雅克·拉康：语言维度中的精神分析》，北京：东方出版社，2006年。
马振方：《小说艺术论》，北京：北京大学出版社，2000年。
梅晓云：《文化无根——以V.S.奈保尔维个案的移民文化研究》，西安：陕西人民出版社，2003年。
瞿世镜主编：《当代英国小说》，北京：外语教学与研究出版社，1998年.
任一鸣、瞿世镜：《英语后殖民文学研究》，上海：上海译文出版社，2003年。
彭刚：《精神、自由与历史—克罗齐历史哲学研究》，北京：清华大学出版社，1999年。
皮埃尔-安德烈·塔吉耶夫：《种族主义源流》，高凌瀚译，北京：三联书店，2005年。
乔纳森·弗里德曼：《文化认同与全球性过程》，郭建如译，高丙中校，北京：商务印书馆，2003年。
乔治·拉伦：《意识形态与文化身份：现代性和第三世界的在场》，戴从容译，上海：上海教育出版社，2005年。
任一鸣、瞿世镜：《英语后殖民文学研究》，上海：上海译文出版社，2003年。
塞缪尔·亨廷顿：《文明的冲突与世界秩序的重建》周琪等译，北京：新华出版社，2002年。
石海军：《后殖民：印英文学之间》，北京：北京大学出版社，2008年。
孙妮：《V.S.奈保尔小说研究》，合肥：安徽人民出版社，2007年。
陶家俊：《文化身份的嬗变—E.M.福斯特小说和思想研究》，北京：中国社会科学出版社，2003年。

特里·伊格尔顿:《现象学,阐释学,接受理论-当代西方文艺理论》,王逢振译,南京:江苏教育出版社,2006年。

V.S. 奈保尔:《米格尔大街》,张琪译,于晓丹校,北京:大众文艺出版社,2001年。

_____《河湾》,方柏林译,南京:译林出版社,2002年。

_____《毕司沃斯先生的房子》,余珺珉译,南京:译林出版社,2002年。

_____《幽暗国度:记忆与现实交错的印度之旅》,李永平译,北京:三联书店,2003年。

_____《印度:受伤的文明》,宋念申译,北京:三联书店,2003年。

_____《印度:百万叛变的今天》,黄道琳译,北京:三联书店,2003年。

_____《抵达之谜》,邹海仑,蔡曙光,张杰译,杭州:浙江文艺出版社,20004年。

_____《奈保尔家书》,北塔,常文祺译,杭州:浙江文艺出版社,2006年。

王成兵:《当代认同危机的人学解读》,北京:中国社会科学出版社,2004年。

王树英:《宗教与印度社会》,北京:中国华侨出版社,1995年。

王岳川:《后殖民主义与新历史主义文论》,济南:山东教育出版社,2001年。

韦勒克·勒内,奥斯汀·沃沦:《文学理论》,刘象愚等译,南京:江苏教育出版社,2005年。

威廉斯·埃里克:《从哥伦布到卡斯特罗:加勒比地区史》,辽宁大学经济系翻译组译,沈阳:辽宁人民出版社,1976年。

威廉斯·埃里克:《特立尼达和多巴哥人民史》,吉林师大外语系翻译组译:长春:吉林人民出版社,1972年。

谢少波:《抵抗的文化政治学》,陈永国,汪民安译,北京:中国社会科学出版社:1999年。

徐贲:《走向后现代与后殖民》,北京:中国社会科学出版社,1999年。

阎嘉主编:《文学理论精粹读本》,北京:中国人民大学出版社,2006年。

杨中举:《奈保尔:跨界生存与多重叙事》,上海:东方出版中心,2009年。

伊夫·瓦岱:《文学与现代性》,田庆生译,北京:北京大学出版社,2001年。

约翰·斯道雷:《文化理论与通俗文化导论》,杨竹山等译,南京大学出版社,2002年。

殷企平等:《英国小说批评史》,上海:上海外语教育出版社,2001年。

张静主编:《身份认同研究:观念 态度 理据》,上海:上海人民出版社,2006年。

张京媛主编:《后殖民理论与文化批评》,北京:北京大学出版社,1999年。

―――《新历史主义与文学批评》,北京:北京大学出版社,1993年。

张旭东:《全球化时代的文化认同》,北京:北京大学出版社,2005年。

张一兵:《不可能的存在之真—拉康哲学映象》,北京:商务印书馆,2006年。

赵一凡,张中载,李德恩编:《西方文论关键词》,北京:外语教学与研究出社,2006年。

周建漳:《历史及其理解和解释》,北京:社会科学文献出版社,2005年。